D0953532

EUPHEMISM, SPIN, AND THE CRISIS IN ORGANIZATIONAL LIFE

Howard F. Stein

Foreword by Seth Allcorn

Q

Quorum Books
Westport, Connecticut • London

Library of Congress Cataloging-in-Publication Data

Stein, Howard F.
    Euphemism, spin, and the crisis in organizational life / Howard F.
Stein : foreword by Seth Allcorn.
        p. cm.
    Includes bibliographical references (p.   ) and index.
    ISBN 1–56720–124–5 (alk. paper)
    1. Organizational behavior. 2. Industrial management—
Psychological aspects. 3. Reengineering (Management) 4. Downsizing
of organizations. 5. English language—Euphemism. I. Title.
HD58.7.S742   1998
158.7—dc21   97–48618

British Library Cataloguing in Publication Data is available.

Copyright © 1998 by Howard F. Stein

All rights reserved. No portion of this book may be
reproduced, by any process or technique, without the
express written consent of the publisher.

Library of Congress Catalog Card Number: 97–48618
ISBN: 1–56720–124–5

First published in 1998

Quorum Books, 88 Post Road West, Westport, CT 06881
An imprint of Greenwood Publishing Group, Inc.

Printed in the United States of America

The paper used in this book complies with the
Permanent Paper Standard issued by the National
Information Standards Organization (Z39.48–1984).

10 9 8 7 6 5 4 3 2 1

Copyright Acknowledgments

The author and publisher gratefully acknowledge permission for use of the following
material:

Howard F. Stein, "Death Imagery and the Experience of Organizational Downsizing:
Or, Is Your Name on Schindler's List?" *Administration and Society* 29, no. 2 (May
1997): 222–247. Reprinted by permission of Sage Publications, Inc., and Gary L.
Wamsley, Editor, *Administration and Society*.

Howard F. Stein, "Trauma Revisited: Mourning and the Unconscious in the Oklahoma
City Bombing." *Journal for the Psychoanalysis of Culture and Society* 2, no. 1 (1997):
17–37. Excerpts reprinted by permissioin of Mark Bracher, Editor, *Journal for the Psychoanalysis of Culture and Society*.

Excerpts from *Nineteen Eighty-four* by George Orwell, copyright © 1949 by Harcourt
Brace & Company and renewed 1977 by Sonia Brownell Orwell, reprinted by permission of the publisher; copyright © Mark Hamilton as the Literary Executor of the Es-
tate of the late Sonia Brownell Orwell, reprinted by permission of Martin Secker &
Warburg Ltd. and A M Heath & Co. Ltd.

Jan Edry, "Letter to the Editor," *The Daily Oklahoman* (Oklahoma City), May 3, 1995,
page 6. Reprinted by permission of Jan Edry.

Dedicated to the Memory of
Abraham Joshua Heschel

Contents

Foreword

This is a book about wizards who do not change lead into gold but, more profoundly, change evil into good. This book is about the art form behind the magic of the wizardry, the spinning of a web of mind- and reality-altering words that change the very nature of what we know and how we experience ourselves, others and events. Stein provides us a patiently developed and thorough analysis of what amounts to a verbal cleansing of awareness, motives, and actions of the darker—indeed, at times, darkest—side of human nature. He challenges us to listen to what we say and hear the true meaning of the words. He asks us what it really does mean to pursue organizational downsizing and provide managed health care. He uncomfortably, but accurately, reveals that the use of euphemisms such as these is not really much different from the euphemisms used by the Nazi German state to dehumanize and then systematically exterminate millions of Jews as well as other "unfit" individuals and races in their pursuit of ethnic purity.

This book makes clear that the verbal sleight of hand involved in the business world is so omnipresent as to not only go unnoticed but much of the time be embraced as buzz words. As I read, I was reminded of "Neutron" Jack, a CEO of a large international corporation who eliminates the people, leaving only the buildings standing, as would be the case if a neutron bomb were used, and "Chain Saw" Al, a corporate turn-around artist who, as fast as possible, cuts out organizational fat (Bennis, 1989). These men and other executives like them are the darlings of Wall Street and popular management magazines (Micklethwait and Wooldridge, 1996). They are also exponents of organizational downsizing and reengineering. In this book we are asked to join with the author in the peeling back of the reality of organizational downsizing and the use of many other words that are used to justify and explain away organizational change that destroys individuals and organizations, words used to justify the actions of the "corporate killers" among us (see the Corporate Killers cover of *Newsweek*, February 26, 1996).

The horrific specter that emerges from this book is that downsizing, restructuring and reengineering are not merely management techniques (regardless of however unsound they have proven to be) that all executives use. They are management techniques only some executives use. The question must be asked: "Why are these methods used by some executives and not others?" Stein leaves us with the grim realization that perhaps (and, worse yet, very likely) the truth is that these management tools, often supported by a cadre of "hatchet men" consultants armed with computers, data, spreadsheets, and analyses of the gains to the bottom line, are an externalization of a CEO's internal world filled with sadistic aggression and paranoia (Kets de Vries, 1980, 1984, 1991).

The use of these management methods and the accompanying consultants seems to invariably create a new, Orwellian-like language within the "targeted organization." Management-speak and consultant-speak, one implicitly understands, if not accepted by organization members, signals that you are not getting with the program (not a "team player") and, therefore, may be greeted by a security guard some Friday afternoon who asks you to remove your belongings before being escorted out of the building. Those on their way out very likely understand that management-speak and consultant-speak are a defensive language that obfuscates what it means to downsize, restructure and reengineer while simultaneously forcing you, the listener, to either agree and make your deal with the devil or disagree and find yourself sacrificed on the downsizing butcher block.

What were once people have become human resources, some of whom—having become, through no fault of their own, bad, unhealthy organizational fat—must be ruthlessly cut from the organization to save it. The workplace suddenly becomes win-lose. The strongest (usually the team players and sycophants) win and the losers are not fired but rather "restructured" out of work and "outplaced." Of particular interest is the near-term, bottom-line nature of these kinds of change that, while driving up stock values in the short run, have by now undermined much of what was good in the business world. The psychological contract with workers has been torn up. These are not insightful, well-thought-through, reflective management methods. They do not offer any solution other than doing more or less of the same thing—what Argyris and Schon (1978) call single-loop learning.

As I uncomfortably read on I was reminded of a recent television program that discussed Robert McNamara's "whiz kid" role of leading the war in Vietnam. He relied extensively upon quantitative operations research methodologies in conducting the war. A commentator and no doubt a critic offered the following phrase that I think captures the essence of management engineering and numbers-driven techniques like downsizing, restructuring and reengineering. Referring to McNamara, he quoted Oscar Wilde, saying, "He knew the cost of everything and the value of nothing." We today seem to live in a world that, lacking values other than making money, has created a reality too harsh and frightening to admit exists, a reality filled with the devaluation of people, groups and the human spirit. It has been said that we live in an age of narcissism (Lasch, 1979). However, we have had our hopes and dreams, our fantasies filled with fantastic images of self-actualization and effortless self-realization if not—let's face it—physical pleasures, smashed to so much rubble. Stein reminds us that we are today also often filled with chronic narcissistic rage. Our fantasy worlds have imploded leaving only disillusionment, alienation and, at our very core, rage that occasionally and more frequently today leaks out in the workplace in the form of workplace violence (Allcorn, 1994; Diamond, 1997). Not only have we all become the victims or potential victims of mindless downsizing and its human devaluation, we have all been victimized by the destruction of our cherished fantasy world, a loss so profound that it is hard to acknowledge and even harder to talk about. Often, husbands and wives must both work to afford a decent meal, not to mention "luxury" items. In a time when we seem to have to work ever harder to make enough bucks to maintain some semblance of our fantasized existence, we are faced with the harsh realities that nothing and nobody count any more—everyone can be restructured out of a job including the boss and the boss's boss. This book eloquently reveals the exceptionally painful and vulnerable side to our work lives and explores them for their true meaning.

Stein, as our metaphorical guide on our journey into the heart of euphemism and the darkness it conceals, reveals the subtle nuances of downsizing the business world and the even harder to understand and detect and, therefore, even better concealed aspects of managed health care where the most cost-effective treatment of a young mother's leg injury is a $5,000 amputation as compared to a $50,000 restoration of the limb. A trip to our doctor is no longer exclusively filled with the hope that our diseased or injured body will be healed. Rather it has become a business transaction filled with economic issues that we often do not understand very well. Today we are not cared for as a human being nor even as a patient. We are now a potential cost to the system, an anonymous member of a panel of patients, one among millions in a pool of covered lives. Our physician's ability to meet our needs has been downsized by treatment paradigms—cookbook medicine—and a system called managed care.

Like all journeys into darkness, Stein's journey into the subtle, but profound, nature of managed care yields to the realization that downsizing and managed care are not so very different from the economic and biomedical attributes of Nazi Germany's final solution to rid the German people of disease-ridden vermin—the Jews and others like them—the despicable, unwanted fat of humanity. It is not too much of an intellectual stretch to understand that these German programs eliminated the most vulnerable members of their society by "scientifically" locating them as a social disease vector that brought Germany to its knees.

The fact that virtually everyone in the United States has been, will be, or may be victimized by downsizing of business, government and health care delivery raises yet another profound question that this book addresses. What does the traumatic nature of this level of victimization really mean? How can it be dealt with, lived through, adjusted to, made sense of? The trauma associated with the Oklahoma City bombing is explored for the many insights and lessons it has to offer. The bombing ripped apart the social fabric of a community, state, and nation. Not unlike the downsizing led by the corporate killers, the bombing destroyed lives and families. Workers are similarly left with but a flimsy shell of their former career aspirations and indeed fundamental ability to care for themselves and their families. And, like the remaining tortured shell of the Murrah Federal Building, one's sense of self-integrity, self-efficacy, self-worth is just as assuredly vastly diminished, imploded within us to create an emotionally walled off and numbing former site of personal growth and well-being. In an era where the demise of communism and socialism, as represented by the disintegration of the Soviet Union, is claimed as an American victory, we feel vindicated that our way of life, including our economic model of capitalism, is the "right stuff." It seems as though we are on top of the world. This book, however, raises disquieting and profound questions about an ethical and moral bankruptcy within our society that is concealed in euphemism. We are faced squarely with the question, If the stock market rewards the mention of the word "downsizing" by a CEO (the larger the numbers, the better), does not our society at its foundation value money more than people and place profit over the human spirit? Might we not all be living in a mind- and reality-altering web of words that hide a painful truth? Perhaps the call for a return to "family values" is itself a euphemism, one that conceals the larger and much more painful possibility that our society, like those that have gone before, may ultimately be without a core of redeeming values. Are we a society where euphemism reigns supreme? Are we all, figuratively speaking, "members of the band on the Titanic" standing on an ever more steeply sloping deck waiting for our long slide into euphemized oblivion? Are capitalism and our way of life to join their foes on the stack of discarded social and economic theory?

This book asks the question "Who is an essential worker?" and the answer that creeps into consciousness with its terror that reverberates within one's soul is—No one. Stein points the way to lifting the blinding mask of euphemism so that we may see the future and stay the course against organizational evil that fills the workplace with unspeakable executive aggression, violence and horror. We must mourn our loss of innocence and reach out to embrace our individual vulnerabilities to offer a hand of mercy to those who have fallen along the way and even contemplate forgiving our corporate killers for the banality of their transgressions. It is in this hope that Stein offers us escape from the trains of cattle cars that metaphorically await to haul us off to a holocaust of the human spirit.

I want to add that, based upon my twenty years of work experience as a chief financial and chief operating officer in three schools of academic medicine, the content of this book rings painfully true. My places of work were often filled with ritualized workplace violence that occasionally destroyed people and families as surely as if they had been hauled off and shot or gassed. I have looked into the bottomless pool of arrogant and frequently misinformed executive decision making fed by ignorance, the search for the "quick fix" and their own deeply felt but unacknowledged aggression toward anyone who was different or dared to ask a tough question (Kilmann 1989).

I recall hearing of a meeting in a large teaching hospital that was called to formally announce that downsizing was about to ensue with the help of a notorious downsizing consulting group. The hospital CEO was speaking to all of upper and middle management, approximately 150 people. He explained the downsizing process this way. "You are standing on a train station platform. You have three choices. You can get on the train that is going where I want to go. You can wait just a little bit before deciding what you want to do. Or, you can get on the second train that is leaving the hospital." Since I studied this downsizing in depth as a researcher (Allcorn, et al., 1996), I can bear witness to the fact that the metaphorical trains both lead to a man-made hell on earth. The truth that lies within this book, even if painful to acknowledge, challenges us all to assume responsibility for the nature of our organizational lives, to take a stand against the presence of evil in our places of work.

Seth Allcorn, Ph.D., M.B.A.
Principal DyAD and Adjunct Faculty and Organizational Consultant
Department of Public Administration
Center for the Study of Organizational Change
University of Missouri–Columbia

REFERENCES

Allcorn, Seth. *Anger in the Workplace*. Westport, CT: Quorum Books, 1994.

Allcorn, Seth, Howell Baum, Michael A. Diamond, and Howard F. Stein. *The Human Cost of a Management Failure: Organizational Downsizing at General Hospital*. Westport, CT: Quorum Books, 1996.

Argyris, Chris, and Donald Schon. *Organizational Learning: A Theory of Action Perspective*. Reading, MA: Addison-Wesley, 1978.

Bennis, Warren. *Why Leaders Can't Lead*. San Francisco: Jossey-Bass, 1989.

Diamond, Michael. "Administrative Assault: A Contemporary Psychoanalytic View of Violence and Aggression in the Workplace." *American Review of Public Administration* 27, no. 3 (September 1997): 228–247.

Kets de Vries, Manfred. *Organizational Paradoxes*. New York: Tavistock, 1980.

———. *The Irrational Executive*. New York: International Universities Press, 1984.

———. *Organizations on the Couch*. San Francisco: Jossey-Bass, 1991.

Kilmann, Ralph. *Managing Beyond the Quick Fix*. San Francisco: Jossey-Bass, 1989.

Lasch, Christopher. *Culture of Narcissism*. New York: W. W. Norton, 1979.

Micklethwait, John, and Adrian Wooldridge. *The Witch Doctors: Making Sense of the Management Gurus*. New York: Times Books, 1996.

Acknowledgments

Many people have helped me to understand, and to break the silence on, euphemism in the workplace and in wider society. If they have given me much knowledge, they have given me even more courage (from the French, *coeur*, "heart"). My gratitude goes to those I have and have not acknowledged by name.

In 1993, Seth Allcorn, Ph.D., invited Howell Baum, Ph.D., Michael A. Diamond, Ph.D., and me to participate in the longitudinal study of hospital downsizing that resulted in the publication of a book titled *The Human Cost of a Management Failure: Organizational Downsizing at General Hospital* (1996). They have been an indispensable home base and "detoxification container" for my further development of ideas on the role of euphemism in organizational management.

My publisher, Eric Valentine at Quorum Books, not only shepherded this book manuscript through to publication, but from the beginning understood what I was trying to say but had not yet been able to write. For me, he was a writer's patient editor and coach.

The International Society for the Psychoanalytic Study of Organizations has welcomed my psychoanalytic anthropological perspective, and has encouraged my exploration of the boundaries between workplace, psyche, family, and society. Among those at the ISPSO whom I wish to single out for my thanks are Rose Redding Mersky, Ph.D., Yiannis Gabriel, Ph.D., Howard Schwartz, Ph.D., Joseph Rosenthal, Ph.D., Harry Levinson, Ph.D., Howard Book, M.D., Harold Bridger, M.D., Shelly Reciniello, Ph.D., Larry Hirshhorn, Ph.D., and Laurence Gould, Ph.D.

Many friends at the High Plains Society for Applied Anthropology have encouraged my presentation on "organizational culture" over the past decade, among them, Arthur Campa, Ph.D., Mary Granica, Ph.D., Susan Scott-Stevens, Ph.D., Deward Walker, Ph.D., Gottfried Lang, Ph.D., and Ed Knop, Ph.D. Medical anthropologists Thomas M. Johnson, Ph.D., J. Neil Henderson, Ph.D., Charles Nuckolls, Ph.D., and Lorna Amarasingham Rhodes, Ph.D., have urged that I continue the "organizational" route of analysis, consultation, and theory building. Organizational anthropologists Ann Jordan, Ph.D., and Pamela Puntenney, Ph.D., have persuaded me that I am (whatever professional identities I also have) an organizational anthropologist.

The annual Forum for the Behavioral Sciences in Family Medicine has long encouraged my organizational forays in Family Medicine and the culture(s) of medicine beyond this specialty's boundaries. Kathy Zoppi, Ph.D., Calvin McGinn, Ph.D., Fay McCutchan, Ph.D., G. Gayle Stephens, M.D., Samuel Romano, Ph.D., Harley Racer, M.D., William Miller, M.D., Milton Seifert, M.D., among others, have steadfastly encouraged me to explore, consult, present, and write on the organizational, now corporate, aspect of American medicine. Fay McCutchan, now program committee chairperson for the annual Forum, has long offered me a clinical behavioral science forum at which to make presentations on clinical teaching, workplace culture, downsizing, managed care, and the Oklahoma City bombing.

The annual Corporate Psychology Conference, Division 13, American Psychological Association, held in Keystone, Colorado, each February, has given me the opportunity to present my ideas on organizational culture and consulting, and most recently to serve as group "process consultant" and interpreter for the entire convention. People such as Timothy Murphy, Ph.D., Michael Atella, Ph.D., John Deleray, Ph.D., Paul Winum, Ph.D., and Kevin Somerville, Ph.D., have trusted me to go more where I was headed than even I knew!

Rear Admiral W. R. Rowley and Chaplain Commander Julius A. Thomas generously invited me to present my ideas on downsizing and catastrophe in their "Stress and Trauma" conference, held on March 27, 1996, at the U.S. Naval Medical Center, Portsmouth, Virginia. I had the opportunity to compare my work with that of professionals who had developed and implemented the Critical Incident Stress Debriefing approach to disaster, including such pioneers as Jeffrey Mitchell, Ph.D., and George Everly, Jr., Ph.D.

Timothy Coussons, M.D., and CEO of The University Hospitals,

Oklahoma City, gave me more of a learning opportunity that I had ever bargained for when, in early 1995, he asked me to serve as long-term, internal consultant on the hospital systems' "downsizing," "restructuring," and preparation for merger with local and national hospital systems. Similarly, Fred Jordan, M.D., Chief Medical Examiner of the State of Oklahoma, his office personnel, and Allene Jackson, M.D., graciously included me in their intimate family in the long-term aftermath of the April 19, 1995, bombing of the Federal Building in Oklahoma City. Our group expanded to include Cynthia Calloway, M.Ed., L.P.C., a gifted grief counselor, and Sergeant Michael Isaac, of the Norman, Oklahoma Police Department. We meet weekly at a local coffee joint, and call our group a "detoxification group," with the apt Oklahoma name "Outlaws." We learn together, we have taught each other, what we need to know and feel.

Richard A. Wright, Ph.D., and Nance K. Cunningham, M.A., both of whom are biomedical and health care ethicists and applied philosophers, have tried to keep me honest and philosophically informed. Ms. Cunningham is also my wife and mother of our 3½-year-old son, Zev Jacob. They have challenged my temptation toward the indirectness of euphemism at home, and forced me to be more plain-speaking and open-feeling than I have been. They have also had to live with the development of this book, an emotionally demanding process about which there is no possibility of euphemizing!

Within the Department of Family and Preventive Medicine, where I teach, Frank Lawler, M.D., a faculty colleague, has been especially courageous in questioning the wisdom of political correctness in naming people and roles: What is lost in understanding suffering and healing, when patients become mere customers, and doctors become mere providers?—he continues to ask at our departmental meetings. He has also helped me to identify euphemisms in sources I would not otherwise read.

Henry Ebel, Ph.D., renaissance man and organizational consultant, has helped me to develop these ideas over a twenty-two-year friendship. Barbara Shapiro, M.D., pediatrician and psychoanalyst, has for several years given me courage to explore the euphemisms of American medicine, and of its wider culture. Roger Fowler, a retired Oklahoma City letter carrier and avid reader, has constantly challenged me on virtually every idea and made sure that even if the ideas were untenable, at least they were grammatically correct.

I would also like to thank B. J. Haywood, M.D., Wesley Andrews, M.D., Robert Like, M.D., and David Rogers, M.D., whose ideas I have quoted or paraphrased.

Mark Lightfoot, B.A., my part-time office assistant (he prefers this over the more gendered term, secretary), has read this text many times for content and has prepared many versions of the manuscript on the computer. He has made this work technologically possible and aesthetically presentable. Sometimes he is my eyes as well as my vision.

A scholar without reference librarians is an outright lie: I didn't do it all myself; I couldn't have! Five reference librarians at the University of Oklahoma Health Sciences Center Bird Library have on countless occasions redeemed me from bibliographic perdition, in this and in earlier books. To Stewart Brower, Jennifer C. Goodson, Edith A. Schneeberger, Shari Clifton, and Roswitha Allin I offer my gratitude for undertaking many a "mission impossible" search on behalf of my writing.

The following acknowledges the sources in prior presentations of much of the material in this book. Earlier versions of the chapter on organizational downsizing (chapter 3) were presented at (1) the Department of Family Medicine Grand Rounds, Wayne State University, Detroit, Michigan, on October 13, 1994, in a talk titled "Family Medicine, Organizational Culture, and the Corporate Downsizing of America"; (2) the Sixteenth Forum for the Behavioral Sciences in Family Medicine, Chicago, Illinois, September 1995; (3) a "Stress and Trauma" conference held at the U.S. Naval Medical Center, Portsmouth, Virginia, March 27, 1996, with a talk titled "Deep Effects of Organizational Change: Downsizing in American Corporate Life"; and (4) the June 14, 1996, Symposium of the International Society for the Psychoanalytic Study of Organizations, in New York City, in a paper titled "Death Imagery and the Experience of Organizational Downsizing."

Many of the ideas in chapter 3 also owe their existence and testing to lengthy telephone conversations with Michael Robin, M.S.W., whom the author gratefully acknowledges. An earlier, and abbreviated, version of this paper was subsequently published in the May 1997 issue of *Administration and Society*. I use that material with permission of the editor, Dr. Gary Wamsley, and of the publisher, Sage Publications, Inc.

Earlier versions of the chapter on managed care (chapter 4) were presented at (1) the Symposium on "Health and Bioethics: Patient-Physician Relationships in the Era of Managed Care," Symposium in Honor of Dr. James E. Hurley (a biologist at Oklahoma Baptist University, Shawnee, Oklahoma), at the University of Oklahoma Health Sciences Center, Oklahoma City, Oklahoma, June 29, 1996; Program roles: faculty presenter and panelist; (2) the Asheville Study Group, Asheville, North Carolina, September 7, 1996; (3) invited presentation on "American Medicine and Managed Care: Why Ethics Now?," Integris Southwest Medical Center of Oklahoma, Oklahoma City, October 2, 1996; and (4) as Featured Speaker, at the Conference on "Rationing of Healthcare: 'Who's Guarding the Hen House?,' " sponsored by the Oklahoma Association for Healthcare Ethics, Metro Tech, Oklahoma

City, October 4, 1996. I dedicate chapter 4 to Dr. James E. Hurley and to his legacy as inspired and inspiring teacher. One member of that legacy is Dr. J. Michael Pontious, a former Family Medicine resident from whom I learned as least as much as I think I taught. He is now my boss and residency director at the Enid Family Medicine Clinic, Enid, Oklahoma, and has a growing legacy of his own. To Seth Allcorn, Ph.D., Michael Diamond, Ph.D., Allene Jackson, M.D., Kathleen Cain, M.S.W., Susan Hickerson, M.S.W., and Richard Perry, M.S., go my heartfelt thanks for their encouragement and careful criticism of earlier versions of this chapter. To David Pingitore, Ph.D., goes my gratitude for his relentless encouragement of my effort to bring psychoanalytic insights into the heart of social criticism and policymaking.

Earlier versions of the chapter on the Oklahoma City bombing (chapter 5) were presented as (1) the Keynote Address, titled "Grief Beyond Debriefing: Living in the Long Shadow of the Oklahoma City Federal Building Bombing," at the "Love of Violence Conference," sponsored by the Ernest Becker Foundation and the Washington Commission for the Humanities, held in Seattle, Washington, October 11, 1996; and (2) Grand Rounds in the Department of Internal Medicine, University of Washington, Seattle, November 14, 1996, in a talk titled "Physicians' Response to Mass Tragedy." Portions of chapter 5 were previously published in the *Journal for the Psychoanalysis of Culture and Society*, and are reprinted with permission of Dr. Mark Bracher, editor.

1

Introduction

Euphemisms are not strange, exotic, rare creatures from foreign lands. They are not the private property of literature and national politics. They are garden variety organizational features and are part of every-day life. The trouble is, we usually recognize—awaken from—them af-ter they have done their damage. Consider the company Acme Widgets (AW). For several years, AW had inexplicably gone into a slump. Pro-duction, profit, quality, morale, all were down. The board of directors decided that things had just gotten too low, especially for a company that (like Northwest Airlines) once was the gold standard of its market. During their search for a new, more dynamic CEO they found one young executive, "a man with a vision," named Hiram Wald.

Wald inspired them into thinking they could recover from their dol-drums and recover their Number One place in the market. They felt like losers who once were the unrivaled winners in their field. Wald vowed to make them uncontested winners again. He would banish their sense of shame. He promised them the "new vision" they were eagerly looking for. His presentations, like his manner, were dazzling, self-confident, state-of-the-art audiovisuals (despite the prominence of misspellings!). His slides and overheads were as impeccable as his wool-and-silk suits. He promised to lead AW back to better than their former prominence. From the initial interviews, the board called him "charismatic." Many said that for them, "Hiram walked on water." He was unanimously chosen.

At the agreement of the new CEO, the board, and upper-level managers, Hiram Wald would be allowed to pursue the organizational vision, to be their visionary, while they tended to daily, more mundane details of running the company and implementing his new ideas. As time went on, there were a few trouble signs, but no one bothered talking with him about them. Wald's enthusiastically declared "open-door policy" simply had no time for them. His door was often closed because he had distinguished out-of-town visitors or was busy at his computer with some master plan. He was often on extended national and international trips in behalf of AW. At the meetings he did have with the managers, he was more speaker than listener. They explained to themselves that he was too busy to be bothered with their petty details or qualms. What they came to call "the black box" of corporate finance was entirely off limits to them. He demanded that they accept on faith that he was looking out for them all. They accepted that they were accountable to him, but he was not accountable to them.

Nonetheless, they were still enthralled with Wald's enthusiasm, his promises, and told themselves and each other that he was "our visionary" and they were his "troops on the ground." For instance: "He thinks way ahead of us. He is a futurist. His job is to guide AW to the distant future. Our job is tomorrow, to handle the day-to-day details. He's way up there in the stratosphere, thinking great thoughts we're sure will pan out and make us great again."

For several years, the CEO himself, those who had appointed him, and the majority of the workers at AW routinely used the words "vision" and "visionary" to describe Wald, his role, his promise, and their reliance on him to turn the company around. The more ambitious and audacious he became, the more dependent and loyal they became. Occasional disaffection with his leadership, or with the growing gap between his words and the company's deeds, was silenced, either by one's own self-doubt and fear, or by peers' rebukes. The nearly unanimous "win-at-any-price" attitude was buttressed by the conviction held by his subordinates that they would indeed "win" big, that the "price" of their total suspension of critical judgment was worth it, and that their leader who flew high above them was really looking out for their collective interests. No one dared to stand up to Wald and confront him with their concern about his expenditures of time and money. Where censorship and silence did not work, some bullied and demoralized employees simply left to find work elsewhere. AW came to be called "Wald's Forest" (in German, "Wald" means "forest").

By the end of the third year of his administration, a ground swell of doubt, second thoughts, and concerns about conflict-of-interest had risen from salaried employees to midlevel managers, senior executives, and members of the board. By the end of the fourth year, Wald was taken to task at fiery meetings with the board and senior executives. He was quietly eased out. All his promises, his salesmanship, sweet talk, enthusiasm, dazzling computerized presentations, and insistence that he needed more time for the vision to become reality no longer worked their charismatic magic upon those who until just recently had so staunchly defended him and AW's need for him to make them great again. Productivity, profit, quality, morale were all lower than before he had taken over.

Toward the end, several managers and board members had the insight and courage to realize that their own organization's neediness and decline, in comparison with the prior "golden era," had made them succumb to Hiram Wald's promises and plans, and had led them to discount their own early misgivings. They believed him because they wanted, needed, to believe him. Four years before, they felt nearly defeated as a company. Wald had promised them a new age of victory. They were ashamed; he vowed to make them proud. They "bought into" what he had to "sell" because their vulnerability corresponded so perfectly with his grandiosity. He had promised to be their company's savior. They, in turn, had wanted desperately to believe in him. They had reasoned away his disrespect, often contempt, for them. He had cavalierly exploited their dependency on him. For a time, they were "made for each other," until they saw through Wald's exploitation and opportunism. (For a theoretical discussion of organizational and larger processes like these, see La Barre 1972; Volkan 1980; Diamond 1993).

The words *vision* and *visionary* now took on a new, dark hue. No more did they serve as the bright lights managers and employees had used to blind themselves from reality. They had served as euphemisms that ruled and distorted four years of AW's history, euphemisms that they could not afford emotionally to see through or decode because they needed to believe in him to restore AW and their pride. *Vision* and *visionary* no longer "worked" as euphemisms. If anything, they became terms of derision, of embarrassment. At AW, they were rarely used again. It came to me of little surprise that in the next corporate search, the kind of CEO sought was a low key, maintenance-style bureaucrat, a "meat and potatoes man," somebody "with his feet on the ground."

RATIONALE

Why a book on euphemism in *workplace* organizations? That is, in businesses, factories, corporations, hospitals, universities, government agencies. What seems at first glance to be so small, so incidental, a subject can take us to the heart of the experience of being a member of an organization, and to vital decision making that organization members engage in and carry out. Euphemism is not a footnote, but is part of the main text of organizational life. A study of language goes beyond language. This book begins with the workplace, but it does not end there. Workplace social units are bounded, but permeably so. Euphemism turns out to be a key to unlock well-kept secrets of organizational behavior, of bureaucratic behavior, of American (USA) behavior, and of human behavior alike.

Euphemism is not the exclusive domain of the linguistic specialist or of the mythic scholar who supposedly has the luxury of living the high road above grubby practicality. As a figure of speech, euphemism is far from inconsequential. It is a figure of intentionality and a distraction from that intentionality. It often has dire consequences for the speaker and those spoken to alike. It is as much a hard fact in decision making as are hard numbers. Whatever else we learn from the century-old Freudian revolution, things are not what they seem, what we need them to seem. Euphemism makes the obscurantism of masking even further into an obscenely fine art: we are commanded to believe uncritically that things are *only* what they seem. Euphemism can be a deadly weapon that passes for a child's toy.

For instance, we do not say directly that organizations fire or lay off large numbers of people. We say instead that we downsized or RIFed an organization (RIF stands for "Reduction in Force"). We say that we trim the fat, even cut down to the bone, to make the workplace lean and mean. And not only the bounded unit of the workplace: the Republican Party's 1994 "Contract with America" was based in part on a political vow to "downsize government," a torch that Speaker of the House of Representatives Newt Gingrich has carried zealously following the triumphant election of November 1994. The boundary between, say, workplace organization, electoral political psychology, and national culture is highly permeable and fluid. When we think and speak in terms of downsizing and reinventing corporate organizations and national government, people become machines and systems of machines, inanimate things, interchangeable, replaceable parts, figures on a spreadsheet. We codify our view of people in the words we use: we reengineer organizations, retool workers, restructure workplaces, delayer hierarchies, and flatten organizations.

There are "human factors" behind the most rarefied technological and managerial facets of organizational life. For that matter, even "engineering" people or organizations (like "reengineering" them) is a way of thinking about people and their work relationships. The material for the interpretations offered in this book is provided in the culture itself (if I may be allowed to reify for a moment, to make the point). The interpretation is in the folklore, in the language, in the best-selling business books, already (Freud and Oppenheim 1958; Dundes 1984). The interpretation about culture and symbolism is not some "add on." It is a matter of seeing and hearing, of feeling, what is there.

For instance, Joseph B. White wrote an illuminating article on Michael Hammer and his popular concept of organizational "reengineering," in *The Wall Street Journal*, November 26, 1996 (front page, right hand, lead article). The article, on Hammer's belated recognition of the importance of "people issues" as well as "engineering issues" in corporate change, gave strong hints at personal issues of Michael Hammer's own behind his organizational doctrines and strategies. In 1993 Michael Hammer and James Champy published the best-selling book *Reengineering the Corporation: A Manifesto for Business Revolution.* Hammer's celebrated 1990 *Harvard Business Review* article was titled "Reengineering Work: Don't Automate, Obliterate." The child of Holocaust survivors, Hammer speaks of "a common sense of mission" among them. "You feel responsible for all those who might have been, but aren't" (in White 1997: A13). Shortly after this quotation, White described Hammer's presentation style,

> Like many a college lecturer, he spices his presentations with one-liners, occasional barnyard expletives and outrageous comments. Talking about what to do with middle managers who undermine re-engineering efforts, he says: "I sort of believe in public hangings for that." Then, assuming the role of corporate sheriff, he points his finger like a pistol and plays out a scene: "What do you think about what we're doing? You don't like it? BANG!" (1997: A13)

It is not "wild analysis" to see in Michael Hammer's role plays and language a replaying and reliving of Holocaust images, here not as victim but as victimizer, as often happens with the terrorized who identify with their persecutors, and who then obligate the next generation to "remember" only by traumatizing them first. The impersonal, depersonalized language of massive corporate change, of change-by-obliteration, of public hangings and point-blank executions is from a man clearly with a mission, in whom the unconscious speaks as clearly as the conscious. I am not claiming from a single newspaper article to know a great deal about the shaman of reengineering; and from psychoanalysis, I know that at the unconscious level, ideologies, like dreams, are condensations of many ideas, wishes, and feelings. But, from this documentary source alone (including its presence as a leading business newspaper's lead article), I can confidently say that, whatever else reengineering is, it is *also* about the symbolism of destruction to live human beings.

There is by now a rich and growing literature that documents how decision making, policy formulation, strategic planning, problem solving, leadership and followership, and day-to-day role performance in the workplace are not governed entirely by rational, objective, pragmatic, conscious, reality-oriented concerns, mission statements, and strategic plans. Mediating—often contaminating, if not sabotaging—these conscious formulations are often unstated values, fantasies, beliefs, ideology, expectations, worldviews, attitudes, symbols, rituals, feelings, affects, agendas, and the like, which unconsciously shape organizational thought and behavior. This transdisciplinary work builds on the writing and research of such scholars as Sigmund Freud, Melanie Klein, George Devereux, Weston La Barre, George De Vos, Melford Spiro, Ernest Becker, Richard A. Koenigsberg, W. R. Bion, Donald Winnicott, Arnold Modell, Thomas Ogden, L. B. Boyer, James Grotstein, Vamik Volkan, Michael Balint, Elliott Jaques, Harry Levinson, Michael Diamond, Seth Allcorn, Howell Baum, M.F.R. Kets de Vries, to name but a handful.

From my experience as organizational consultant and participant observer in academic medical settings for twenty-five years, the role played by *euphemism* in organizing workplace thought, feeling, and behavior remains a little-charted, largely neglected, landscape. With this book, I seek both to help "fill the void" in the management, business, and behavioral science literature, and to identify, through theory and in-depth case studies, how immense and dangerous a mental "territory" euphemism in fact occupies in the organizational culture of the 1990s. Chronologically, this study is a sequel to *The Human Cost of a Management Failure: Organizational Downsizing at General Hospital* which I co-authored with Seth Allcorn, Howell Baum, and Michael A. Diamond (1996). What I have learned about the prominent place euphemism plays in downsizing applies in many other, less noisy, facets of organizational behavior.

Similarly, we do not talk directly of rationing or limiting medical care. We speak instead of managing healthcare. In fact, there is little that we Americans do not try to "manage" (which is to say, force under human control as functions, not as whole people). *Management* or *managing* is a key to organizational and wider cultural behavior that includes industry and business, but is far from limited to these social units and institutions. In medical care institutions, for example, it is becoming customary to speak of a "panel of patients" and "production quotas" per unit of time in an outpatient clinic. The shadow of Frederick Winslow Taylor's (1911) principles of scientific management, and of interpersonal atomism, is long.

There is an intimate link between euphemism and suffering, a link that euphemism itself denies. When we as Americans speak of "violence" or "anger" in the workplace, we usually think of guns, knives, bombs, and of equipment sabotage. We do not consider the destructive power of words, declared or thought, of murderous glances or laughs, of exclusions from meetings, of exclusion from access to the most up-to-date computers or information. Yet, words and their associated feelings and gestures hurt, maim, induce "physical" and "mental" symptoms, injure, even kill. If it seems strange to the reader that I consider euphemism to be a form of violence and anger in the workplace, I hope this bewilderment will only be temporary (see also Allcorn 1994). Perhaps even managed care and downsizing, as much as a spray of machine gun fire or a bomb, can be construed as part of our "violence in the workplace," albeit psychological rather than physical violence. They injure the soul, are as hurtful as injury to the body.

Further, in an era in which anger and violence in the workplace are increasingly important subjects for study and consultation, the part played by euphemism as a handmaiden of human destructiveness deserves closer and more comprehensive scrutiny and analysis. Finally, the analysis of euphemism in workplace structure forces us to look at its psychosocial dynamics beyond the organizational unit, and to explore the permeable boundary between organizational culture in a mixed capitalist society, and the wider national, if not international, cultural currents.

EUPHEMISM AND MYSTIFICATION BY LANGUAGE

Euphemism is a deft, elusive, and powerful trickster we use to deceive ourselves, to hide our own motives and feelings from ourselves. It is evasion we make to look like directness. In its beguiling way, it is frightfully precise. Euphemism can serve as a fundamental organizing principle of workplace and other culture. On National Public Radio's "All Things Considered" evening program on December 23, 1996, the respected news commentator Daniel Schorr presented an entire essay on current and recent American political euphemisms (ranging from House of Representatives Speaker Newt Gingrich to President Bill Clinton to former President Richard Nixon), which he called "Scandal-speak." Far from being a trivial footnote about words, their meanings, people's intentions, and use of language in organizational life, the study of euphemism is about how we humans devise a deliberately slippery language to justify to ourselves and to others, if not to impose on them, the degradation of categories of people, if not the literal extinction of their lives. The mystifying, official political language called "Newspeak" in George Orwell's 1949 novel *1984* is a widely referred to symbol and classic text of euphemism. The science fiction–environmental thriller movie *Soylent Green* (MGM, 1973) paints an even bleaker view of the euphemism-dominated, imagined future. But no euphemism, no language, has an independent biological life of its own. We—people—invent, use, and choose words to suit thought, feeling, wish, and defense.

Part of the sinister work of euphemism is that we are so much in its thrall that we are certain we are talking about reality, when we are in fact talking about our imagination we have legislated into reality. Through euphemism, we replace, we override, and reinvent reality, by the magic of language. In contemporary corporations, desperation and greed are often expressed and disguised as "the bottom line." By cultural imperative, there is no "bottom line" (that is, account or meaning) beneath "the (business) bottom line" of short-term profit. Sometimes the means toward achieving this bottom line is "downsizing" or "reduction in force" or "RIFing" (verb, noun, gerund, and acronym in one, testimony to the dexterity of language and wish).

Yesterday's faithful, valuable, often long-standing, co-workers, if not friends, become tomorrow's "fat" to be "trimmed" and forgotten so that the company will be "lean and mean." They are now disposable waste. Organizations dominated by images of "reengineering" and "restructuring" are lured into reducing people and whole lives into machinery parts and mechanical functions. People become a "workforce" of functions, machines, and computers who work machines and computers. In some workplaces, notions of "open-door policy" and "participatory workplace" or "management" are authentic; in others, they are sham. Where they serve as oppression and deception, they are euphemisms.

To understand euphemism in workplaces and beyond, we must be prepared to question everything we take for granted. To borrow a widely used image: *fish must start asking questions about the water in which they swim*. We must begin by defamiliarizing the familiar, by making the "normal" the subject of critical inquiry. We must wonder of it, "How bizarre!" Consider next that all-encompassing word *manage* (manager, management, managed, managing, managerial). What, for instance, does it mean to "manage" workers, to "manage" people and their health problems, to "manage" resources, to "manage" caring, and so on? Within and beyond the institution of biomedicine where I teach, the use of *to manage* as a verb, *management* as a noun, and *managed* as an adjective have become so widespread in daily discourse as to suggest that their referents are not primarily medical or business, but far more broadly cultural. That is, the more the inner and outer worlds feel hopelessly "out of control," the more we press to restore that control via the idiom of "managing" everything and everyone. When we say "manage," we think we know (at all levels) what we are talking about; the trouble is, we don't. Whatever else *manage* is, it is a euphemism, and as I hope this book will demonstrate, an especially toxic one.

At a national level in Nazi Germany, the systematic collection and annihilation of a people become phrased as "The Final Solution to the Jewish Problem," and in the war-soaked Bosnia-Herzegovina of the 1990s, "ethnic cleansing." It does not require any stretch of the imagination to see, in the management and administration of genocide, a similar translation and simplification of all life-anxiety into a problem of total *control*. One magically regains control through the elimination of those who are defined as the source of the loss of control. Renewal of the life of the national "body" is achieved via massive sacrifice (death). In a certainly less literal manner, this is also the American mode of staying in business, of survival, of keeping one's corporation "viable," "competitive." What we in our mixed capitalist economy insist is "only business, so don't take it personally," is in fact a subtle act of war.

For some persons and some organizations to survive, others must die, at least symbolically. As groups of people, workplace organizations, like religions, ethnic groups, and nations, try desperately to purchase (temporary) immortality through endless rounds of sacrifice. The conscious logic is: "If we cut enough we will survive; we will become profitable." But the unconscious meaning is far different: too often that sacrifice is organizational self-destruction. If euphemisms are lies, they are also desperate lures.

In any case, through euphemism, persons become transmuted via language into disposable categories of things, and their disposal is well veiled and rationalized. Thus in workplaces and in other social units, euphemism comes to serve as a governing force that justifies action and sustains power. It is far mightier than one is supposed to think: therein lies its subtle power and danger.

SITUATING THE AUTHOR IN THE STUDY

This book situates the author and the author's work-history as organizational consultant and "member," in relation to the subject under discussion. I did not set out to study euphemism as a "subject." It is only via the wisdom of the "retrospectoscope," one of physicians' favorite tools of understanding, that I can visualize the theme that emerges from all the variations I have seen. Via the rear-view mirror, I can look back through my life and professional activities and recognize: "Yes, *that* was a euphemism." Professional is always also in some way personal: it is from having been run over by a freight train, so to speak, that I become vitally interested in trains, train wrecks, and train safety! Perhaps we can learn from what we could not recognize at the time, but now, retrospectively, can—and inflict less suffering in the future. Further, not only does every subject or topic have an author, but the author's own roles, experiences, and his or her emotional response (countertransference, in psychoanalytic language) are crucial tools of understanding: they can distort and illumine.

Just as this is a book, then, on what I have learned about organizational language, and about how I have learned about that language, it is likewise a book about the redemption of language—and of workplaces—from destructiveness and self-destructiveness we engage in via euphemism. It is about the reclamation of language from lie, from deception and self-deception. It is about the annihilation and renewal of meaning in the workplace. It is about understanding subtle violence in the workplace and the search for the emotional wellsprings of that violence.

To situate an author, any author, relative to the subject is to inform the reader about both. I have learned much about organizational membership and consulting from my own sense of helplessness, my own rage, and my own unconscious and later conscious guilt over my inability to prevent, or even comprehend, psychological torture and its acceptance as modus operandi, individually and institution-wide, in workplaces where I have been employed and where I have consulted. Euphemism has often been the seemingly innocent vehicle of that quiet terror. My long struggle for my own voice, and against my frightened voicelessness, thus found in the study of organizational euphemism the convergence of the private and the public. Personally and professionally—and ethnically, as a Jew—I know the high price of mystification.

Let me offer a brief, quite ordinary, example. About a decade ago, I consulted with a large healthcare corporation whose ambitious, controlling, micromanaging, voraciously intrusive leader had driven off about a half-dozen midlevel managers who had been fiercely loyal to him. They felt betrayed and abandoned, "chewed and spit out" by him, as one manager said, after they had unquestioningly filled his needs and he reneged on career promises he had made to them in exchange for their loyalty. Many demoralized, bitter people throughout the organization referred to their departure as "the exodus." Several years later, the same CEO triumphantly concluded a revival-style upper management retreat by saying something similar to this: "When several managers left the company around the same time three years ago, many people called it 'the *exodus*.' I would like us to think of it from here on as the *liberation*!" With that, participants left the room for the parking lot and their cars, as if a sports team or troops had just been given a pep talk by their coach or general and were headed out renewed onto the field of play or of battle. I felt sickened, disgusted, tricked, and betrayed by a master-manipulator of dependency, shame, pride, and guilt.

I knew the history of deceit he and many of his subordinates were trying to erase by relabeling it and making that relabeled story an organizationally obligatory lie. In small ways I tried to help a number of organizational staff to retain the courage of their own memory and perception. Still, this moment and the CEO's shrewd and bold "rectification of names" or historical revisionism was a lesson in euphemism I would never forget. I witnessed the birth, rapid growth, and institutionalization of a dangerous, if consoling, lie that immediately became obligatory organizational truth. Namely, that we had been rid of rubbish, and not thrown away gold. The moment was a template for many to come.

EUPHEMISM AND ORGANIZATIONAL DESTRUCTIVENESS

In *The Anatomy of Human Destructiveness*, Erich Fromm (1973) describes "the technical-bureaucratic nature of modern large-scale destructiveness" (348), ranging from airplane "crews who drop bombs," those who "processed" millions of people to their deaths in concentration camp gas chambers, and the more ordinary marketplace logic in which everything is a commodity to be used, and used up. Consider, for instance, the widespread use of such notions as "human resources" and "labor," less a person than a thing or commodity. We treat the living as though they were, and should be, dead, inanimate objects to be consumed. Such "treatment" (or mistreatment), via euphemism's magical powers, comes to feel reasonable and morally justified. Specifically, Fromm notes "the technicalization of destruction, and with it the removal of the full affective [that is, emotional, conscious and unconscious, HFS] recognition of what one is doing. Once this process has been fully established there is no limit to destructiveness because nobody *destroys*; one only serves the machine for programmed—hence, apparently rational—purposes" (1973: 348, emphasis in original). We become—identify with—machines, computers, spreadsheets, bottom lines, so as not to know what we are doing, and why we are compelled to do it.

Managed care and downsizing are expressions of a vast *cultural revolution* akin to those we usually associate with China in the 1960s, the U.S.S.R. in the mid-1930s, and Cambodia in the 1970s. If our purges are bloodless, they are purges nonetheless, no matter how "merely" metaphorical and euphemized they are. Ours as well as theirs have casualties, except that we hide ours better. The differences notwithstanding, what they have in common and share with our symbolic revolutions is the thoroughgoing destruction of meaning, the rewriting of history, and the elimination (by various means) of any and all opposing voices.

In all such cultural revolutions, a "rectification of names" and a "rectification of language" are an inherent part of the process of falsifying both past and present. Our own organizational, and more widely, cultural, totalitarianism requires the euphemism. In the United States, our euphemized, sanitized, impersonal, culturally stylized solution is the spreadsheet! Euphemism is a crucial protagonist in this drama of destructiveness. It is one of our most potent "covers" or "smoke screens" for our intentions.

The *timing* of this study of organizational euphemism is part of the very *content* of the study. Content and context are inseparable. The abject depersonalization, regimentation, degradation, and dehumanization of "the workplace" in American life is now occurring at precisely the time that employed people ("workers" of all collars) invest increasing time and emotional expectation in the workplace. It is the era of two-income families, of sixty-and-more-hour workweeks, of the expectation that workers will give increasingly more of themselves for less. If social institutions beyond the family have always built on childhood-rooted family relationships, fantasies, wishes, and sentiments (La Barre 1951, 1954; Stein and Fox 1985), the workplace now is heir to the burden of even heavier hopes and transferences. For many, "work" at a money-paying "job" is more "like family" than "home." We Americans often expect the workplace to be the home and family, the intimacy, that we never had. Its function is thus reparative (to fix, repair our lives, now if not retrospectively), as well as income-generating. Turning from the fragile family to the workplace for emotional nurturance, we find in its place a rejecting, brutalizing, abandoning, annihilating, isolating style among leaders, managers, and co-workers alike, and nowhere left to turn. If we can (and should) acknowledge that it is unrealistic for us to expect any institution to bear this much emotional freight—especially one in which we are expected to produce "work"—we can also say that workplaces are also a major source of contemporary degradation of the human spirit.

Two psychologically opposing fantasies now collide: (1) the wish for far too much emotionally from a workplace organization, and (2) the fear that one can expect absolutely nothing from the organization. Yet one is expected nonetheless to give the organization everything of oneself, to the point of allowing oneself to be consumed by the devouring organization.

Concurrent with this collision, or divergence, is the additional fact that the supposedly caring professions (health and mental health professionals, and the host of allied health workers), pressured by the corporate organizations that employ them, are becoming less and less interested in their traditional role of "relieving human pain and suffering," and more in short-term profit. Worse, at the same time that this withdrawal of institutional support for health coverage and well-being is occurring, workplaces, via mass firings and endless disorienting reorganizations, and further via the decrease of health insurance coverage offered to employees, are if anything inflicting even greater pain and suffering than before. Put colloquially, there are even more train wrecks but even fewer rescue squads to cover them.

The pain and suffering (to continue the commonplace pairing of terms that purport to distinguish between "objective" data and "subjective" experience, a false dichotomy) are not, to our eyes, as flagrant as was the brutal treatment of coal miners and steelworkers early in the twentieth century. But the assault on the human spirit such as is currently happening is no less brutal because it cannot be measured the same way—or because we are unwilling to see it in front of us. It at first seems odd, but is not, that a study of massive social change in American workplace culture should in fact also be a meditation on what theologians and philosophers have long called the problem of evil (see Alford 1990, 1997).

ROADMAP FOR THE BOOK

The reader deserves a reliable roadmap of this book from the outset of the journey. This book is organized into six chapters. Chapter 1, the Introduction, situates euphemism in language, defines euphemism, explores its rhetorical and unconscious operations, and describes its place in organizational and broader social thinking, decision making, policy, and action. The Introduction also draws upon George Orwell's novel *1984*, and the Nazi Holocaust, as illustrations of the ominous social power of euphemism. Chapters 2, 3, and 4 are the core of the book, consisting of three case-like studies: in chapter 2, of downsizing; in chapter 3, of managed care; and in chapter 4, of the many sentimentalizing terms used immediately after the bombing of the Alfred P. Murrah Federal Building (itself a workplace and site of many workplaces) on April 19, 1995, in Oklahoma City—a place that is part of the Great Plains' indomitable work ethic. The final chapter, the Conclusion, not only discusses implications of this study for recognizing and unearthing organizational euphemisms, but also offers approaches to dispelling euphemisms' clench-hold—without the magical thinking of rescue fantasy or the reversal of time.

I conclude this book with a paradox for workplace organizational communication—indeed for communication in any group. What cannot be talked about must be talked about. What must not be talked about must be talked about openly. What cannot and must not be felt must be given its hearing. We must have the courage to break the spell of our cherished workplace self-protectiveness. And such self-honesty, such reflection, is more difficult in groups than individually, one-on-one (dyadically) (see Bion 1959). The mask of euphemism must be removed in order to reveal the disavowedly hidden face(s) behind it. To recover from the pain, we must first feel it. If we all will suffer anxiety, shame, and guilt a little more, if we can bear to internalize or "own" our own aggression and feelings of disappointment, we will suffer less from the prodigious effort and time required to keep our euphemisms in place. As the mask of euphemism lifts, so will the oppressive weight of destructiveness also be lifted. There are no guarantees. But we are doomed to increased workplace accidents, absenteeism, alcoholism and drug use, illness, and violence, and to diminished morale, productivity, and profit, if we keep trying to solve the wrong (unconsciously misdefined) problem (see Stein 1996).

YES, BUT . . . (SOME RESERVATIONS ABOUT THIS APPROACH)

At the outset, I wish to anticipate and briefly address a number of the reader's legitimate concerns, reservations, or skepticism about my arguments. I will even admit that I had to persuade myself to adopt so foreign, so culturally counterintuitive, a view of three major areas of traumatic organizational change: downsizing, managed care, and the bombing of the Federal Building in Oklahoma City. I had to do much rethinking and soul searching to persuade myself that we, as a nation, were in the throes of a moral crisis, even a spiritual crisis, in the guise of a strictly business crisis. To begin with, much, though certainly not all, of my research, consulting, and teaching—which is to say the source of my data—come from health care and academic medical organizations. Is there any evidential basis for a wider cultural statement or claim beyond those organizations that are service-based, nurturing types? Is downsizing (etc.) as emotionally devastating and dislocating in steel, automotive, or dishwasher manufacturing industries as it is in hospitals and clinics? With the intensive case study and the comparative method as a foundation for scientific generalization and testing, what may I legitimately generalize and conclude about the experience of downsizing and corporate members' well-being?

Surely, one might surmise, the work of doctoring and of healthcare administrators is not the same as building computers or washing machines. There are at least two types of "work" for a livelihood: one is where "My work is my life, or at least my way of life, not just a paying job"; and the other where "My work is just a job, just a paycheck." At the inner level of experience, "a job" with high pay and no security is surely not the same as "my work [career] is my life." I have heard members of three-generation families who work in a steel mill say, "I am a steelworker." This means that steelworking is a vital part of personal identity, not only role function, as in "making steel," something one does rather than is.

To continue this line of argument: for-profit, entrepreneur-driven organizations have—ostensibly—different values and interpersonal styles from not-for-profit organizations. Surely organizations that run on driven, aggressive, cold-blooded, entrepreneurial surplus-seeking logic are not the same as those driven by mission statements of service, nurturing, caring, and less-is-enough. Surely the difference between these institutional types is qualitative and not merely quantitative— so that mass layoffs, constant worker reshufflings, and diminished healthcare benefits in the former would be experienced as far less devastating than those in the latter. Presumably, values between the institutional types differ vastly; people expect factories to be less humane work environments than hospitals.

But things here are not what they seem. Our categories and reality far from match perfectly. "Sameness" between institutions is often illusory, and is often a matter of the level of abstraction—that is, how and where we are looking. Biomedicine has claimed to be far more personal a business than, say, coal or iron ore mining. But biomedicine has always been an entrepreneurial, even fiercely competitive, business, even prior to the mid-1980s' era of open advertising. The age of corporate, for-profit medicine has made this explicitly and publicly so. Under grueling, if not also cruel, working conditions, mines and mills nonetheless became a family tradition and occupational way of life for two-, three-, and four-generation father-son successions (not unlike the family farm, where work and family were fused). For a steel mill to close, as has become epidemic in the northeastern U.S. "rust belt," is for whole communities to lose a cherished way of life and to reel into often frozen mourning—not only for an individual to lose long-term employment and a paycheck.

Many cynical, opportunistic people of the younger, so-called, "Generation X," now in their twenties and early thirties, work hard at their jobs, give their skills, but not their hearts and loyalties, to their workplaces in modern corporations. They have learned to expect no long-term reciprocity of commitment from the company in return. Giving on both parts is full of withholding. The young already know they are expendable quasi-soldiers, capable of being sacrificed for the organization at a moment's notice. They are social castaways, adult latchkey children, who trade their skill but not their soul. The prior "social contract" of loyalty in exchange for job security, which had characterized industries and businesses for at least two-thirds of a century, has been rescinded and violated in countless trades and professions. Today, one often reads of the deprofessionalization and fragmentation of complex roles and worker identities into supposedly constituent, and cheaper, parts. Fragmentation is met with, defended against by, further fragmentation. A reciprocity resting on dependency, if not mutual dependence, has given way to mutual exploitation, crass opportunism, and depredation. In colleges and universities, where "teaching" was once an honored career and inseparable from the idea of "teacher," courses and whole curricula are being made into so much piecework. From part-time, gypsy-like, "adjunct" university professors who are paid without benefits per course, to salaried, highly skilled, full-time corporate computer and information specialists who can be terminated at any time, we are becoming once again a nation of pieceworkers. The temporariness is built into the job, as is the lack of long-term obligation on anyone's part.

Anyone can be occupationally and culturally orphaned anywhere now; it is our expectations and values that discriminate between, say, healthcare and computers. Even such a term as the "industrialization" of medicine somewhat misses the mark (though it is correct with respect to role fragmentation), because the same callous impersonality that has come to represent businesses and industries in recent decades has culturally diffused into the supposedly caring professions and communication businesses. Even industry is psychologically de-industrialized in spirit! Across the board, leaders and CEOs know bottom lines far better than they know the product and process of their company.

When managers and employees of numerous businesses describe to me their workplace experience of the past decade in the language of the Holocaust, I have learned not to dismiss and discredit their analogy as trivialization, but instead to listen carefully to the idiom of suffering and horror that is being evoked. The sense of imminent danger, of free-floating dread, of helplessness and hopelessness, and of extinction—if from "merely" symbolic rather than "real" danger—makes the metaphor emotionally plausible, even as the analogy is imperfect.

How do we know? For purposes of what Fred Eggan called "controlled comparison" (1954) of social units, consider the following observations from American popular culture. The mid-1990s witnessed a series of feature or cover stories and lead articles, in weekly newsmagazines and national newspapers, all severely reappraising the received wisdom about the human costs, the ethics, and even the assumed profitability of downsizing, restructuring, reengineering, and related concepts and managerial methods. In this world, "managed" health care becomes only a mask for profit; "care" has been cast out. Clearly, the second thoughts are not only about health care, but about the logic of the entire business ethos.

During this same time, Scott Adams' newspaper comic strip "Dilbert" and his 1996 book *The DILBERT Principle* and its successors depicted, mocked, and caricatured the dominant management and organizational change styles in vogue. "Dilbert" as an art form can been seen as culturally pathognomonic or diagnostic for the way of life it evokes and rebukes. Its wide appeal, measurable by syndication and book sales (not to mention its presence in photocopy form as social commentary on break-room bulletin boards and refrigerator doors), cross-cuts a wide array of organizational types, "aggressively capitalist" and "nurturantly service-oriented" alike. Adams' genius in his characters' words, gestures, and facial expression is to reveal the viciousness and brutality behind supposedly inexorably good business sense. His ever-present image of the workplace "cubicle" depicts the austere, lifeless, mental geography of confinement and constriction. In this world, work is prison with pay. "Dilbert" at once parades our euphemisms before us and exposes them. The cartoonist is in fact a moralist.

A few examples (without full benefit of cartoon) must suffice. In a 1995 "Dilbert" cartoon, Dogbert, acting as a downsizing consultant, demonstrates how to notify employees that their jobs will be outsourced by having his consulting partner, Ratbert, bend over. At the edge of a desktop, Dogbert kicks Ratbert in the buttocks into the trash can. In the final scene, the "Pointy-Haired Boss" asks Dogbert, "How do I get them all stooped over?" Dogbert recommends "a program of very bad ergonomics."

In a 1996 cartoon, Catbert, the Evil Human Relations Director, advises Wally, a stressed-out worker, to start smoking cigarettes, since in that way he would "have frequent company-sanctioned breaks throughout the day." Wally asks: "This is your strategy for downsizing, isn't it?" In another 1996 "Dilbert" cartoon, Catbert's tail is twitching, which is his sign that it is time to write more evil company policies. This time the directive is: "Employees must wear shoes that are one size smaller than their feet." Later, "This is my favorite part: 'We must do this to be competitive.'" Finally, to the inquiry as to whether anyone has complained about the "footsizing" program, Catbert replies: "I haven't listened to a single complaint."

Finally, in 1997, "Dilbert" features a sequence of three worsening medical scenarios, each presided over by the "Pointy-Haired Boss" and representing corporate bad news being announced by the boss: In 1985, "We're replacing the company doctor with a registered nurse"; in 1990, "We fired the nurse and put the aspirin and tourniquets in the vending machine"; and in 1995, as the boss stands with a mallet concealed behind his back, "We've been asked to increase vending machine revenue by fifteen percent."

The success of "Dilbert," in sum, is a reliable social barometer or index of mass discontent. It resonates with the cynicism, the mistrust, the dread in the workplace—many workplaces. Adams' comic strip is popular humor's closest approximation to social protest. "Dilbert" tells us as well as, if not better than, any essayist of our time that people are nonpersons, only "workers" and "producers." They are only as good as they are useful, so long as one can exact work from them—then toss them aside as disposable, expellable waste. If the reader objects that I, the author, make too much of a mere comic strip and its creator, I can only reply that the meanings I infer are those mass culture has created. The data are already there; I am only pointing them out. In a sense, American culture has created Scott Adams and the "Dilbert" characters in which we recognize ourselves—and pay to recognize this portrait of ourselves. Or, to put it differently: we give voice (and dollars, checks, and credit cards) to one who serves as our voice and mouthpiece.

My argument about euphemism, language, and corporate identity is thus widely generalizable precisely because "Dilbert" speaks to, gives form to, a whole way of life that has come to be regarded as rational business-as-usual. "Dilbert" unmasks our self-deceptions and smoke screens. Adams refuses to go along with the crowd. He tells us what we know but are afraid to admit directly: things are as bad as, if not worse than, they seem. His is one rare voice and pen that does not aspire to "put a [different] spin" on organizational life—to use a popular phrase—but to expose the cruelty of this way of life. This well-oiled cruelty helps us also to understand the wide appeal of the Holocaust metaphor by those experiencing downsizing, managed change, and other forms of corporate WorkSpeak. Through hyperbole, Adams shows the destructiveness behind the euphemisms we use.

Consider, for my final observation, the very term "spin" itself—and its appeal as a popular rhetorical form (as in, "Let me put a different spin on the problem . . ."). *Spin* is one of those slick, slippery, cunning, mind-numbing euphemisms against which "Dilbert" tacitly rails. To "put a new spin on" some subject is, on the surface, nothing more than to offer a new perspective, a novel, illuminating viewpoint. Here, *spin* is but a new word for an old concept. But in the world of cunning "spins," words are subtle weapons of manipulation, of gaining advantage over another, not of truth telling or of the search for truth. Rhetoric becomes reduced to "sales," and all meaning becomes subordinated to selling, which is conquest-by-business.

To "spin" is to persuade by deception in the guise of telling the truth. Spin, then, is the ultimate euphemism—and diagnostic symbol of euphemism—of our age. There is no reality, only "spin," and my spin at that. "Spin" is a masterful idiom of expression for our socially fragmented, worldwide Balkanized planet as well as workplace. Each faction asserts that "spin" (its spin) is truth—extreme relativism and postmodernism become corporate, business, ethic, national policy, politics, and economy. "Spin" is hidden agenda that must be heard as open and honest. "Black-is-really-white" is "a different spin" or "a positive spin." With enough "spin," anything can be made to look good.

"Spin" is at the core of a contemporary style of entrepreneurial survivalism (everyone for him- or herself), where there is no sense of communal, let alone global, responsibility. For example, a legislator invokes the wish to "balance the budget," as a euphemism for pitting young versus old. There is little sense of "we're in this together; let's try to find a common solution." There are competing factions, each acting as though it were a society, a species, even a planet, unto itself. George Orwell, author of *1984* and *Animal Farm*, would have recognized, and labeled, our "spin" as *propaganda*, where critical thinking itself becomes forbidden, where only official positions are allowed, and where one says something only by indirection.

In "spin," euphemistic thinking is operationalized and culturally canonized. In it we glibly, slickly turn one thing into another—the medieval alchemists' dream of making gold. Clients, far too worshipful at the altar of expertise, pay for the euphemisms they need to hear. It should be clear to the reader by now that the cunning of "spin" and the lure of euphemism cross-cuts specific business types. In organizational presentations in varied settings, "spin" serves a covert purpose while the presenter can protest that everything is entirely "up front."

It is my intuitive wager, then, that insights into the role of euphemism in health care settings, and on health care issues, can illuminate a cultural landscape far beyond the clinic, the hospital, and the health sciences center. The remainder of this book will be devoted to offering extended examples that study organizational euphemism in much detail.

REFERENCES

Alford, C. Fred. "The Organization of Evil." *Political Psychology* 11, no. 1 (1990): 5–27.

———. "The Political Psychology of Evil." *Political Psychology* 18, no. 1 (1997): 1–17.

Allcorn, Seth. *Anger in the Workplace*. Westport, CT: Quorum Books, 1994.

Allcorn, Seth, Howell Baum, Michael A. Diamond, and Howard F. Stein. *The Human Cost of a Management Failure: Organizational Downsizing at General Hospital*. Westport, CT: Quorum Books, 1996.

Bion, Wilfred R. *Experiences in Groups*. New York: Ballantine, 1959.

Devereux, George. *Basic Problems of Ethno-Psychiatry*. Chicago: University of Chicago Press, 1980.

Diamond, Michael A. *The Unconscious Life of Organizations: Interpreting Organizational Identity*. Westport, CT: Quorum Books, 1993.

Dundes, Alan. *Life Is Like a Chicken Coop Ladder*. New York: Columbia University Press, 1984.

Eggan, Fred. "Social Anthropology and the Method of Controlled Comparison." *American Anthropologist* 56 (1954): 743–763.

Freud, Sigmund, and D. E. Oppenheim. *Dreams in Folklore*. New York: International Universities Press, 1958.

Fromm, Erich. *The Anatomy of Human Destructiveness*. New York: Holt, Rinehart and Winston, 1973.

Hammer, Michael. "Reengineering Work: Don't Automate, Obliterate." *Harvard Business Review* 68, no. 4 (July 1990): 104–113.

Hammer, Michael, and James Champy. *Reengineering the Corporation: A Manifesto for Business Revolution*. New York: HarperBusiness, 1993.

Heath, Dwight B. "The War on Drugs as a Metaphor in American Culture." *Drug Policy and Human Nature: Psychological Perspectives on the Prevention, Management, and Treatment of Illicit Drug Abuse*. Warren K. Bickel and Richard J. DeGrandpre, Editors. New York: Plenum Press, 1996: 279–299.

Koenigsberg, Richard A. *Hitler's Ideology: A Study in Psychoanalytic Sociology*. New York: Library of Social Science, 1975.

———. *The Psychoanalysis of Racism, Revolution, and Nationalism*. New York: Library of Social Science, 1986 [1977].

La Barre, Weston. "Family and Symbol." In *Psychoanalysis and Culture: Essays in Honor of Géza Róheim*. George Wilbur and Warner Muensterberger, Editors. New York: International Universities Press, 1951: 156–167.

———. *The Human Animal*. Chicago: University of Chicago Press, 1954.

———. *The Ghost Dance: The Origins of Religion*. New York: Dell, 1972.

Nuckolls, Charles W. *Culture: Problems That Cannot Be Solved*. Foreword by Howard F. Stein. Madison: University of Wisconsin Press, 1997.

Stein, Howard F. "Substance and Symbol." In *Recent Developments in Alcoholism, Volume 11: Ten Years of Progress*. Marc Galanter, Editor. New York: Plenum Press, 1993: 153–164.

———. " 'She's Driving Us Nurses Crazy': On Not Solving the Wrong Problem as a Consulting Organizational Psychologist." *Consult-*

ing Psychology Journal: Practice and Research 48, no. 1 (Winter 1996): 17–26.

Stein, Howard F., and Dan Fox. "Work as Family: Occupational Relationships and Social Transference." In *Context and Dynamics in Clinical Knowledge* by Howard F. Stein and Maurice Apprey. Charlottesville: University Press of Virginia, 1985: 182–197.

Taylor, Frederick Winslow. *Principles of Scientific Management.* New York: Harper and Brothers, 1911.

Volkan, Vamik D. "Narcissistic Personality Organization and 'Reparative' Leadership." *International Journal of Group Psychotherapy* 30, no. 2 (1980): 131–152.

White, Joseph B. " 'Next Big Thing' Re-Engineering Gurus Take Steps to Remodel Their Stalling Vehicles." *The Wall Street Journal,* November 26, 1996: #1, A13.

2

A Survey of the Work of Euphemism

EUPHEMISM AND LANGUAGE

The study of euphemism in the workplace and beyond must begin with at least some brief comments that situate the nature of euphemism and its use in language. Such a position is a necessary parallel exercise to understanding, say, metaphor in organizations (Lakoff and Johnson 1980; Stein and Apprey 1987; Stein 1994). I shall defer until the next section a definition of euphemism. All language *abstracts* from perception and experience, *structures* perception and experience, and *overlays* perception and experience of reality, internal and external alike. There has long waged a debate as to how thoroughgoing this is, and whether thought can be said to exist (among humans and other animals) in the absence of language. It is useful to revisit that still-unresolved controversy. Indeed, postmodernist thought can be seen as a direct descendant of one extreme pole of this conflict.

Early in the twentieth century, Edward Sapir and Benjamin Whorf formulated the hypothesis that language determined thought, that there is no pristine perception of reality unmediated by thought's categories and classifications. This model was an updated reading of Immanuel Kant's subjectivist philosophical argument about knowledge

and knowing—a viewpoint that is also a vital part of psychoanalytic
theory. The "object" is always known via the "subject," and that knowing is via language. Not only can subjectivity not be eliminated, but all
knowing is subjectively mediated by the very existence of the knower.
With euphemism, then, as with all language, the question is what generates the language, what potentiates the use of certain kinds of language or taxonomy during certain situations? If everything comes from
language, where does language come from? And if we are prisoners of
language, what does that mean? Evidently, something is behind language—the issue is what, and how to gain access to it. This is, of course,
complicated by the fact that words—via reification, the mental process
by which ideas are magically converted into real things—"become" (are
experienced and defended as) and substitute for things and experiences. Our classifications of the world "become" perceptually fused with
the world; via language, we say that, culturally, we live in distinctly
different worlds, whether ethnic or corporate. Words mask experience,
yet we experience words as unmasking, revealing the depths of experience. The question—to borrow shamelessly from George Orwell's
novel *Animal Farm*—is whether or not some words are more equal than
others!

The next linguistic issue is classification or taxonomy. If language is
abstraction in the form of symbolism, where does euphemism fit? What
kind of symbol is it? To begin with, all euphemisms are symbols, but
not all symbols are euphemisms. If all symbols mask and reveal, and
do so in different ways, they are difficult to distinguish between absolutely. The simile "Our new manager is like a wolf" is at the purely
abstract level, different from the metaphor "Our new manager is a real
wolf," since ostensibly, manifestly, the metaphor blurs the boundary
between signifier (manager) and signified (wolf), while the simile allows
at least some potential distance between person and wolf. Yet, use is
another thing. The subordinate who likens his or her new manager to
a feral animal may in fact treat and test the new arrival as if he or she
were an infrahuman, aggressive predator, and provoke the very wolf-
ness that is perceived and feared. Further, a person, as symbol, can
also condense many symbolic meanings.

If we have learned anything in the century-old Freudian revolution,
it is that the world of thought, feeling, fantasy, wish, and deed is murky,
self-mystified, and not at all clear or rational. Things are not what they
seem—a viewpoint that will soon become apparent as we explore euphemism at work. Even something as seemingly rational and goal ori-
ented as "strategic planning" may be rife with euphemism, metaphor,
and simile, which is to say, with hidden, unvoiceable agendas wending
their way into policy. A pure euphemism or metaphor cannot be easily

isolated from other symbolic operations or functions that condense with, or contaminate, it. This, alas, is the nature of thought. Figures of speech can, at the level of language, work very much like unconscious defenses: several usually work in concert, rather than one alone.

Having said this, I want to specify how I shall use organizational euphemism in this book, while at the same time recognizing that euphemism, too, serves multiple functions, consciously and unconsciously. My use of the term shall draw upon classical Greek etymology or origin of this figure of speech, its rhetorical use, and its meaning. It is important early on to state this linguistic foundation.

Consider the issue via another term: *tragedy*. Many colleagues in corporate management and medical practice have described the downsizing and managed care revolutions as "tragedies" or as "tragic." From their use of these terms, I have no doubt that they were not referring to the tragedic plays of Sophocles or Euripides in the classical age of Greece. They were, I am sure, not evoking as explanation the hidden gods and fates who conspire behind the scenes. Nor were they describing psychologically the conspiratorial work of the unconscious to make true our worst fears. Instead, the noun or adjective was updated to far more current usage: *tragic* meant terrible. A tragedy is a very bad, awful (not full of awe, but bad), or unfortunate (without the connotation of the gods of fortune or misfortune) event. *Tragic* refers to the magnitude of the badness, not to its source.

In the spirit of effort toward clarity and meaning, I explore workplace euphemism via the Greek roots of the term. Perhaps the best we can aspire to is for our words to reveal more and to conceal less. If we cannot know all hidden meanings, we can strive to hide less from knowing. That is my hope for this study of euphemism.

EUPHEMISM AND RHETORIC

My next step in defining euphemism and exploring its organizational uses is rhetoric, that is, principles or rules of speaking and writing. A euphemism can be understood to be a subcategory of metaphor (whole for whole) or of metonym (attribute or part for whole). According to *The Compact Edition of the Oxford English Dictionary* (1971: 903), *euphemism* derives from the Greek "to speak for." It is "that figure of speech which consists in the substitution of a word or expression of comparatively favorable implication or less unpleasant associations, instead of the harsher or more offensive one that would more precisely designate what is intended." It is "a less distasteful word or phrase used as a substitute for something harsher or more offensive." What could be said more directly is put instead indirectly (euphemize). An example offered is "A shorn crown [as] a euphemism for decapitation," whereby something dreadful-sounding becomes less dreadful.

From an earlier source, *The Century Dictionary* (1914: 2027), euphemism can be understood as the use of "a good for a bad, an auspicious for an inauspicious word"; "uttering sounds of good omen, abstaining from inauspicious words." "In *rhetoric*, the use of a mild, delicate, or indirect word or expression in place of a plainer and more accurate one, which by reason of its meaning or associations or suggestions might be offensive, unpleasant, or embarrassing." For politeness' sake, one says "plain" rather than "ugly," "gallantry" rather than "licentiousness."

Further, according to *The Century Dictionary* (1914: 2020), the frequently used Greek prefix "eu-" is used to form adjectives, the second element being a noun or verb root, and the compound being an adjective meaning "with good," "having good," "well." "Eu" is the opposite of "dys," such as in the words *eulogy* and *dyslogy*, or *eupepsy* and *dyspepsy*.

Description (phenomenology, careful hermeneutic attention to the declared text) is a starting point to understanding motivation. At first glance, one might conclude that the substitutions described and illustrated above point toward the wish to be kind, to avoid humiliating the person euphemized, to be considerate of the listener (after all, "beheading" conjures blood and gore, while "shorn crown" suggests mostly an abrupt end to a leader's reign!). Yet, the kindness, the auspiciousness, hint at the aggression, the violence, which is meant to be hidden. To label an ugly person plain softens at first blow, but reveals the fist inside the padded glove. Such defenses as reaction formation, isolation, and undoing might be involved in some degree.

The act and motive of aggression are attested to in the very act of obscuring it, but conscious attention is supposed to be directed only to the obscuring. Motivationally, to call an ugly person plain only seems to sweeten the condemnation. The recipient of the description is expected to be able, without thought or articulation, to reverse the translation: "plain" highlights, intensifies, "ugly." And everyone knows that Mozart's "gallant" Don Giovanni was a "rake." If euphemism and euphemizing disqualifies or negates an unsettling image or feeling, it also attests to the underlying intensity of the image or feeling.

At a funeral, for instance, the speaker *eulogizes* the deceased, musters images of all the virtues the recently dead possessed. One would not even think of delivering a *dyslogy* at the chapel or graveside! Yet, can't we imagine someone whispering to another after the service, "Well, he/she wasn't *that* virtuous"?

Euphemism diminishes and distances. It dehumanizes in the specific sense of making someone less than fully human. Through euphemization, reification, and part-for-whole logic, people are made smaller and less than life. In biomedical practice, sick people become "cases," things; they are known as a disease ("the oat cell carcinoma in room 123") or by organ ("the gallbladder in room 234"), not as persons. A surgeon who works in a large urban hospital saw fully clothed a patient upon whom he had operated only a few days before. She had returned to work. Upon recognizing her (of sorts), he said to her: "You were last Tuesday's breast."

In corporate medicine the term "medical supplier" or "provider" of a "product" called "healthcare" is coming to supplant the term "doctor" or "physician," just as the term "customer" or "subscriber" is coming to replace the term "patient." Connotation (of vulnerability, of suffering, of intimacy) shrinks to denotation of role (specific skill, technique, task).

Furthermore, just as employers "terminate" employees instead of "firing" them, physicians and other healthcare professionals often say that "life terminated" rather than speaking directly of "dying." Death and aggression are disguised as something else so that, consciously at least, the act no longer feels aggressive or destructive. In all these instances, the fact of human suffering, and the common fate of all of us— solitariness, decay, loss, ugliness, and death—remains. The new denials affirm it in the very act of negating it by euphemism.

My point in this brief review of the figure of speech euphemism-as-rhetoric is that the idea and work of "euphemism" is far from simple, that it is founded on the idea of opposition and negation, and that the act of substituting one thought for another is full of dynamic significance—in workplace organizations and elsewhere.

GEORGE ORWELL'S *1984* AND THE LANGUAGE OF EUPHEMISM

George Orwell's novel *1984* is at once a vivid description, evocation, and tacit condemnation of euphemism. The "friendly fascism" the Hippies warned us of three decades ago was given its most compendious linguistic landscape by Orwell even two decades earlier in a depiction of English Socialism. The circumstances and ideologies differed, but the political and linguistic foundations, and the psychological totalisms, remain the same. Euphemism serves the creation and maintenance of some kind of utopia: desperate drive toward social perfectionism, total control, and untrammeled grandiosity through human engineering. Nothing, not even thought or word, must be left to chance. Obsessive prohibition and inhibition become the foundation of language. What must be thought is inseparable from what must not be thought. Often, "must not" becomes "cannot." In his *Afterword* to the book, Erich Fromm writes:

Another important point in Orwell's discussion is closely related to "doublethink," namely that in a successful manipulation of the mind the person is no longer saying the opposite of what he thinks, but he thinks the opposite of what is true. (265)

I shall not paraphrase Orwell on euphemism. He begins his "Appendix: The Principles of Newspeak," as follows:

Newspeak was the official language of Oceania and had been devised to meet the ideological needs of Ingsoc, or English Socialism. . . . It was expected that Newspeak would have finally superseded Oldspeak (or Standard English, as we should call it) by about the year 2050.

The purpose of Newspeak was not only to provide a medium of expression for the world-view and mental habits proper to the devotees of Ingsoc, but to make all other modes of thought impossible. It was intended that when Newspeak had been adopted once and for all and Oldspeak forgotten, a heretical thought—that is, a thought diverging from the principles of Ingsoc—should be literally unthinkable, at least so far as thought is dependent on words. (246)

As with all euphemism,

Newspeak was designed not to extend but to *diminish* the range of thought, and this purpose was indirectly assisted by cutting the choice of words down to a minimum. (247, emphasis in original)

For example,

He [the Party member] knew what was meant by *goodsex*—that is to say, normal intercourse between man and wife, for the sole purpose of begetting children, and without physical pleasure on the part of the woman; all else was *sexcrime*. In Newspeak it was seldom possible to follow a heretical thought further than the perception that it *was* heretical; beyond that point the necessary words were nonexistent. (252, emphasis in original)

Under the dominion of euphemism, what could be thought and expressed was often directly opposite from what was meant, but the original is now unthinkable:

No word in the B vocabulary [words deliberately constructed for political purposes] was ideologically neutral. A great many were euphemisms. Such words, for instance, as *joycamp* (forced-labor camp) or *Minipax* (Ministry of Peace, i.e., Ministry of War) meant almost the exact opposite of what they appeared to mean.

Further,

> It was perceived that in thus abbreviating a name one narrowed and subtly altered its meaning, by cutting out most of the associations that would otherwise cling to it. (252–253)

In euphemism, appearance is everything, at least consciously. Totalitarianism—fictionalized and real—requires the prettification of all social aesthetics. Ugliness, satire, mixed feelings are all vilified. One recalls, for example, how the great composers Dmitri Shostakovich and Sergei Prokofiev were repeatedly condemned by the brutal Stalinist government and music critics for their supposedly un-Soviet, "formalistic," "decadent" music, when only "Socialist Realism" fit the official bill.

> In Newspeak, euphony outweighed every consideration other than exactitude of meaning. . . . The intention was to make speech, and essentially speech on any subject not ideologically neutral, as nearly as possible independent of consciousness. (253)

EUPHEMISM: DEFINITIONS AND DYNAMICS

With Orwell as my foundation, let me clarify how I shall use the word *euphemism* in this book. Like all symbols, it stands for, represents, something else. It is a substitute and compromise. It condenses many meanings and feelings and intentions, conscious and unconscious, into a single image. It (which is a shorthand way of saying *our* use of it) directs our attention toward some things and away from others. What distinguishes euphemism from other symbols is *how* it represents that something else, and *why* people select it rather than other kinds of symbols, such as simile and metaphor.

Euphemism is a specific form of symbolic operation. Euphemism constitutes a form of masking, of massive deception. It cunningly affirms and loudly negates. Affect (conscious and unconscious emotion) is almost entirely split off from the concept presented in the euphemism. Those concepts that serve as euphemisms have consciously only the narrowest of permissible meanings. (For instance, "the bottom line" is permitted to be only about economic profit and loss.) If hyperbole exaggerates, euphemism understates, so much so that it entirely redirects attention from the wish, feeling, and deed, to an entirely sanitized, anesthetized, intellectualized version of the original wish, feeling, and deed.

Euphemism entirely redefines them such that the original is scarcely recognizable (e.g., Orwell 1949). Large becomes small, tiny, insignificant. Euphemism reverses thought into its opposite: just as hyperbole magnifies, euphemism reduces. What isn't, is; what is, isn't what you think. Things cannot and must not be called, or felt, what they are. To do so would bring on overwhelming guilt, anxiety, and remorse. So, in euphemism the mask is the obligatory face that must be seen. The face is hidden, disguised. For instance, to cite an extreme example, the Nazis' wish to get away with the mass murder of Jewry is transformed into a dispassionate scientific treatise on the public health campaign against insects, infectious disease, vermin, infrahuman parasites—embodied in that colossal euphemism: "The Final Solution to the Jewish Problem."

If euphemism *makes murky* what is clear, it paradoxically also *clarifies* in a macabre way. Seth Allcorn (personal communication, July 27, 1996) writes that "euphemism is, in a way, sending a very clear communication about what *cannot* [may not] be discussed. In a sense, at one level it redirects attention away [from some idea or feeling] but at an undiscussable level it sends a clear message about what *can* be discussed" (emphasis mine, HFS). Euphemism is an amazingly dexterous way of thought and speech! It simultaneously directs and distracts attention. It mystifies and clarifies.

Euphemism draws heavily upon such defense mechanisms as denial, isolation (the splitting off of emotion from cognition), reaction formation, dissociation, repression, rationalization, and intellectualization. In terms of social (group) defensive processes, euphemism is formidably buttressed by family, workplace, and larger societal beliefs and ideologies. One can think and do in groups what one could not imagine or do alone. If one could begin to feel and comprehend what one was doing under the shield of euphemism, one could not tolerate the anxiety, guilt, and shame. One would likely turn the aggression inward.

A market and marketplace ideology, together with the language of rational contracts, utterly dissolve the issues of meaning and suffering into simple business decisions (David Armstrong, comment, Symposium of the International Society for the Psychoanalytic Study of Organizations [ISPSO], New York City, June 14, 1996). The breadth and depth of human meaning disappear into black holes. "Managed care," like the "downsizing" and "RIFing" with which it is strategically associated, denies as even relevant what is toxic to think and feel about: sickness, vulnerability, aggression, decay, dread, despair, death. It "manages" (rationalizes) them out of existence. "The merchandising of meaning fills suffering's void"; "euphemisms are black holes into which meaning disappears" (Yiannis Gabriel, comment, ISPSO, New York City, June 14, 1996). We need to ask squarely, "What do we do when we want to be [organizationally] lean and mean?" (Shelley Reciniello, comment, ISPSO, New York City, June 14, 1996). The unchallenged idea of "Somebody's got to do it!"—that is, the tough, masculine, ostensibly unwanted job of firings, cuts, exclusions from medical care—"is not always or necessarily true," unless we are in the thrall of the euphemism (Robert Young, comment, ISPSO, New York City, June 14, 1996). That is, we cannot stop ourselves from "doing it" because we have euphemism's perfect alibi to rationalize what is already a compulsion.

Nor may we innocently blame only upper management or shareholders for the dominion of euphemism. Its little-contested reign and its success are as much horizontal (peer consensus) and bottom-up as top-down. To a large degree, organizational and national leaders and upper-level management can only take their people where they already wish to go.

ORDINARY EUPHEMISMS OF THE CORPORATE WORKPLACE

I wish to emphasize and illustrate the *ordinariness* of euphemisms in modern corporate workplaces, businesses, government, the military, education, and medicine. Their use is far from limited to the magnitude of crisis, trauma, large-scale catastrophic change—the Holocaust, for instance (although for those who conducted and condoned it, it became quite ordinary, too). Ordinary euphemisms are like the air we breathe, like old furniture that has sat in one place for decades: they are "there," almost axiomatic givens; they are automatic, ritualistic ways of thinking. Terms that immediately come to mind are "the bottom line," "team" and "team player," "empowerment," "competitive," the world as "marketplace," a boss' "open-door policy," a company's "suggestion box," "strategic planning" and "mission statements," a "panel" of patients or customers, and often opportunistic name changes of work units and even entire organizational names. Four common concepts will illustrate the ordinariness of euphemism in the workplace: "team," "open-door policy," "empowerment," and "survivor."

Consider, first, the now-widespread concept of *teams* as collective work units, responsible to complete certain tasks. Closely associated with the team concept is the notion and role of being a *team player*, that is, a person who works for the good of the group, and not for personal gain in a direction opposite from the group will. Teams often have *quarterbacks* and *quarterbacking* as leadership. At the level of official, espoused speech, teams represent an effort to bring greater voice to individual participants, to make organization less authoritarian, less arbitrary, if not more democratic. The team concept is closely related to the notion of empowerment (see below). It is supposed to connote a cooperative, collegial atmosphere, one not dominated by hierarchical coercion. In principle, everyone works in behalf of the team goals and the team ideal. Ideally, such a concept reduces individual competitiveness, the struggle for domination, and authoritarianism, and creates a friendly, productive environment. A recent and widely current synonym for *team* is "self-managing work group."

In the era of mass layoffs and the combination of workers into units consisting of people with whom they have not worked before, there is a flowering of "multidiciplinary teams," of people who are expected to work together and complete tasks as if they had been together for years and as if there were no hierarchy or superiority of "turf" within the group. The previous status hierarchy in the organization is supposedly superseded. The "department" one is from, or the "profession" in which one has trained and is credentialed (surgeons or family doctors, engineers or accountants), is supposed to matter far less than what one is able to contribute to the whole, to production, to profit, to saving money. Everyone is now officially equal and is supposed to have equal input into the group process of decision making.

In reality, members of such groups, especially those members in supervisory or executive positions in the larger organization, will sharply rebuke, if not threaten, a dissident member for not being a *team player*, which means not submitting to group or official leadership's will. Authority and power still count, but their sting is driven underground by official euphemism. The quarterback is supposed to listen to everyone, and everyone is supposed to have the opportunity to serve as quarterback, as decisions are based on the merit of ideas—but in reality the quarterback is often less open, or is at least perceived to be less open, than can be said publicly. Further complicating team and leadership roles, these units are defined from the outside, and members define their own group, at the same time that new lines of authority within the organization are created and people are uncertain as to their roles, statuses, and to whom to report in the larger picture. What occurs, then, is that hierarchical authority is exercised, insisted upon, nonverbally or informally manipulated, but the fact of such exercise of authority is denied.

Whenever there is conflict between horizontal (peer) and vertical authority, the hierarchical prevails, wins out. The egalitarian, individualist, consensus-for-the-greater-good principle works so long as the values, priorities, and agendas of the hierarchy (explicit and implicit) are met under democratic guise. The default "team" mode is dominance and compliance with the "chain of command." Within the *operational* team function—especially during conflict or crisis—some members must report to others *within* the team. The idea of a post-bureaucratic, post-hierarchical, rationally bounded, virtual organization is a delusion. To be a team player, then, is to submit, but the submission cannot be acknowledged or named. One must act as if equality is true, even when it is not. One must act as if sham is sincerity.

Consider next the concept of an *open-door policy*, which upper management and leaders often espouse. It ostensibly means that anyone who works for a particular leader, manager, or administrator should feel free (unintimidated) to come to the supervisor's office or work station, by drop-in or appointment, and discuss a subject of concern, presumably about the job or the workplace. Furthermore, it implicitly means that suggestions and criticisms are welcomed and will not be punished. In a highly hierarchical and bureaucratic institution, this policy is officially meant to diminish the social distance in the "vertical integration," and in making the boss(es) more accessible, to create an atmosphere of friendly feelings to help compensate for the inevitable distance and mistrust in complex organizations.

Implementation of the "open-door policy," and its ready contamination with hidden, often unconsciously laden, agendas, is a different matter. The espoused policy is often a sham. Under such circumstances, if it is taken at face value, the employee jeopardizes his or her dignity, status, and even job. Consider the corporation Acme Widgets (AW), which we met in the opening vignette of this book. The CEO insisted from his first day that he had a truly open-door policy, that his co-workers were invited to drop by and visit, that they truly were welcome. Yet many secretaries were soon seen leaving his office in tears after they had taken the offer literally; they were "chewed out" (a common term of rebuke) instead of listened to. Many middle managers who succeeded in coming by unannounced or in securing an appointment found the CEO to be verbally abusive, intimidating, or later vindictive for any questioning of his authority or policy. If they were not fired or could not be directly forced to resign, they were sufficiently bullied and deprived of resources that they left sooner or later. "Open" meant closed, off-limits. "Present" meant absent or unavailable. Still, everyone was expected to disavow what he or she knew to be true: that people were unwelcome. In many cases, the disavowal was internalized because many junior managers felt dependent on the CEO for their careers. One middle manager said to me what sounded like a quotation from Lewis Carroll's *Adventures of Alice in Wonderland*: "Now, how is it supposed to go? When he's not here, he's here. When he's here, he's not here. When his door is open, stay out, or you'll get reamed. When his door is shut, you're supposed to act as if it's open. Go in and you still get reamed." Many employees spent much of their time during corporate meetings and afterward trying to second-guess and decode his baffgabble, to figure out what he was "really" saying.

The architecture and personnel configuration of the CEO's administrative suite told the same story in space ("isomorphically"). His office suite was virtually a fortress. Between the outer door from the long corridor to his office, several doors and rooms intervened. Secretaries, their desks, computers, printers, fax machines, postage machines, and photocopying machines were arranged in phalanxes of barriers, from the outer offices to the inner offices. One had to pass between several secretaries and much furniture before reaching the door to the CEO's office. Several people independently described to me the scenario as "castle walls and moats," "minefields," or "battlements," around his office. The sham "open-door policy" isolated the executive from his personnel, and them from him. What protection he secured was more than offset by the deficit in information they both had. The employees learned for the most part to stay away. Only as they accepted that, as euphemism, *an "open-door policy" was precisely its opposite, and an opposite that could not be acknowledged* could they diminish the cognitive and emotional dissonance (see De Vos 1975) that existed between official pronouncement and reality.

Third, consider the now-popular organizational term *empower (-ment, -ed, -ing)* and its plasticity as euphemism. At face value, empowerment is supposed to bestow on a subordinate a greater sense of power (the ability to bring an idea or wish to fruition), authority, value, or self-worth. Empowerment is supposed to make the upper tiers of a structural hierarchy less remote, to make superordinate/subordinate, employer/employee relationships more equal, more democratic, more open to change from the grass roots. Differences of viewpoint are supposed to enrich, rather than threaten, organizations and their chain of command. Empowerment is supposed to help people to function together more independently, more cohesively, more harmoniously, as teams. It is supposed to put teeth into the process of delegation of power, task, responsibility, and the like, at both the personal and group level. In the current era of organizational "de-layering," "flattening," and the replacement of specialty "departmental" or other professionally bounded units with "multispecialty teams" in medicine, industry, and government, these empowered multispecialty professional groups are supposed to function more cooperatively, more collaboratively, and less rancorously because no one's "turf" is superior to anyone else's. Groups are freed to be more creative, and presumably more productive and profitable. Through downsizing and outsourcing (large-scale firing and contracting with outside organizations to perform tasks once performed by people and units inside the organization), members of a smaller organizational group are put together as "functional units" or "teams" whose members are expected to function at optimal levels unencumbered by seniority or long-standing relationship histories. Everyone is at least more equal than before (although equally more vulnerable as well), and such equality is supposed to increase personal and team empowerment.

But empowerment, like power "itself," is no simple, unambivalent matter. To bestow decision making capacity upon another, one must be prepared to relinquish some of it oneself, and mean it. One must nurture and cherish the separation, the conflict, the uncertainty, the ambiguity of all roles. Viewed from the subordinate employee's perspective, one must be prepared, willing, and eager to accept greater responsibility, to take greater initiative, to relinquish some dependency, and to take blame for failures as well as credit for successes (that is, to forgo placing some of the blame upward for workers' own poor decisions or poor planning).

Power and empowerment are heir to all the unconscious issues of parent-child relationships, including fears of annihilation, aggression, separation, loss, castration, abandonment, mutilation, guilt, and shame. Even under the best of workplace circumstances, with good faith and self-awareness on the part of leaders and workers, empowerment involves far more than bestowing and accepting a mantle. It requires hard work, as much on relationships as on the completion of tasks. Under the worst of circumstances, empowerment is an illusion, a sham, an obligatory doctrine (not unlike Total Quality Management, Continuous Quality Improvement, participatory management ideologies) to be enunciated but not meant to challenge the "vertical integration" of the organization. Nor, for the most part, can the disparity be acknowledged with impunity. Often, everyone is expected to act as if he or she is empowering others or is empowered by others, when neither is the case.

Two organizational structures, values, and self-images coexist within one. The result is appeal to an ideal no one really believes in but feels obligated to espouse, that is, to speak and act as if empowerment were true even though they know it is false. Corporation members who act on the empowerment doctrine come to be ignored, ostracized, punished, or ridiculed as "wave makers," even though they are complying with the manifest message. "Be more independent" means "Be as dependent as before, but act as if you are feeling better because you are more independent, more an equal."

The conflict core of empowerment, of teams, and of executives' open-door policy is not recent, but long-standing in American culture. As Spiegel (1971) points out, Americans have long touted the individualistic ethic, but have repeatedly installed oppressive governmental and industrial hierarchies they secretly admire: for example, the "Daley

Machine" in Chicago, the "Robber Barons" of late nineteenth-century industry, the audacious financial corporate raiders of the 1980s, or the aggressive high financiers of corporate mergers, hostile takeovers, and leveraged buyouts of the 1990s. Today, as organizations "de-layer" and become organized around "functional units" or "teams" drawn from several areas of an institution, empowerment will become even more problematic a euphemism for the espousal of individual worth and the default practice of lineal or vertical leadership. Despite the popular organizational rhetoric of empowering all participants and units in production, some remain more empowered than others. Corporate raiders claim to "add value" (itself a common euphemism) to companies for the sake of investors or shareholders by buying large companies, downsizing them, and selling off the most immediately lucrative-appearing pieces. Under such circumstances, a few people are "empowered" at the cost of the sacrifice of many. Here, "empowerment" is sham and crass opportunism. Equality, individuality, and freedom make for better myth than they do for organizational reality. Here is some of the most fertile soil in which euphemism flourishes.

Fourth and last, consider the unlikely word *survivor* as corporate euphemism. In this era of large-scale layoffs, those who somehow manage to keep their jobs often call themselves, and are called by others, "survivors." Like employment itself, it might only be temporary, but at least one has "survived" as opposed to having been symbolically killed off. Survivorship is a military honor in civilian clothing. When it is a sham, it is being used as a euphemism. Consider this personal example. Several years ago I attended a social function where I saw a senior administrator of the health sciences center where I have been employed nearly twenty years. He came over and, with a broad smile and firm handshake, said to me: "Howard, you're a real survivor!" I am sure he consciously meant it to be a compliment. Indeed, among many Oklahomans and other prairie folk, to be called a "survivor" is to receive the ultimate and rarely bestowed praise. It is a badge of membership and admittance to membership. It is a sign of being a *real* man or *real* woman. Outer circumstances such as the Great Depression, the Dust Bowl, wild swings of the international wheat and cattle market, and the fickleness of the weather, all contribute to the virtue of hardiness, of uncomplaining realism, of unflappable stoicism ("I can take it"; "It's nothing"). These are all summed up by the phrase "true grit." Despite everything, one has endured and not whined about it.

But external focus and locus of control are given more weight than they are due, perhaps in order to direct attention away from more immediate family, occupational, community, political, and inner, unconscious oppressions. Being an organizational survivor or meteorological survivor is often a death-defying badge of courage, of victimhood cultivated in a sadomasochistic dance. One repeatedly requires the conditions of near death to have the right to claim the prize of survivorship. Or one congratulates the corporate survivor for enduring his or her own reign of terror. It is an extreme form of patronage.

The executive who bestowed the compliment on me was also the one who had made the degrading conditions of work which I endured and had "survived." His was a Godfather's benediction to one whom he claimed to "protect" but in fact had—along with many others—terrorized. His was a classic terrorist's gambit, inspiring horror, greater dependency, and the cruel comfort of identification. When he said it to me, "something" felt wrong, like I had just swung my bat at a curve ball. Only several years later could I find the right words (and the rage that had kept me from the words) to classify my uneasiness. "Survivor" was a grim organizational euphemism for those victimized by him, but who still managed to be around on the job. It takes time and emotional work to begin to recognize something to be a euphemism, because such basic issues as a sense of safety, security, and freedom from annihilation trigger automatic unconscious acceptance of the sham as the REAL.

Once a euphemism is internalized and comes to be shared intersubjectively, that is, at a deep level, among co-workers and leaders, it comes to be taken for the normal. Psychological brutality comes to be expected as ordinary; we calibrate the world according to its "norm." Tragically, and sometimes comically, when we are treated respectfully, nicely, decently—or at least seemingly so—we respond as if such civility, even kindliness, were exceptional or extraordinary, as though somehow we only deserve the worst. We come to assume that "normal" is a psychological state of siege, attack, and protective withdrawal. Corporate office party extravaganzas at Christmas—from abundant flavored popcorn to lavish, executive-sponsored, family-like buffets for employees—are rarely recognized for the living euphemisms they usually in fact are. The threat of being fired and of being on the street tomorrow, or of one's job constantly being "redesigned" or "reinvented" utterly without one's active participation, is the "ordinary" face of these garish once-a-year feeds. "Starvation" and "homelessness" are the unstated counterplayers of holiday office food cornucopias in the temporary palace of home.

EUPHEMISM AND THE NAZI "PUBLIC HEALTH" EXPERIMENT OF THE HOLOCAUST

In this section, I turn from the ordinary euphemisms of today's corporate organizations to the extraordinary web of euphemisms that constituted the German National Socialist ideology that made the

Holocaust possible. I do not invoke the Holocaust for rhetorical effect, for hyperbole: to us, the whole episode might be macabre, unthinkable, extraordinary, but to them, those who designed and administered it, it was as ordinary as going to work. Just as "managed care," "downsizing," and much of the response to the Oklahoma City bombing cannot be understood apart from the language and psychology of euphemism, we would also do well to see what we can learn from that most vile and thoroughgoing experiment in the exploitation of euphemism, German National Socialism (1920s–1945) and the Holocaust it manufactured. Without committing the error of equating the two, one can learn much about the social uses and abuses of euphemism in American downsizing, managed care, and the Oklahoma City bombing from examining its place in Nazism's path of destructiveness. Whatever else the Holocaust was at the level of nationalism or of state politics, it was also a meticulously integrated *organizational* effort in the industrialization of death, one in which the Nazis were more successful than in their war effort on three fronts. It is well documented that, in addition to being a form of nationalism, Nazi Germany was also a form of work organization. "The Nazis are an example of a workplace culture that attempted to fulfill an organizational vision and mission" (Seth Allcorn, personal communication, August 12, 1996), we would say in current, American managerial teams. In the Holocaust, the extraordinary systematic collection, transport, and annihilation of a people became quite ordinary.

We—executives, managers, administrators, workers—rightfully squirm at facile analogizing between organizational behavior and the efficient, impersonal brutalities of much of the Holocaust (see, however, Daniel Jonah Goldhagen, 1996). However else we might approach Nazism as an integrated national ideology (for instance, as a repetition on the political scale of child brutality), German National Socialism was an example of the ingenious and complex coordination of workplace culture that individually and collectively attempted to fulfill an organizational (and rational) vision, mission, strategic plan, and set of tactics for implementation. How they organized their efforts, and the social organizational Darwinist ideology that rationalized getting rid of an entire population who did not serve the vision or mission—these differ little from overarching principles of thought that govern our own corporate, hospital, government, industrial, educational, medical, and other workplaces. Further, as an organizational form, Nazi Germany is a well-documented era that can shed light on our own (Kren and Rappoport 1994; Dawidowicz 1975; Hilberg 1985, 1992; Staub 1989). Far from being mere hyperbole or false imagery, the Nazi doctrine and its meticulous implementation in social policy can cast light on our own still-veiled efforts to expel people from workplace organizations with utterly no concern for their future.

At the outset of her monumental study, *The War Against the Jews, 1933–1945*, Lucy Dawidowicz writes:

> "The Final Solution to the Jewish Problem" was the code name assigned by the German bureaucracy to the annihilation of the Jews. The very composition of the code name, when analyzed, reveals its fundamental character and meaning to the Germans who invented and used it. . . . The "Jewish question" was, at bottom, a euphemism whose verbal neutrality concealed the user's impatience with the singularity of this people that did not appear to conform to the new political demands of the state. (xxi–xxii)

Later, she discusses the institution that was developed for introducing the "euthanasia" program in 1939. First its members killed "racially useless" children, then the adult insane. The group was called the Reich Committee for Scientific Research of Hereditary and Severe Constitutional Diseases (*Reichsausschluss zur wissenschaftlichen Erfassung von erb-und-analagebedingten schweren Leiden*). Its program to kill insane adults operated out of an office in Hitler's chancellery at Tiergartenstrasse 4; its code name was "T-4."

> The names given to these institutions for killing, as well as the words used later to designate the killing of the Jews, were originally intended as camouflage to conceal from the general public these systematic programs of murder. This neutral bureaucratic terminology for various methods of murder no doubt later reinforced schizoid and delusional traits among the killers. (177 ftn.)

Among the euphemisms, the following enumeration offers a sense of the scope of what was desired and what was at all costs concealed: for instance, (1) Hitler's insistence early on, as in a letter to Adolf Gemlich, on "Rational Anti-Semitism" to separate it from the popular image of rowdy, emotion-based crowd behavior (Dawidowicz 1975: 204); (2) *Endlösung der Judenfrage* ("The Final Solution to the Jewish Problem"); (3) *Aktion(en)* ("Action[s]," usually designating killing procedures as in "Self-Cleansing Actions"); (4) the "Special Tasks" assigned to *Einsatzgruppen* ("Special Duty Groups") in Eastern Europe (groups who engaged in mass killings, their designation attesting to the vagueness of many terms associated with the killings [Dawidowicz 1975: 152]). The phrase "*Abgereist, ohne Angabe der Adresse*" ("Moved, without leaving

forwarding address") was stamped on mail returned to sender after
Jews were rounded up and deported to France via freight cars from the
states of Baden, Palatinate, and Saar on October 22, 1940 (Schwab
1992: 204). Ambiguous words flowered, signifying removal and cleanup,
for example, *Entfernung*, *Aufnaumung*, *Beseitigung* (Dawidowicz 1975:
204).

The very institutionalization and bureaucratization of the Holocaust
was shrouded in scientific, medical, euphemism. Mass murder was re-
imagined as *Rassenhygiene* ("racial hygiene"); extermination was an
experiment in applied human biology and in public health. After a visit
to the Holocaust Museum in Washington, D.C., Alford writes, "Overwhelming is the perverse rationality of it all, the elaborate categories
of being to be destroyed, the Institutes for Racial Hygiene, the Offices
of Purification of the Reich, the Departments of Special Procedures. The
Holocaust was science, industry, and bureaucracy driven by images of
doom, impurity, and dread, the stuff of precategorical evil" (1997: 13),
phrased in the sanitized, anesthetized language of euphemism. Adolf
Eichmann, whose task was to coordinate the trains to run at peak capacity to the labor and death camps, was Minister of Migration.

In its singularity of human scale and meticulously "rational"mode of
destructiveness, Nazism has taught, and continues to teach, both about
an era and about far beyond that era. If German National Socialism
and the Holocaust it created have often been misappropriated, they still
are a deep well from which we can continue to draw, if we dare. Whatever else they illumine of our own more ordinary hells, they show how
the art and science of euphemism was brought to unsurpassed perfec-
tion in political ideology, propaganda, and ordinary language. They illustrate how wish and fantasy can be revealed and concealed, how an
act can be sanctioned and justified by making it into something quite
ordinary: a scientific, medical problem to be defined, diagnosed, treated,
and cured.

Since the 1950s writers and quite ordinary people have asked repeatedly out of revulsion and innocent horror: "How could the Holocaust have been possible? How could anyone do such a thing as create
and mobilize an entire industry of death in a modern nation? How could
so civilized a nation as produced Goethe and Beethoven also have produced gas chambers and crematoria for human beings? How could *they*
have done such a terrible thing?" I have come to the conclusion that
these questions tell us far more about the ones posing the question(s),
about limits upon the imagination and unconscious of the questioner,
than about the events themselves. Why should the creation of hell on
earth be extraordinary rather than ordinary? Listen to our backward
schizophrenics and paranoiacs, and they will tell us our stories in
theirs—but we will call them bizarre, because their form is so "weird."

But if they tell us the secrets of our hearts and inspire us to follow them in our common quest, then we will call this political philosophy or ideology. Hitler is a singularity in history, but not only a singularity.

The whole linguistic web of euphemism was an indispensable part of the "success" of the Nazi aim of making the world free (cleansed) of Jews and of making national mobilization toward that goal—one more vital than the German war effort itself—palatable. If Beethoven, Bruckner, and Wagner could easily be conscripted into Nazi service, why could not the great German biological science, and scientists from Rudolph Virchow to Robert Koch, be summoned as well? And mighty German industry? Is not God on our side (*"Gott mit uns"*), and religious institutions as well? Why not science, industry, and the arts also? If any psychoanalytic insight during individual therapy can be turned almost immediately into resistance to another, more frightening, insight or feeling, why should this not be true of the social use of science, music, religion—for that matter, anything—by individuals alone and in groups?

Euphemism without the vigilant watch of the conscience, ever ready to condemn and strike the vulnerable ego, is unthinkable, because unnecessary. Euphemism is a dodge to the conscience—in classical psychoanalytic terms, an alliance between superego and id to trick the ego. Rationalized by euphemism, one may commit the immoral, the unethical in the name of the "highest" morality. People commit atrocity in the name of good, in the service of what they are certain is virtuous.

But that certainty of goodness and virtue wobbles—which is why euphemism is required to steady its course. Among the Nazis, for instance, the very fact of killing, the justification for killing, the mode of killing, and its scale, all needed to be affirmed and disguised. A precise coordination of army, special forces, Gestapo, SS, medical practitioners, train scheduling, chemical manufacturing (of Zyklon B, by IG Farben), government bureaucracy, and propaganda were essential to the success of the final years of the Holocaust: both to bring it about and to attempt to keep it a secret by covering its bloody tracks via linguistics and via a myriad of oral orders that were not to be written down.

To the Nazi cause, the destruction of Jews, the purification of Germany (its people, its blood), was an even more vital mission than the conduct of a two-front war. Hitler long insisted that the world would thank him for what he—almost—did to the Jews. Resources were necessarily diverted from the "external" war effort to the "internal" war effort: to rid the organism that was the body of Germany of its bacteria, cancer, lice, vermin (all widespread images of Jews). The January 20, 1942, secret Wannsee Conference, at which "The Final Solution to the Jewish Question" was articulated and began to be implemented, marks both continuity and discontinuity with the earlier (1933–1942) eugenics, sterilization, hospital gassings, and mass shootings by the *Sonder-kommandos*, *Einsatzgruppen*, and SS. The latter were the "clean-up crew," so to speak, who followed the *Wehrmacht* (the regular army) to destroy all Jews in the newly conquered territory. The ultimate goal remained the same: but the depersonalized, anesthetized, euphemized, industrialized, mechanized form of death removed the last barriers of common humanity between Germans and Jews. Now, anything was possible. Yet, its secrecy still had to be maintained, and oral, not written, orders given. Germans participating at any level had to create a taboo even against self-knowledge, one which took the form of dissociation and denial: No one knew what was really going on! The question, then, "How was this possible?", a question born of self-protective disbelief, moral outrage, denial, reaction formation, and a little self-righteousness, begins to be more easily answered.

The secret was one that millions of Germans shared and enthusiastically endorsed. It was publicly articulated in the idiom of disease (typhus and other infectious disease, cancer), treatment, hygiene, and heredity. The murdered dead were not corpses or bodies, but public health *Figuren* (disembodied pieces, parts, statistics). Glass writes:

> The Germans invented a new language to describe actions undertaken in relation to Jewish bodies. For example, the tattooing of numbers removed the real victim from the *kultur*-group's perception of the victim; annihilating a number is an entirely different operation from annihilating a person. (1997: 133)

Biological purification took the form of obsession with heredity and genetics. Glass writes: "An entirely new vocabulary had been added to the practice of medicine and legal administration" (1997: 133).

In a similar vein, in his study of medical science under the Nazis, Robert Proctor describes the medicalization of anti-Semitism. It consisted of:

> the attempt on the part of doctors to conceive the so-called Jewish problem as a medical problem, one that required a "medical solution." The medicalization of anti-Semitism represents only part of a larger attempt by the German medical profession to medicalize or biologize various forms of social, sexual, political, or racial deviance; Jews, homosexuals, Gypsies, Marxists, and other groups were typecast as "health hazards" to the German population. When the Nazis herded Jews into the ghettos of the occupied East, public health provided the ideological rationale: concentration was justified as "quarantine." (1988: 7)

In a 1993 study of the town of Storm Lake, Iowa, anthropologist Mark Grey reports that IBP, Incorporated, the world's second largest pork-packing plant, opened in 1982, had a daily "kill capacity" of 13,400. IBP's annual production was around three million (Grey 1993: 33). By way of comparison, Milton Meltzer (1976: 130) reports that by 1944, when Germany was already losing the war, rail transports to Auschwitz came to over 10,000 Hungarian Jews and 20,000 Jews from the Lodz Ghetto. At Auschwitz, bodies were burned in open pits because the crematoria (ovens) could not handle the quantity of corpses. The peak and record at Auschwitz was 34,000 people gassed and burned in a twenty-four-hour period via continuous "shiftwork." Put differently, Auschwitz, the singular goal of which was to produce human death, outproduced by 2½ times the labor-, technology-, and capital-intensive effort at IBP. And Auschwitz was working toward a different "profit" in its relentless industrialization of death.

All this—to repeat—was shrouded in official secrecy and euphemism, and in public denial: "We never knew," as the tall stacks spewed and belched the stench of burning human flesh, and rained mysterious ash. Even for those devoid of olfactory intelligence, one could not help but wonder—at some level of the dynamic mind—about the fate of those tens of thousands herded into cattle cars, none of whom came out alive. The need for secrecy and euphemism gave the lie to how "secret" it all was. Here the euphemism filled the void of thought, doubt, and conscience, and fulfilled the sinister wish of sacrifice: For Germany to live, all Jews must die. If Jews, Slavs, Gypsies, the retarded, the mentally ill, the infirm, and other outcasts could be redefined and experienced as subhuman (as deadly bacteria, as lice, as vermin, as cancerous growth in the healthy body), then the "solution" to the "problem" followed inexorably: to exterminate them as such. The creativity and ambiguity of language provided the excuses: *Entjudung* was to get rid of Jews; *Judenrein* meant a world cleansed, purified of the presence of Jews; *Vernichtung Lebensunwerten Lebens* meant the making-into-nothingness human "life unworthy of life."

If, in the shadow of Robert Koch's 1890s bacteriology and of all German science, Jews could be regarded, redefined as a pathogenic disease, as some form of psychosomatic illness, then the treatment and cure of the sick body, and its restoration to health, consisted logically of the location, isolation, and eradication of the disease. Further, in terms of social role, it is "merely" an extension of the disease-and-cure metaphor that physicians were involved in the clinical decision making over worthwhile and unworthy life forms, from the earliest sterilization of the mid-1930s to the "selection" at the labor-death camps of who should be allowed to live and who should die immediately—the infamous "go left"/"go right" orders.

Further, it should come as no surprise to see, for instance, in a 1935 celebration of Hitler's birthday, April 20, a picture of a smiling Hitler bending over toward a smiling little girl who is reaching toward her leader—all this with large-lettered caption "*Adolf Hitler als Arzt des deutschen Volkes*" ("Adolf Hitler as Physician of the German People"), "*Die Volksgesundtheitwacht*" ("The People's Search for Health," *Oster-mond*, 1935, p. 3, in Proctor 1988: 51). And a 1943 political cartoon depicts a large optical microscope in the foreground, while the background consists of a large white circle—the field of magnified vision on a glass slide—with the Star of David (Jews), dollar signs (capitalists), hammer-and-sickles (communists), triangles (homosexuals), and the American dollar sign and the British pound sign as the identified infecting bacterial diseases. The cartoon is titled *Krankheitserreger* ("Infectious Germs," *Die Stürmer*, April 15, 1943, p. 1, in Proctor 1988: 163). Beneath the cartoon is a poem in German, which translates: "With his poison, the Jew destroys/ The sluggish blood of weaker peoples."

Hitler and his fellow propagandists, some belonging to a generation or two earlier than his, converted the fierce, passionate hatred for Jews into a public-health policy based on nineteenth-century science, medicine, and reason: "Rational Anti-Semitism," as Hitler called it. Biological logic, not hate, would be the final linguistic solution to the German problem with their—and everyone's—Jews. In this way, the human-strength Zyklon B became the functional equivalent of Zyklon A and C. Jews became a different kind of challenge, a different kind of bug to kill in enclosed space. In this section I have tried to draw attention to the less emotional, and the more deliberate, side of National Socialism: how, via the language of euphemism, the nearly successful effort to slaughter every Jew on earth became an exercise in applied human biology, a public health campaign designed, led, implemented, and administered to eliminate people diminished to insect- and bacterium-like threats to the German immune system. In that light, what more apt and culturally "logical" a plan than *extermination*, a process that required the careful coordination of countless corporate and other workplace organizations?

SUMMARY AND LOOKING AHEAD

In this chapter, I have described euphemism in terms of its rhetorical properties, and I have drawn from Orwell's novel *1984* to illustrate its political psychology. I have defined it and its complex interpsychic and group dynamics. I have offered illustrations of its use in day-to-day corporate America, and shown how the Nazi Holocaust would have been impossible without it. In the next three chapters—the descriptive and experiential core of the book—I shall portray and evoke three distinct, yet interrelated, systems of thought governed largely by euphemism: downsizing (chapter 3), managed care and corporate biomedicine (chapter 4), and the response to the 1995 Oklahoma City bombing (chapter 5).

Taken as a unity, together with the overviews I have offered in this chapter and in chapter 1, these three chapters develop the following overarching formula or "symbolic equation," the symbolic logic of which is central to our culture: (a) "Passing away" is to "dying," as (b) "plain" is to "ugly," as (c) "downsizing" is to "mass firing of people," as (d) "managed care" is to "letting people suffer and die," as (e) "closure" (to the official period of mourning following the April 1995 bombing of the Federal Building in Oklahoma City) is to "shutting off one's own and others' grief over the mass catastrophe and returning to normal," as (f) "The Final Solution to the Jewish Problem" is to "the systematic, industrialized effort to round up and kill off every Jew on earth." The relationship is not analogic, but isomorphic. To say that the first member of each pair bears the same kind of relationship to the second member of every other pair as it does within its own (and vice versa) is to shed light on something common to all. The element or process common to these is *the denial through euphemism of what really is happening, of how and what one really feels, and of what one really means.*

Downsizing and managed care are not "the same as" the Holocaust. But Nazi "applied human biology" in the service of public health, and our cult of the computer spreadsheet, of the bottom line, and of business administration are two culturally distinct ways, processes, of doing the same thing: magically preventing death by producing it, one way or another. The study of organizational euphemism in late-twentieth-century America will show, unmistakably if astonishingly, how the American way of business has become the American way of death.

REFERENCES

Alford, C. Fred. "The Political Psychology of Evil." *Political Psychology* 18, no. 1 (March 1997): 1–17.

The Century Dictionary. New York: The Century Company, 1914.

The Compact Edition of the Oxford English Dictionary. Oxford, England: Clarendon Press, 1971.

Dawidowicz, Lucy. *The War Against the Jews, 1933–1945.* New York: Holt, Rinehart and Winston, 1975.

De Vos, George A. "Affective Dissonance and Primary Socialization: Implications for a Theory of Incest Avoidance." *Ethos* 3, no. 2 (1975): 165–182.

Glass, James M. "Against the Indifference Hypothesis: The Holocaust and the Enthusiasts for Murder." *Political Psychology* 18, no. 1 (March 1997): 129–145.

Goldhagen, Daniel Jonah. *Hitler's Willing Executioners: Ordinary Germans and the Holocaust.* New York: Knopf, 1996.

Grey, Mark. "The Failure of Iowa's Non-English Speaking Employee's Law: A Case Study of Patronage, Kinship, and Migration in Storm Lake, Iowa." *High Plains Applied Anthropologist* 13, no. 2 (1993): 32–46.

Hilberg, Raul. *The Destruction of the European Jews,* Revised and Definitive Edition. New York: Holmes and Meier, 1985 [1961].

———. *Perpetrators, Victims, Bystanders: The Jewish Catastrophe 1933–1945.* New York: Aaron Asher Books, 1992.

Kren, George M., and Leon Rappoport. *The Holocaust and the Crisis of Human Behavior.* London: Holmes and Meier, 1994 [1980].

Lakoff, George, and Mark Johnson. *Metaphors We Live By.* Chicago: University of Chicago Press, 1980.

Meltzer, Milton. *Never to Forget: The Jews of the Holocaust.* New York: Harper and Row, 1976.

Orwell, George. *1984.* New York: Harcourt Brace Jovanovich, 1949.

Proctor, Robert. *Racial Hygiene: Medicine under the Nazis.* Cambridge, MA: Harvard University Press, 1988.

Schwab, Henry. *The Echoes That Remain: A Postal History of the Holocaust.* Weston, MA: Cardinal Spellman Philatelic Museum, 1992.

Spiegel, John. *Transactions: The Interplay Between Individual, Family, and Society.* New York: Science House, 1971.

Staub, Ervin. *The Roots of Evil: The Origins of Genocide and Other Group Violence.* Cambridge: Cambridge University Press, 1989.

Stein, Howard F. *Listening Deeply: An Approach to Understanding and Consulting in Organizational Culture.* Boulder, CO: Westview Press, 1994.

Stein, Howard F., and Maurice Apprey. *From Metaphor to Meaning: Papers in Psychoanalytic Anthropology.* Charlottesville: University Press of Virginia, 1987.

3

Death Imagery, Euphemism, and the Experience of Organizational Downsizing

INTRODUCTION: DOWNSIZING, ECONOMICS, AND AMERICAN CULTURE

My first extended organizational study or "test case" of euphemism is "downsizing," which is to say the mass layoff and firing of employees. Here, experiential realities of downsizing, reductions in force, restructuring, outsourcing, and cognate terms are often at wide variance with their touted and expected promises of increased productivity, profit, rationality, realism, efficiency, teamwork, and role interchangeability. Vignettes cited suggest that downsizing is often not primarily about economics or business, but instead myth and ritual. Downsizing is explored as a symbolic form and action, rationalized and masked by euphemism. Downsizing implements devastating planned social change, one that takes the form of sacrifice to purchase organizational life via symbolic death. Downsizing is experienced as a metaphorical Holocaust, one driven by the need to perform sacrifice in order (a) to separate "bad" from "good" parts of oneself, and (b) to secure organizational rebirth through the expulsion of death. The link between the popular 1993 movie *Schindler's List* and organizational themes in the language of the Holocaust is explored and takes us to the heart of the conscious and unconscious emotional experience and meaning of downsizing.

Whatever the ideological chasms between positivism, modernism, constructivism, and postmodernism, they at least agree on the position that things are rarely what they seem to be, or are officially declared to be. Life is more than meets the eye or ear or nose. It is the additional, and disturbing, legacy of the century of the Freudian revolution to teach us that our thoughts, feelings, and decisions are made from unconscious material to which we have rare and ambivalent access, let alone over which we exercise complete control. We act, but we do not know wherefrom we are acting—though we insist we are consciously and rationally in charge of our thoughts and destinies. In a sense—and I shall say this over and over again in different ways about the subject of "downsizing"—our depths and breadths of meanings and emotions elude us because we unconsciously wish them to do so.

Here is precisely where a psychoanalytic perspective on workplace and wider cultural organization is essential: both retrospectively over the past decade and prospectively toward the millennial year 2001. The contribution of the present study will be to show how an apparently rational action such as downsizing is being driven by unconscious motives. I conclude that if we paid more attention to unconscious motives, we could avoid much grief and long-term social costs, as well as economic costs. Yet, it is of the very nature of unconscious resistance, especially when buttressed by group consensus, to wreak havoc on reality testing in the name of preserving psychological—and including organizational—structure.

I shall make an effort to reclaim more of the story of downsizing than Americans find comfortable. Although I am a citizen of American culture, I cannot turn away from what I have learned through a decade of consulting and writing on the triad of social change, loss, and grief in workplace organizations, including one of its most widespread manifestations, the mass firing of workers.

In this chapter on American downsizing, I situate "economics" within culture rather than outside as its "engine." That is, I locate it within a broader ideological structure of what life is all about, and within the shared unconscious substrate of such ideological systems, rather than uncritically accepting economics as the driving force of our society. In many circles, this is secular heresy. However, I come to this interpretation inductively and inferentially—not deductively from theory— from twenty-five years of ongoing fieldwork inside biomedical training institutions and from consulting. My views take exception from much of our received, official, and even obligatory wisdom about American's healthcare institutions, corporate decision making, and their link to the wider national culture.

I do not ask the reader to accept this counterintuitive, against-the-cultural-grain view on faith, but on data—data different from spreadsheets and computerized profit/loss/production statements. I shall question our own business-related cultural presuppositions, most of which are not articulated in mission statements and strategic plans— *To wonder why getting rid of people on a large scale in the workplace via upper-management decision making is the first and final solution (the latter, a term upper management often uses) we now offer and implement to organizational problems of profit, loss, productivity, and global competition.* Why this? Why now? I ask these on a large cultural scale, much as a physician wonders why a patient develops a particular disease at a particular time, and why the patient comes to the office or to the hospital emergency room at this time instead of some other.

I should state my premises from the start. Downsizing, reductions in force (RIFs), restructuring, reengineering, rightsizing, outplacement, outsourcing, placing offshore, and trimming fat, to cite but several core euphemisms, are not primarily business decisions determined by economic rationality, enlightened self-interest, pragmatism, realism, empiricism, and objectivity—although our American cultural rule is that we *should* if not *must* see them as motivated this way and only this way (see 't Hart 1991). I hope to show through seven vignettes that *downsizing* and cognate terms are cultural maps and euphemisms. Through them we direct ourselves and are directed by others toward some things and away from others. These maps make some things explicit and blur others. I describe how downsizing and related ostensibly business terms are deeply embedded in unstated values (workers as machines and expendable units of production), perception of time (short term rather than long term), and unconscious conflict (e.g., about aggression, dependency, and identity). I argue that downsizing as a mode of decision making and of induced social change is opaque to comprehension if we do not first recognize that it rests upon unstated values placed on human life, well-being, and loyalty, to name but three dimensions.

Far from being the pinnacle of rational, enlightened self-interest and objective judgment, downsizing is driven by destructively irrational forces. Even *The Wall Street Journal* and *The Washington Post* (e.g., Grimsley 1995) now feature articles that raise skeptical "second thoughts" about the heady promises advocates of downsizing made in the 1980s era of corporate leveraged buyouts, raids, takeovers, and mergers. The cover story of *Newsweek*'s February 26, 1996, issue is titled "Corporate Killers." David M. Noer's recent book (1993) is tellingly titled in euphemism-free English: *Healing the Wounds: Overcoming and Revitalizing Downsized Organizations.* Sometimes sacred, culturewide solutions turn out to be recognized as problems in disguise—or at least safely so in retrospect.

In our zeal to "de-layer" and "horizontally flatten" workplaces (a paradoxically "vertical" act), and to brand those "cut" ("axed," as many newspaper and magazine cartoonists depict) as nonessential "fat," we forget that in the 1970s and 1980s we regarded increasing administrative, managerial vertical layers as solution rather than as problem. We could not produce and hire MBAs (masters of business administration) fast enough. We once believed in the "fat" we now disdain, cut, and discard. They were to be our organizational "muscle," a police (externalized superego) to help corporations gain better control. Now "bloating" is our enemy, and "anorexia" is our salvation: yet both are our own organizational ideologies.

Downsizing is an inescapable reality and has been a constant threat in the United States during the past decade. There is scarcely any American whose life has not been directly touched, or at least threatened, by it, often multiple times. Many executives as well as workers have been through two, even three, mass layoffs. Many now hold two, three, even four jobs to make ends meet for themselves, their families, and their life-styles. Downsizing as reality, as memory, as anticipated event, as emotion-charged fantasy casts many shadows. Having said this, I wish also to be clear that I am not engaging in "downsizing-bashing." The culprit is not a specific mode of organizational change, but is rather unrecognized and disavowed influences that drive workplace life. Following upon the pioneering work of Diamond (1984, 1985, 1988) and Diamond and Allcorn (1985), I argue that business and other workplace organizations in our mixed-capitalist economy, like larger ethnic groups and nations, are largely unconsciously constituted and constructed. Downsizing is a special, and current, instance of this process. Business, policy, economics—from day-to-day bureaucracy to upheavals—are not sufficient unto themselves; they rest upon volcanoes.

What downsizing *is* is inseparable from what it symbolizes and what it feels like to all involved. In a formula: downsizing (and related terms) is a cultural idiom of problem definition and problem solving in the language of economic necessity. If in the 1960s, the image of abundance and generosity prevailed in political economy, in the 1990s, the image of scarcity and deprivation dominates. There is not enough of anything (resources, money, love, caring, commitment) to go around in order to survive: this is the central unstated dread of our time.

Downsizing is a single institutional form taken by bloodless as well as bloody *domestic, internal wars* now occurring between groups inside the United States (Stein 1990a, 1994a, 1995a). Since 1990, the Cold War is ended, the "evil empire" of the Soviet Union is but memory. The aggression, though, that the bipolar world contained is now let loose among us. In an essay on the United States' defense budget, Stephen S. Rosenfeld astutely ties current pressure to increase military defense to free-floating anxiety:

Leading congressional Republicans have seized upon his [President Bill Clinton's] discomfort to define a post–Cold War global environment of pervasive danger and struggle. In this fevered vision, a fear of chaos replaces the old fear of communism. The outcome is a similar sense of embattlement and crusade, and a certain increased readiness to spend more on the military. (1995: A25)

We all live in Bosnia now. Our equivalents to "ethnic cleansing" and Balkanization are conducted in gang wars, in racial and ethnic strife, and in ruthless business competition, to name but three ways we strive to keep a sense of goodness inside and to expel badness outside, to create decisive local boundaries in an era of collapsing global boundaries.

Historically, I would situate downsizing as one expression of our domestic internal wars against a myriad of internal enemies. These wars erupted in the wake of the end of the Cold War and the emotionally destabilizing effect of the loss of the Soviet Union as our "shadow," or evil double, that served so well as a focus and vessel of Americans' disavowed aggression (Volkan 1988; Stein 1993, 1994a, 1995a, 1995b, 1995c). With the boomeranging return of the repressed, and of what we had dissociated and projected outside our national group self in order to feel good and whole, we now shatter into alliances and oppositions, corporate and clinical camps of enemies and allies, as well as ethnic and political ones. "We" are now uncomfortably "they" as well—unsure of our internal boundaries, as we continue to try to expel the "bad" from ourselves in groups as well as individually. In corporate businesses and academic biomedicine alike, our computers and spreadsheets conduct bloodless wars. But death and thoughts of death abound—as the vignettes below illustrate vividly.

SCHINDLER'S LIST AS PARABLE OF THE DOWNSIZING OF AMERICA

This chapter takes its inspiration from a movie, Steven Spielberg's 1993 *Schindler's List* (Spielberg, Molen, and Lustig 1993). For all its historical inaccuracies and understatement, this movie was a box office success and won an Academy Award in 1994 for best picture. It disturbed and fascinated me enough to see it three times—not only because it allowed me, an American Jew, to safely visit once again a still raw historical trauma. The more I watched it, the more I saw it also as allegory for our America of the 1990s, not only as a quasi-documentary of Europe between 1933 and 1945. Are there any "essential workers" left in America? "Business," ours or that of dandy-porcelain industri-alist Oskar Schindler, is high drama, opera, cinema, and grueling re-ality.

Now, I am aware that for an employer to lay off a large number of employees is not the same as to murder them by firing squads and in gas chambers. Symbolic murder is *not* actual murder. Equivalence at the unconscious level is *not* identical with equivalence at the level of reality. I only ask that the people whom I quote here be heard in their own voices, that we begin to wonder why so many people articulate their experience in the catastrophic symbology of the Holocaust, and that we not be quick to dismiss their idiom as exaggeration. If an entire nation uses downsizing as a preferred way to problem-solve, many peo-ple will be unemployable, uninsurable. Many will be left out in the cold—placed at great risk, to disappear, to go away and die. The presence of the Holocaust as a constant occupant of the inner repre-sentational world makes psychodynamic sense. Further, its presence can be discerned at the most global and the most concrete levels. Kren and Rappoport write that "insofar as the Holocaust is seen in general moral terms, it stands as the ultimate expression of the human capacity for organized evil and has come to serve as the standard to which all lesser or proximate evils are compared" (1994: 4). In organizational downsizings, the common invocation of images of Jews, Nazis, Gypsies, roundups, selection, trains, disposable people, and of the imminence of death transcends the lures of vulgarization, trivialization, and mer-chandising of the Holocaust.

Certainly "older" workers (those nearing or over fifty years) are among those at high risk for being regarded as expendable. They are the ostensibly less "fit" in a Social Darwinist sense, culturally and bi-ologically. What are experience, loyalty, the sense of organizational his-tory—for example, what has been tried before and succeeded or failed?—informal networking, and the girth and cumulative wisdom of one's Rolodex if one is viewed by management and younger co-workers as "dead meat" or "corporate fat"? Yet, are the "lean and mean" younger, less expensive competitors any more secure when upper man-agement begrudges them all benefits and perks? Nothing matters ex-cept the performance of the more and more narrowly defined task.

So what if knowledge of who counts, of how to work in a place, of how to solve problems, and of how to get something done in an organization are all lost through massive layoffs and reorganizations? In the new frame of reference that discounts all memory and history, that lives and works only in the immediate present, knowledge of intricate infor-mal human "systems" and of their history is obsolete. It does not matter that organizational thought, planning, and decision making are done on an increasingly irrational and self-destructive basis. The increasingly counterproductive destruction is obligatory. (Do we not ask today, retrospectively, how much Germany in the years of the Third Reich might have accomplished if it had kept its Jews on the German side and not banished them beyond the pale of humanity?)

Experience, a sense of institutional history, the availability of organizational memory "housed" in people, the value of knowing the "shadow organization" as well as the official organization—these are abruptly discounted, devalued, and repressed. The organization's loss of memory is in fact the conscious and unconscious banishment of memory by terrorism, by identification with the aggressor, and other defenses that also allow and encourage raw aggression to be expressed. All conventional wisdom about "how this place works (worked)" is suddenly declared null and void; value is itself transvalued. Everyone knows the wisdom stored in intermediate and even lower-echelon personnel about who to know and how to accomplish things. But suddenly, everything must be done "by the book," in terms of the formal organizational chart, the official structure, following the bylaws and charter, and so on. To speak of the calculated slaughter of meaning is not to indulge in poetic license, but to recognize the systematic degradation and murder of the human spirit. To say "What you know no longer matters" is to insist on the greater power and truth of a great lie. It is to wish dead the person(s) whose knowledge is now dismissed.

In this chapter I try out my fantasy that as an American culture we have become our own death camp, one where we hope some CEO Oskar Schindler or Daddy Warbucks (the industrialist in the Broadway musical *Annie* popular a decade and a half ago) will protect us with our jobs, our health insurance, and our dignity. But in the movie, even a person with the proper documentation, "papers," an "essential worker," could be summarily pulled out of the work-line and shot point-blank dead in the head. In our movie fantasies, we are now all Jews, wandering the corporate halls, industries, and campuses. Even upper management, whom we might fantasize as Nazi torturers and butchers, is not exempt. We are both Jews and Germans; we vacillate between poles of victim and victimizer. There is no place to hide. We who protect ourselves one day by consuming others might soon become the consumed. Spreadsheets and profit-loss figures are symptoms in the guise of impersonal solutions. Downsizing is bloodless, but we know that we have created a trail and a pool of blood. Symbolic murder harbors the wish to kill.

Schindler's List is parable. What the Nazis did to the Jews is allegory for what we Americans now do to our own. Sometimes cinematic and other artistic fiction is truer than official sociological fact. In the Vietnam War, the memory of which still haunts us over twenty years later, we Americans did not know who was friend or foe. All Vietnamese be-

came potentially dangerous "Gooks"—things, not people—depersonalized menaces. Today in our American hospitals, corporations, banks,
research and development institutions, industries, universities, and
even government, we do not know from one day to the next who is ally
or enemy. Many upper-management personnel have said to me: "The
person or board whose firings I execute today could fire me tomorrow,
no matter how productive or loyal an employee I have been." The living
are all disposable waste.

The scale of destructiveness is emotionally overwhelming even to
consider, as a Department of Human Services announcement describes:

> If the 1980s are remembered as the decade of mergers and acqui-
> sitions, the legacy of the 1990s will be the decade of downsizing
> and reorganization. The trend toward downsizing began in the
> late 1980s, but increased substantially in the 1990s, and widened
> its focus from blue-collar jobs to include white-collar jobs. The re-
> sult has been a virtual epidemic of job loss due to downsizing
> across all industries and forced career changes, especially among
> professional and white-collar workers. It has been estimated that
> two-thirds of all large firms in the United States (U.S.)—more
> than 5,000 employers—reduced their workforces in the latter
> half of the 1980s. From 1983 to 1988, approximately 4.6 million
> U.S. workers were displaced, with 2.7 million (57.8%) resulting
> from plant closings. An estimated 300,000 jobs will be lost in the
> banking industry alone in the 1990s, and over 200,000 jobs are
> being eliminated as part of the federal government's *"Reinvention"*
> effort. ("Prevention of Stress" 1995: 3)

Questions that come immediately to mind are why for nearly a decade we as a nation have been in the thrall of the beliefs (1) that the
primary motives behind downsizing are economic, and (2) that the only
victims have been those who have lost their jobs, and further, (3) why
we as members of workplace organizations have been so slow to notice
that in the workplace and outside, downsizing is everyone's business.
It is culturally significant, and disturbing, that we are surprised by how
widespread the suffering might be. Our self-blindedness—not unlike
tragic Oedipus' own—takes us to the heart of the matter. *"The bottom
line" (as culture) is not only about "the bottom line" (as economics)*. As
a way of thinking, "the bottom line" cries out for careful dissection.
Schindler's List is a warning about what our All-American bottom line
is coming to—a point to which I shall return in the vignettes.

We must listen carefully to people's images, words, metaphors, and
feelings as they describe downsizings and their roles. They are not in-

consequential, epiphenomenal, "icing" on the cake. If organizational RIFings are indeed bloodless, if borrowing from what Lucy Dawidowicz (1975) called "the war against the Jews" is allegorical, we must still take seriously the fact that *annihilation by Holocaust is a recurrent frame of reference by which people undergoing downsizing articulate what it feels like to experience RIFing.*

Ultimately, no one is secure from damage in this devouring process. No one is truly exempt, and everyone in some way becomes complicit. Boundaries are unclear and constantly shift in the liquid world of downsizing. Everyone is a potential Jew and a potential Nazi. Everyone is at risk. Perpetrators, victims, and bystanders (Hilberg 1992) are not fixed categories. Much of the Holocaust's systematic degradation, dehumanization, of non-"Aryans" (non-us; persons manufactured into disposable nonpersons, "them") commends analogizing precisely because at the unconscious logical level, if not at the behavioral level, the two had similar goals.

There is still another level one might characterize as the phenomenological level: the way people *experience and make sense of* the event and process of downsizing and of being downsized. *To live through downsizing, to witness it firsthand, is so horrible, so devastating, so inducing of regression, that the only consistent image that can do it justice is the Holocaust.* The first question is: "Was it *real?*" "Did this really happen at our organization, to us? Did *we* really do this?" To answer in the affirmative—whether one be consultant, outside observer, or employee—one must be able to experience enormous guilt, shame, anxiety, even terror, rage, remorse, and sadness. One must feel regression's disorganization and desperate effort to reorganize the inner and outer worlds. The next question is: "What image(s) condenses and sustains those feelings, wishes, fantasies, and the defenses against being overwhelmed by them?" Those who insist on analogy with the Nazi Holocaust have much to teach us about removing the shroud of euphemism and unreality from the face of downsizing. Use of the Holocaust metaphor commits the fallacy of misplaced concreteness only if we take the metaphor literally. An extension to this question is the "why" of motivation behind the selection of the Holocaust as the central story line, and of Nazis and Jews as the inseparable protagonists. I shall address this latter question of *analysis* via the vignettes and following them.

DOWNSIZING AND ITS VICTIMS

What happens to the morale, the spirit, the soul of an organization when it is guided by such imperative mottoes as "No margin, no mission," "The only bottom line is the bottom line," "Don't tell me what you did for me yesterday; tell me how you're going to benefit the company tomorrow"; or when, after a major series of layoffs, an executive or midlevel manager upbraids a worried worker: "What are you whining about? You weren't RIFed! You've still got your job! You should be relieved, grateful, not worried. Forget this nonsense and concentrate on productivity. We've a job to do." What happens to profit and to productivity when morale is assaulted by the degradation of "survivors"? What are the consequences of calling oneself, or of being called, a "survivor"? What happens to profit and to productivity both in reality and in expectation?

As in a drama, enter now, from the wings to center stage the downsizing corps of consultants and consulting teams who live out the prevailing military metaphor and competitive, war-like, atmosphere. These corps serve the symbolic function of "SWAT" teams and "Special Forces," even "hired guns." Economic and military metaphors condense. Business comes largely to be a military operation in disguise, one in which only the fit survive. The creation of a new, radically different future takes the unmistakable form of annihilation to prepare its way.

Downsizing in business, industry, health care, education, and government is a "logical" cultural extension of the widespread *eradication of all pasts* and of an *arrogant monochromatic and foreshortened vision of the future*. This new vision is one often imagined and imposed by upper-level executives isolated and self-isolated from the rest of the organization. Further, often the owners or largest investors consist of high-risk leveraging financiers who are virtually unacquainted, and who have little interest in becoming familiar, with the day-to-day details of the very industry or type of work done in the place they have acquired.

Downsizing is an institutionalized solution that is in turn embedded in a worldview that defines human life as nothing more than a globally competitive marketplace. It is a Hobbesian image of all social life (not only the workplace) as driven by sudden-death economics. It is also Social Darwinism in corporate rather than (or in addition to) nationalist guise. The reified body with whom we symbiotically fuse our own fate is the workplace. In the fantasy underlying this work-world, there are no people here, only products, producers (robots), and wished-for profit in the shadow of dread loss and death.

What is the view of the world in which downsizing and restructuring make sense and become orthodoxy? If I propose downsizing to be a problem rather than a solution—or as well as a solution—my point of departure is to understand the view that downsizing and reengineering are the *preferred* solution. Can a whole society be wrong? (See La Barre 1972; Edgerton 1992; Endleman, 1995; Stein 1994a.) And wrong in what ways? Is downsizing itself inherently evil (dehumanizing, degrading, destructive), or is it the way it is implemented that is evil? We are creating by result, if not by design, an emotionally vulnerable, unprotected, starved, regressively dependent, and enraged workforce, and we are rationalizing the entire process by insisting that it is necessary for organization economic survival.

Downsizing's Orwellian "Newspeak" euphemisms and cognates include an entire, obligatory vocabulary of self-deception. The emotional reality is of abrupt firings, staged as surprise attacks, layoffs, betrayal, abandonment of everyone, and plummeting morale. Downsizing is one contemporary expression of what I have come to call "murder of the spirit," a ubiquitous but little-explored, nonphysical act of violence in the workplace in which people are experienced and experience themselves treated as things, as commodities, as objects, producers of products, and themselves parts of production lines. Those unnecessary for the performance of functions are simply thrown away. For all the official, facile rhetoric of Total Quality Management, the 1990s come closely to resemble Frederick Winslow Taylor's early twentieth-century ideal of a totally controlled, impersonally efficient, American industry governed by principles of "scientific management." More so now than ever before in my experience, medical practice buildings, their standardized architecture and decor, and their human interactions are coming to resemble nothing so much as a *factory*.

In downsizings, who are the victims? Of course, the answer hinges on how victimhood is defined, and by whom. Ostensibly, it is those who are fired. On the other hand, officially, often by fiat, it is no one. There are no victims, only market forces. In today's entitlement-ridden society, virtually no one is left who does not claim some sort of victimhood: ethnic, national, racial, age, class, gender. I would insist that everyone is involved, from the CEO, CFO, COO, midlevel managers who do the actual face-to-face firing, the surviving rank-and-file workers "in the trenches," to the security guards who are summoned to escort those fired to their cars. Upper management might "only" be the psychological casualty of its indifference, its psychic numbing, rationalization, and denial, but more often than not, even upper management is eventually consumed by its own relentless revolution. Some of the most decisive, accomplished, arrogant, swashbuckling, intimidating CEOs and CFOs I know were fired by the very corporate board and stockholder supporters who had hired them to do the axings in the first place.

THE EXPERIENTIAL REALITY OF DOWNSIZING: SOME VIGNETTES

Vignette 1

Leaders, researchers, and consultants alike cannot help but be struck by the ubiquity of death imagery and feelings experienced and articulated by people going through downsizing. For this first vignette, I draw upon an example a consultant colleague told me at an organizational consultation conference. He had been working at a prominent national research and development (R & D) laboratory in the early 1990s. The widely shared image of the RIFing within the corporation was "sudden death." The image took and spread like a prairie grassfire.

The hapless supervisors who did the actual firing were called "angels of sudden death," a bitter twist on the celestial realm: expected mercy becomes unexpected terror. In this context, it will be remembered that the infamous Nazi concentration camp physician, Dr. Josef Mengele, who had "experimented" on thousands of Jews, had been known as the "Angel of Death" (Lifton 1986).

Those who were laid off were fired summarily. They were given absolutely no preparation or anticipation (except, of course, rumor). Security guards escorted the RIFed persons to their cars or other vehicles in the parking lot after they had cleaned out their offices and desks immediately that same day as they had been notified of their firing. Out of upper management's fear that computers and other vital equipment would be sabotaged or stolen, none of those fired were let back into the building after the security guards had led them this one final time to their motor vehicles, and their company keys were turned in. The manner or style of the firings was itself traumatizing. Soon its memory, amplified in further fantasy and dread, came to terrorize the R & D laboratory, even as everyone aspired and was exhorted to return to business-as-usual, only with redoubled effort. This style of forced "recovery" based on the "inability to mourn" (Mitscherlich and Mitscherlich 1975) makes inner recovery difficult if not impossible.

Vignette 2

Organizational metaphors and similes serve as a path to understand how members of a work-group imagine themselves and their situation, what it is like to be there (Stein 1990a, 1990b, 1994b, 1995a; Stein and Apprey 1987). They also serve as one "Royal Road" to an organizational unconscious, to widespread fantasies and affects that underlie and organize recurrent images.

Organizational metaphors express and reflect shared intrapsychic social reality (Diamond 1993). "This is what it feels like to work here" is what management and workers say through their metaphors. "Downsizing," "RIFs," "rightsizing," "restructuring," "reengineering," "outplacement," and "outsourcing" are widely used metaphors for causing, or participating in, great suffering and at the same time gaining vast emotional distance from that suffering. Through euphemisms in the idioms of mechanics and architecture, we can borrow our conscience from others, cede personal responsibility to "The Organization," diminish the feeling that we are causing harm, and therefore diminish our own sense of responsibility, anxiety, guilt, and shame (Alford 1990). Socially shared and justified defenses do not feel like defenses at all: they feel like reality. We "restructure" people whom we have first made into the image of cold, dead, things, not real, whole people.

At one Roman Catholic–sponsored urban hospital long known for its service to the poor, upper management announced and unilaterally executed large-scale firing without including department heads or chiefs of hospital services in the decision. Many employees called these layoffs "Pearl Harbor"—and this in an institution whose entire hierarchy had professed the Vatican II values of dignity and subsidiarity (that is, allocating decision making authority and responsibility not only to the top leaders of church, parish, or hospital, but to the bottom as well). Issues of economics and job security became inseparable from the sense of sham and betrayal and from the consuming rage and despair that shadowed the hospital's future among those who retained their jobs.

In a nutshell, the secular R & D organization in Vignette 1, and the sacred church hospital I just briefly described, were equally suffused by the same narrowly "bottom line" official ethos that made downsizing compelling and unquestioned. But images of the devastating surprise attack of Japanese airplanes on Pearl Harbor on December 7, 1941, and of sinister angels of sudden death—and its implicit allusion to the Nazi doctor Josef Mengele—tell a different narrative tale, one we dismiss at great peril.

These metaphors are not difficult to detect. They are difficult to recognize only if we defend ourselves from taking them in and taking them seriously. For example, as I read a transcript of interviews from a study of the downsizing of a large urban hospital (in Allcorn, Baum, Diamond, and Stein 1996), I wrote down a succession of metaphors and similes.

Rumors are running amok

I'm afraid that when problems arise, my department will be scapegoated

"Am I the one?" [targeted to be fired]

Hospital as the target

Black Friday

D-Day [invasion]

How long can a gun be held to someone's head before they say "shoot"? [reductions]

It was important to hear that the ship was not going down and a message like, "This too shall pass"

Flatten the organization [administrative layers]

Everyone was herded like cattle to slaughter into the auditorium [to announce the layoffs]

It is almost like the university and the medical center are in a glass bubble—people do not know what is going on in the outside world [boundary issues]

Everyone is feeling vulnerable—there is the feeling that we will never let this [the layoffs] happen again, like the Holocaust

The reader might say that, in so enumerating and isolating core metaphors, I am taking them out of their narrative context. I agree. I do not discount the more obvious sequential, narrative context of the detailed interviewing of hospital managers. On the other hand, the official context can be seen as a kind of "smoke screen" to divert attention from the "fire"! The fire is itself clearest when we consider only the metaphors by themselves, as closest to the underlying, unconscious context. It is emotionally draining to read the above list—because it feels so overwhelming. There is nowhere to hide. There is no protection from total vulnerability. Perhaps that is what it feels like to work at this hospital.

Vignette 3

At one large urban, academic health sciences center that consisted of a confederation of a dozen specialty hospitals, it was widely rumored in late 1994 that some 400 people would soon be fired from the hospital system, and 400 additional unfilled hospital staff positions (clinical and administrative) would be eliminated. One entire hospital building was to be closed, and position transfers to other hospitals would not be permitted. The campus learned of this decision and of its imminence through the local newspaper in mid-January 1995. I was invited by upper management to work with the department of human relations, the personnel department, and nursing administration of the hospital system to help a task force prepare the campus for this process and help them deal with the extended aftermath. My consulting role continues through the present.

During an initial two-hour meeting in late January, members of one planning committee said many things that resonate with what was said and felt at the hospital I discussed in Vignette 2 above. The comparative study of accounts of organizational disaster such as downsizings will help consultants and theorists alike to identify and distinguish between local and universal themes, and to learn how to be helpful. Among my field notes from the meeting appear a number of poignant phrases spoken by staff members:

> I'm planning a funeral for somebody who's going to die but doesn't know they're going to die. . . . As a manager I feel it's like World War II. The Nazis have come in and tell us, "Point out all the Jewish people" so we can get rid of them. Then tell us the Gypsies, then the Poles. . . . That's what it feels like. . . . We're asked to plan a funeral and we don't know who's going to be attending. . . . This is my home [the hospitals; spoken with tears in her eyes]! They are my family! . . . Nursing is nurturing and difficult to let people go. So how does a nurse tell another nurse she's fired? I'm a manager. How do I work with a shorter staff (and still be nurturing)? If I survive this time around, how do I know I'll be here the next cutback? . . . I have vast concerns that I will not be employed here long, and I'm one of the people in charge of the program for the people who are being fired now.

Vignette 4

The material in this example is taken from field notes that I made during and after a postdownsizing meeting of a large hospital's middle administration in April 1995. Although hospital administrators did not question the need for large-scale layoffs, they invited my participation as consultant to try to minimize the human suffering from the outset, to try to help the immediate and long-term process to be more humane. The meeting took place after participants had conducted four two-week "displacement training workshops" for groups of people who had been laid off. Holocaust imagery pervaded the discussion:

> People [at the hospital] are just waiting for the Nazis to come and demand the next trainload of Jews to ship to the camps. We've been through three downsizing displacement training workshops now. What will hospital restructuring do to us? No one tells us. Decisions come down from the top, and we're supposed to carry them out. We might be the next to go, no matter how well we do our jobs. . . .

During the four downsizing workshops at St. Gregory's Church, we held a job fair, helped people to prepare resumes, to fill out forms to collect unemployment compensation. We had consultants give excellent career counseling; it wasn't just touchy-feely. We were totally ignored by everyone in the hospital. It was as if we weren't there, as if the RIF hadn't taken place. Nobody talked about it; nobody talked to us. It's like they didn't want to know, even though people in our departments knew full well what we were doing all those weeks. Couldn't a doctor have offered to buy or bring the *pizza* [emphatic, anguished] for a lunch, for the staff or for displaced people? We go around here [the hospitals], and they [other employees] act like they don't even know us. Nobody else sees what we do. They don't want to know.

Vignette 5

The data in this vignette are taken from field notes I took during a middle-management hospital postdownsizing meeting about seven months after 500 people had been laid off from a workforce of 3,500. Here, a veteran nurse, now in nursing administration, speaks about the atmosphere in personnel (the unit where we were meeting). She had had to walk through the department to get to our conference room:

Personnel used to be up-beat, where you could go in the hospital to feel good. Not up-beat now. It is worse in personnel than in other hospital departments. There is a feeling of helplessness, hopelessness, powerlessness. You want to scream and say: "I'm affected, too! Not only the people who are no longer here. . . ." There were no raises in personnel except the *internal auditor* who showed [to the upper hospital management council in charge of the layoffs] what could be done on the computer. *He* got a raise. "Just get them out [the ones being laid off]" was the message we got. "And we don't want to hear about it." No one got any pay or even a compliment for the kind of work we did [two-week-long "work fairs" in which they provided support and information for each group whose jobs had been eliminated].

Vignette 6

This sixth vignette is a composite of countless mini-events and mini-vignettes that occurred, the theme of which I recognize only retrospectively. The narrative line from these conversations and consultantships is stereotypical. According to a common organizational story line, unspeakably terrible as the bombing of the Federal Building in Oklahoma City was, it is the idiom or medium through which one could at last speak of how unbearable was one's own experience of downsizing and/or the swift onset of the age of corporate medicine. The ordinary could only be expressed through the extraordinary, yet the ordinary felt worse.

For myself, as observer, listener, and consultant, it took many hearings to fathom that executives, managers, workers, doctors, nurses, and hospital administrators would think, let alone tell me, so emotionally counterintuitive an idea that the bombing served as a *liberation* from their emotional isolation. For through it, they could at last talk about how harrowing it was to live and work in their downsized and medically minimalist organization via talking about the bombing—and finally wend their way somewhere in the conversation back to their own organization.

In art, such displacements are everyday occurrences. For instance, the great nineteenth-century Italian composer Giuseppe Verdi bypassed the Austrian censors by staging his deeply nationalistic Italian operas in other nations and at other times: for example, the Babylonian captivity of the Jews in *Nabucco*; *Un Ballo in Maschera* (*A Masked Ball*), was depicted alternately in eighteenth-century Sweden or colonial New England. Verdi could write, and his fellow Italians could passionately sing, about their oppressed homeland without ever mentioning its name. Likewise, in corporate, bureaucratic Oklahoma workplaces, one could avoid censure if one spoke about how terrible the Oklahoma City bombing was, but the bombing was a code word for the heartbreak of downsizing and for fewer and fewer workplace health benefits.

In the months after the bombing of the Federal Building in Oklahoma City, many clinical, administrative, manufacturing, and corporate colleagues throughout Oklahoma have told me essentially "the same" scenario, one adapted to, and told in the language of, their specific work environment. (This is a process parallel to that in folklore and mythology in which there are numerous variations on a central folk tale or myth.)

> The move toward managed care in health, and the long-term recovery from downsizing, are more devastating than you can imagine. Nobody wants to hear of it. It might sound like a sin to say so, but for a lot of us [in Oklahoma City, in organizations throughout Oklahoma], what we went through and still go through in downsizing and endless restructuring feels far worse to us than the bombing felt. Downsizing and managed care *are our* bombing.

Horrible as it is to say, when the bombing took place, we finally had a way we could talk about what we had been going through for several years. My office partner and I were discussing recently the bombing and the layoffs and their relation to one another. There really shouldn't be, but there was. And it sounds ridiculous. All in all, both of us believed that we had been more affected by the layoffs and the endless reorganization, and awaiting another corporate takeover, than by the bombing itself, as ridiculous as that idea seemed. Yet the bombing was only ten miles away. The idea wouldn't go away. The bombing seemed to present us all with a socially acceptable way to mourn our own "loss of innocence" [a term many people on the prairie used to describe the emotional effect of the bombing] that now felt like it had more faces than the bombed-out Murrah Building. Maybe what we feel from the layoffs is not as crazy as we originally thought. After all, when we went through our corporate layoffs, we in the EAP (Employee Assistance Programs), in personnel, and in security were the rescue workers. We helped the people fired and the people who stayed on to pick up the pieces and go on with their lives. We were the people working long shifts, going the extra mile, holding hands, giving hugs, bringing in food and holding day after day of seminars to help people get back on their feet. And we're not alone in our huge firm. We go to regional meetings and conventions with people in our line of work and we hear the same thing. We feel less isolated and less crazy when we find out they're feeling exactly the same thing.

Vignette 7

My seventh and concluding vignette is drawn, not from individual conversations and consultations, but from popular media representations of downsizing and related management doctrines of organizational change. Not surprisingly, magazine and newspaper articles and cartoons (and cartoonists) present in public forms the same sentiments and images presented in more private, individual and group forms. In mass society, no less than in small scale, preliterate society, folklore, mythology, and metaphor tell us the secrets of our hearts. Culturally popular and widespread iconography should corroborate the themes found in organizational consultation and study.

For instance, the widely cited, and controversial, cover story of *Newsweek*, February 26, 1996, was titled "Corporate Killers." Bright red lettering stood boldly upon a black background. The photographs of the faces of four corporate executives were captioned with their name, their company, and the number of jobs they had "cut." The inside headline of the story is "The Hit Men"; and the large-lettered preamble reads: "It used to be a mark of shame to fire workers en masse. Today Wall Street loves it" (Sloan 1996: 44).

On the page containing the table of contents, the theme of the magazine's cover story is illustrated by an ax head with its sharp blade in the foreground, captioned: "Stocks are soaring. The economy is healthy. Yet the streets are littered with the bodies of white-collar workers. Firing people is trendy in Corporate America. Now, with workers' woes becoming a hot issue in the presidential campaign, it's backlash time" (*Newsweek*, February 26, 1996: 3). It requires little explanation to link this popular "news" culture language and imagery with that evoked in previous vignettes.

Finally, consider the phenomenal popularity of newspaper cartoonist, and now book author, Scott Adams' character "Dilbert" (1996). The United Feature Syndicate character and ruthlessness of decision making style are distilled literally into an art form. CEO Dilbert, his consulting partner, Ratbert, the Evil Human Relations Director, Catbert, and others are relentlessly, sadistically inventive in ways to get rid of people, to get them to destroy themselves, to torment and torture them, to distort and distend their workers' very bodies. For example, in one cartoon, Catbert orders all employees to wear shoes one size smaller than their feet: "We must do this to be competitive"; the practice is called "footsizing" (1996 cartoon). The grimace of acknowledgment on our faces recognizes the pain: from the *Newsweek* cover story to the popularity of "Dilbert" business cartoons, brutality, indifference to suffering, the pleasure in inducing pain, the writing off for dead large numbers of people—all tell in media language the identical story line told in person in workplace organizations from hospital to university to corporation to government.

INTERPRETATION, IMPLICATIONS, AND CONCLUSIONS

What do we—as leaders, managers, consultants, social scientists, vulnerable mortals—make of these vignettes, and of the meanings of downsizing in whose shadow they stand? Do they help illumine the effects, the process, the meaning, the symbolism, and the catastrophic emotions brought to and evoked by downsizing? Do they convey something vital about American culture, about human nature, and about what we ought to do with their message? Do we—as scientists, clinical practitioners, managers—shrink from responsibility for cultural change by taking a schizoid flight to the moon to find refuge and revenge? Do we secretly obtain vicarious pleasure from the destruction of human lives? Is downsizing a modern, highly abstracted, form of human sacrifice: That is, if one lives, another must die? Is downsizing or RIFing our equivalent form of, say, Aztec bloody rites to assure the return of the sun? In downsizing, do we literally try to "buy time" for ourselves and our organization's "survival" through the symbolic death of others? (The notion of workplace or other organizational "survival" is itself a reification, projection, and anthropomorphization [see Alford, 1990], an example of the logical "fallacy of misplaced concreteness," for no workplace organization is a literal biological organism that goes from birth to death.)

The ethnographic data here suggest that the answer is a grim *yes* to all of these questions, and no amount of death suffices to assure and regenerate life. The corporate immortality project (Becker 1973, 1975) of downsizing must fail, but it cannot be interrupted. There is always some "fat" and "dead meat" that can be cut or trimmed (condensing numerous primitive anxieties from annihilation, to separation, to castration).

Can we acknowledge the enormous loss and grief—the emotional price and cost—this specific form of induced social change has caused? Can we not retreat into psychology-as-smoke-screen, but use psychology as lighthouse to show us where we have done evil, and where we can repent, console, and make amends?

The seven vignettes in this chapter constitute frequently encountered narrative accounts and metaphors offered by people involved in downsizing. As images and story lines, they are thematically representative of lived worlds, although not necessarily statistically so. That is, they serve as cultural exemplars of events and processes that extend far beyond themselves. They tell the story of modern America as refracted through dominant business language and practice.

In this chapter, I have tried to keep to the phenomenological level, that is, the world as experienced and articulated by the interviewee and client, rather than the one mostly interpreted by the participant observer. I have tried to let the vignettes mostly "speak for themselves," rather than force an interpretation upon them, or attempt to dissect them in terms of a preferred psychoanalytic and anthropological theory (for instance, classical topographic or structural theory, object relations theory, self psychology, textual deconstruction). Still, as Freud and Oppenheim (1958), Koenigsberg (1975), Dundes (1984), Paul (1987), and Stein (1994a) have argued, myth, folklore, fairy tales, political ideology, and legend all contain the outlines of their own interpretation. From folklore we could reinvent everything we have learned from clinical psychoanalysis via the couch, free association, and the dream.

In a sense, although Freud's topographical model of mental functioning—that of the vertically organized dynamic process involving the triad of unconscious, preconscious, and conscious thought—is immensely useful, it is also at times a misleading fiction. For "the depth" can often be readily seen and heard at the cultural surface. Those whom in business and other organizations we observe and with whom we consult are telling us the secrets of their hearts even as they are disguising them.

Experience and interpretation or analysis (explanation) are inseparable. Why, for instance, do people liken downsizing to a Holocaust rather than to other cataclysms? Why are we making everyone into Jews to be gassed, or into Nazis? What makes managers blind to the real economic costs, in rational terms, of downsizing—not to speak of the human costs? Why is sacrifice invoked and implemented as the obligatory mode of problem solving? At least the beginning and direction (content) of answers to these linked questions—"Why sacrifice?" (solution), "But why *these* symbol choices (metaphorical Holocaust, Jews, Nazis)?", and "Why now?" (timing)—come from the downsizing interview and work-group narratives themselves and from their wider cultural reverberations. *The subject of the Holocaust drama is sacrifice, the wish to purify and magically restore one national "body" by purging it of another (indeed, of all others) felt to threaten and defile it.*

In the West, Jews have been history's perennial scapegoat or victim, an always-available "other" or foil through whom other ethnic, national, and religious groups attempt to solve their group identity panics (Erikson 1963). When "we" become threatened with dissolving boundaries, we are in turn menaced by what those boundaries contained and kept safely from us: for instance, the hitherto repressed and dissociated "bad" parts of ourselves such as unacceptable sexual and aggressive wishes, death, and separation/dependency conflicts. At the level of social interaction, Jews as real people and as image (internal representation) become the "them" through which "we" can redefine, revitalize, and restore ourselves as "good" once again—an identity struggle likewise played out throughout Jewish history in conflicts over assimilation, separatism, accommodation, and other temporary adaptations.

In *The War Against the Jews, 1933–1945*, Lucy Dawidowicz writes that " 'the Holocaust' is the term that the Jews themselves have chosen to describe their fate during World War II. . . . The word derives from the Greek *holocauston*, the Septuagint's translation for the Hebrew *olah*, literally 'what is brought up,' rendered in English as 'an offering made by fire unto the Lord,' 'burnt offering,' or 'whole burnt offering.' The implication is unmistakable: once again in their history the Jews are victims, sacrifices" (1975: xxiv). Since World War II, many religious and ethnic groups have adapted the term *Holocaust* to depict the cataclysmic destruction visited upon themselves as sacrificial victims in their histories as well. For one to live, another must die, is the magical formula through which a person or group offers another person or group up to a savagely demanding deity and conscience in order to purchase immortality, or at least some more time on this side of death's divide.

A culturally clinical formula comes into play: "We are dying" is the diagnosis; "sacrifice" is the treatment. If "we" feel we are dying, "infected" with death (as introject), then, under the pull of regression and the catastrophic dread of annihilation (Devereux 1955), "we" initiate the sacrifice of "them" as a sacred ritual of purification in order to restore "us" to life, to enable "us" to be reborn as a group, by expelling and "killing" death. Through sacrifice, "we" bring order (life) out of the chaos (death). Sacrifice is the designated means toward this end. The identification, segregation, and elimination of metaphoric Jews from the workplace is the symbolic action by which organizations expect to be magically renewed, cleansed, and born again by the casting out of death (that is, symbolically putting one's own death into others, and then eliminating them, as in scapegoating).

What now invokes the archetypes (Jung) or unconscious fantasies (Freud) of sacrifice? What creates the need for metaphoric Nazis and Jews in the workplace and beyond? It is the collapse of previously internally and intersubjectively stabilizing boundaries, the conflation of "good" (inside) with "evil" (outside), the regression in the face of overwhelming anxiety, and the desperate effort to reorganize the inner world by radically segregating "good" from "evil" in order to contain evil once again outside oneself and one's social units ranging from workplace to nation (via projective identification, see Klein 1946).

At least in part due to the end of the Cold War, the clear-cut polarity of good and evil, of victim and aggressor as inner representations (Meissner 1978), of sacrificer and sacrificed, has been denied not only to Americans, but to the rest of the world as well. The boundary between oppressor and oppressed is unclear. It fluctuates from one moment to the next. Distinctions blur, and with it free-floating anxiety and the search for enemies erupt. Jews and Nazis, as conscious images of the oppressed and oppressor, boomerang to become uncomfortably a part of us (introjects or internal objects, that are indigestible, unassimilatable, haunting presences, in psychoanalytic terms). If the sacrifice of Jews has been an historical solution to restore the purity of the social body, to restore magically the symbiotic fusion of infant with "good" mother (Koenigsberg 1975), this same solution is fraught now with anxiety, shame, guilt, and even identification. In World War II, Americans waged "the good war" against the Nazis, and (together with other Allied armies) liberated the Jews from the death camps—only to have now internalized the war against the Jews and the fear of victimization within the boundaries of the United States. We want to sacrifice; we are the sacrifice. We wish to be and to do good; no matter what we do, we are evil; we carry out our own or others' evil. Even to be a loyal Nazi or bureaucratic servant is no assurance of personal or corporate survival. As the above vignettes poignantly attest, we oscillate between both extremes, even as we contain both and further consciously identify with Jews and counteridentify against Nazis. But we are inescapably both: innocent sacrifice (victim) and guilty tormentor. We are Nazis or zealous bureaucrats one day, Jews the next.

In business and other organizational contexts, *we strive to buy time, if not survival and immortality, through continuous sacrifice* (a sacrifice that attempts to get rid of the "bad" all at once and at all developmental levels: both pre-oedipal and oedipal, from ridding ourselves of disavowed primitive parts of the self, to killing off the competitive parent of the same sex and the rebellious child who wished to kill). The idiom or language of this sacrifice is that of economics or business: we wage continuous, relentless economic competition to save and revive our institutions. Through sacrifice, we believe that if—by endless cycles of cuts and belt-tightenings—we trade enough death for life, we will survive and gain in profit, morale, and productivity. That is the magical wish and deed. But the miracle never happens, or happens only over a brief short term. The organization and the nation are consumed by dread and hate.

Psychodynamically, "bad objects" are not clearly put and kept "out there"; we are virtually possessed by them, in here, everywhere. We act such that all "good objects," all decency, all love, all kindness, all generosity, and all civility have been or should be destroyed, because there is no way we can live up to them (and be loved by them) as ego ideals, as sources of love, as culturally shared symbolic "objects" of value. We cannot be rid of our Jews fast enough, and there are never enough Jews to be rid of. Like World War II Germany, we consume ourselves in our frenzy to rid ourselves of Jews. But even the choice of what Erikson called the "negative identity" (1968), the negative ideal, is insufficient, because we both wish to be and not to be Nazis, and both wish not to be and yet become Jews. No symbolic solution is "final," unambivalent, or secure.

From the historical fear of being Jews (even Jews struggle with their cultural identity), we have come to the point that we are all Jews potentially, imminently. "We" don't sacrifice "them"—or if we do, it is only for a time; "we" are "them," as everyone becomes a sacrifice. We cannot be rid of the bad whether we are Nazis or Jews; and there is no way, or even hope, of restoring the good. Put differently, the false self triumphs with the utter exile and despondency of the true self. Nothing we—as imagined Jews or Nazis—do will save us, though we act as if we can and must save ourselves, or at least our institutions. We condemn ourselves to be the condemned.

We cannot, and may not, stop ourselves. In this Schindler-less world, there is no goodness or benevolence; there is no longer any long-term social contract; everyone is a "temp" (temporary worker). In short, the Holocaust, Jews, and Nazis all condense—as in groups' dreams dreamt in wakeful hours—into a single image and epic story line where wish, motivation, fantasy, defense, relationship, and real world all define what downsizing is about and why it is obligatory.

If, by listening carefully enough to individual patients and clients (both individuals and groups), therapists and counselors learn how to treat them and how to consult, when to speak (e.g., interpret) and when to remain a silent presence, the same ought to apply to our work as researchers and consultants with organizations, especially those where images of disaster prevail. By attending carefully to people's expressed and lived-in worlds, we will learn what to do. This is not to repeat the old and wrong-headed anthropological dictum that "the native [of the group under study] is always right"; rather, the more carefully one listens, the more clearly will the complex texture of the story emerge. Conversely, it is precisely the *neglect* of the inner and intersubjective experience of downsizing that has us as a nation in the difficulty in which we find ourselves. Our slaughter of innocents comes from *not* attending to meanings and feelings—those of others and our own. Downsizing, which has long looked so appealing as a *solution*, is emerging instead as an enormous emotional as well as economic *cost* and *casualty* of our war with ourselves.

As of mid-August 1997, we congratulate ourselves in news stories as a nation that the rate of unemployment is at its lowest in a quarter century. People *can* find jobs, albeit with less pay, fewer benefits, and far less security than in the past. It turns out that even our most reliable economic indicators are (or can be used as) euphemisms!

We have made certain that no one is safe for very long, if at all. In *Schindler's List* lies our contemporary wished-for and dreaded biography of a few good and lucky women who make it as "essential workers"—and even they come to know how precarious their safety is. Ours is no American triumphant self-creation through hard work. The relentlessness with which downsizing is often executed tells us that fathomless rage, sadism, envy, greed, and revenge—among other emotions and motives—are the "bottom line" designated to eradicate every previously espoused element of American culture, a kind of cultural scorched-earth policy we practice upon ourselves. Downsizing is part of a social aesthetic that has no place for dandy-capitalist-turned-wily-rescuer Oskar Schindler, his protective list, or a protected cadre of "essential workers." In this ethos devoid of the sentiment of mercy, there are, mercifully, signs of increasing *resistance*—not in the Freudian sense, but in the sense of "underground," on the part of Americans who are coming to have a healthy disgust and even healthier regret for the nightmare we have created in the name of good business, efficiency, and streamlining, without so much as spilling a single drop of blood.

In the West, since the Calvinist days of the Protestant ethic and the spirit of capitalism (Weber 1930), we have single-mindedly believed that success from one's work was a sign of God's smile in this world, that personal effort would result in upward social mobility, and that ultimately, hard work would set us free of our past and present station. It was the sinister achievement of the Nazi era to transvalue this work ethic, to welcome its condemned slave labor to their labor-to-death camps with the large-lettered sign *"Arbeit macht frei,"* "Work will make you free." It was the special despair—joined with identification with the aggressor—of the doomed inmates, to believe their captors' lies.

It is the special horror of our time in America to have created a latch-key world for ourselves and our descendants, in which no one can make it onto Schindler's list, even if a benevolent CEO or chairman promises that some elect will be spared. The relentlessness of downsizing, RIF-ing, and its lengthy train of euphemisms bears the same message as presided over the gates of Bergen-Belsen and other Nazi slave labor camps: *Arbeit macht frei,* and one dare not question its sincerity. In this world of computerized, stylized, bureaucratized, and economically ra-tionalized hate, *work is only good for the production of death*. One could not be further from the work ethic by which every aspiring Horatio Alger believed he or she could pull him- or herself up by the individu-alistic bootstraps.

In the workplace and larger society governed by downsizing and the constant threat of further disruption, the turn toward frenetic work and productivity as "freeing" represents not only an identification with the aggressor, but a short-term adaptive denial of reality. It is a denial that diminishes paralyzing psychotic anxiety. It fuses omnipotence of thought with omnipotence of deed: "If I work hard enough, if I am pro-ductive enough, it won't happen to me," one tries to persuade oneself, to resolve the cognitive and affective dissonance. One desperately tries to un-know what one already knows. These work beliefs serve regres-sively as magical thinking that bribes the ego into thinking that through hard work one will be spared one's destiny, despite the over-whelming evidence to the contrary that virtually everyone is disposa-ble, expendable. A "text" more parallel with the beliefs held by many doomed Jews in the labor camps in Europe during the Nazi era could not be found. There is, of course, sad irony to this adaptation. A defense that "works" for the short term is powerless to influence the long term to which it submits and, more ironically, is complicit in bringing it about.

Personnel departments and outplacement organizations are espe-cially saddled with (that is, psychologically speaking: delegated, projected onto) this task: how to dispose of people, and only secondarily how to find work for disposable people. Those who perform the selections must somehow emotionally adapt to doing their odious task, rationalizing the very nature of their work (including their own aggressive impulses). They know full well they are performing in behalf of upper management and "the organization" the symbolic equivalent of digging mass graves for the soon-to-be-dead. Both love and the quiet voice of reason are banished, exiled from this Promised Land. Short-lived organizational rebirth and profit draw their nourishment from death, even if "only" symbolic.

Despite the screen of rationality, of dispassionate objectivity, of necessity, and of computerized impersonality, the selection of who is to be kept and who is to be fired is always personal choice and never mere number. Stylized apologies such as "don't take it personally" and "nothing personal," offered to those being laid off, are self-deceptions to distance oneself from one's deeds. Senior executives, midlevel management, and consulting firms all appoint or recommend certain people, and not others, to serve on employee selection committees. The process is not entirely alien to that employed by death camp physicians who decided who, in the long lines of people just disembarked from the trains, should go to the left and who to the right, who would live and who would die.

Despairing since the 1960s that the American Dream, the national ideal as embodied in the martyred Kennedys and Martin Luther King, Jr., was forever unreachable, even approximately, most Americans have all but thrown it away. The land of opportunity has now long become replaced by a land of frantic opportunism (Stein and Hill 1977). We have no Zyklon B cyanide gas chambers, no crematoria and tall smokestacks to belch human flesh's ashes upward, no barbed wire and tall watchtowers around our death camps. But make no mistake about it: downsizing is not primarily about economic competition and survival. Its hardened heart is about death, the dominion and triumph of death (Lifton 1979; Wangh 1986). It is about endless cycles of sacrifice to keep "the organization" alive, cleansed, profitable, and competitive, while consuming, one way or another, everyone in its midst. There is the unmistakable stench of burning human flesh in the air.

REFERENCES

Adams, Scott. *The DILBERT Principle: A Cubicle's-Eye View of Bosses, Meetings, Management Fads and Other Workplace Afflictions.* New York: HarperBusiness (HarperCollins), 1996.

Alford, C. Fred. "The Organization of Evil." *Political Psychology* 11, no. 1 (1990): 5–27.

Allcorn, Seth, Howell Baum, Michael A. Diamond, and Howard F. Stein. *The Human Cost of a Management Failure: Organizational Downsizing at General Hospital*. Westport, CT: Quorum Books, 1996.

Becker, E. *The Denial of Death*. New York: Free Press, 1973.

———. *Escape from Evil*. New York: Free Press, 1975.

Dawidowicz, Lucy. *The War Against the Jews, 1933–1945*. New York: Holt, Rinehart and Winston, 1975.

Devereux, George. "Charismatic Leadership and Crisis." *Psychoanalysis and the Social Sciences* 4 (1955): 145–157.

Diamond, Michael A. "Bureaucracy as Externalized Self-System: A View from the Psychological Interior." *Administration and Society* 16, no. 2 (1984): 195–214.

———. "The Social Character of Bureaucracy: Anxiety and Ritualistic Defense." *Political Psychology* 6, no. 4 (1985): 663–679.

———. "Organizational Identity: A Psychoanalytic Exploration of Organizational Meaning." *Administration and Society* 20, no. 2 (1988): 166–190.

———. *The Unconscious Life of Organizations: Interpreting Organizational Identity*. Westport, CT: Quorum Books, 1993.

Diamond, Michael A., and Seth Allcorn. "Psychological Responses to Stress in Complex Organizations." *Administration and Society* 17, no. 2 (1985): 217–239.

Dundes, A. *Life Is Like a Chicken Coop Ladder: A Portrait of German Culture through Folklore*. New York: Columbia University Press, 1984.

Edgerton, R. *Sick Societies: Challenging the Myth of Primitive Harmony*. New York: Free Press, 1992.

Endleman, R. *Relativism Under Fire: The Psychoanalytic Challenge*. New York: Psyche Press, 1995.

Erikson, E. H. *Childhood and Society*, revised edition. New York: Norton, 1963.

———. *Identity, Youth and Crisis*. New York: Norton, 1968.

Freud, Sigmund, and D. E. Oppenheim. *Dreams in Folklore*. New York: International Universities Press, 1958 [1911].

Grimsley, K. D. "The Downside of Downsizing: What's Good for the Bottom Line Isn't Necessarily Good for Business." *Washington Post National Weekly Edition*, November 13–19, 1995: 16–17.

Hilberg, Raul. *Perpetrators, Victims, Bystanders: The Jewish Catastrophe 1933–1945*. New York: Aaron Asher Books, 1992.

Klein, M. "Notes on Some Schizoid Mechanisms." *International Journal of Psycho-Analysis* 27 (1946): 99–110.

Koenigsberg, Richard A. *Hitler's Ideology: A Study in Psychoanalytic Sociology*. New York: Library of Social Science, 1975.

Kren, George M., and Leon Rappoport. *The Holocaust and the Crisis of Human Behavior*. New York: Holmes and Meier, 1994 [1980].

La Barre, Weston. *The Human Animal*. Chicago: University of Chicago Press, 1954.

———. *The Ghost Dance: The Origins of Religion*. New York: Dell, 1972.

Lifton, R. J. *The Broken Connection: On Death and the Continuity of Life*. New York: Simon and Schuster, 1979.

———. *The Nazi Doctors*. New York: Basic Books, 1986.

Meissner, W. W. *The Paranoid Process*. New York: Aronson, 1978.

Mitscherlich, A., and M. Mitscherlich. *The Inability to Mourn: Principles of Collective Behavior*. New York: Grove Press, 1975.

Noer, David M. *Healing the Wounds: Overcoming and Revitalizing Downsized Organizations*. New York: Jossey-Bass, 1993.

Paul, Robert A. "The Question of Applied Psychoanalysis and the Interpretation of Cultural Symbolism." *Ethos* 15, no. 1 (1987): 82–103.

"Prevention of Stress and Health Consequences of Workplace Downsizing and Reorganization" (Announcement 572). Atlanta, GA: Department of Health and Human Services, Public Health Service, Centers for Disease Control, National Institute for Occupational Health, Summer 1995.

Richards, A. I. *Chisungu*. London: Faber and Faber, 1956.

Rosenfeld, S. S. "Where to Cut Defense." *Washington Post*, November 17, 1995: A25.

Sloan, Allan. "The Hit Men" [of layoffs]. *Newsweek*, Business section, February 26, 1996: 44–48.

Spielberg, Steven, Gerald R. Molen, and Branko Lustig, Producers, Steven Spielberg, Director. *Schindler's List* [Film], 1993. (Available from Universal Pictures, 100 Universal City Plaza, Universal City, CA 91608.)

Stein, Howard F. "In What Systems Do Alcohol/Chemical Addictions Make Sense? Clinical Ideologies and Practices as Cultural Metaphors." *Social Science and Medicine* 30, no. 9 (1990a): 987–1000.

———. *American Medicine as Culture*. Boulder, CO: Westview Press, 1990b.

———. "Organizational Psychohistory." *Journal of Psychohistory* 21, no. 1 (Summer 1993): 97–114.

———. *The Dream of Culture*. New York: Psyche Press, 1994a.

———. *Listening Deeply: An Approach to Understanding and Consulting in Organizational Culture*. Boulder, CO: Westview Press, 1994b.

———. "Domestic Wars and the Militarization of Biomedicine." *Journal of Psychohistory* 22, no. 4 (1995a): 406–415.

———. "When the Heartland Is No Longer Immune: The April 19, 1995 Bombing of the Oklahoma City Federal Building." *Psychohistory News: Newsletter of the International Psychohistorical Association* 14, no. 3 (1995b): 2–4.

———. "The Rupture of Innocence: Oklahoma City, April 19, 1995." *Clio's Psyche* (A Quarterly of the Psychohistory Forum) 2, no. 1 (1995c): 1, 12–15.

Stein, Howard F., and M. Apprey. *From Metaphor to Meaning: Papers in Psychoanalytic Anthropology.* Charlottesville: University Press of Virginia, 1987.

Stein, Howard F., and Robert F. Hill. *The Ethnic Imperative: Exploring the New White Ethnic Movement.* University Park: Pennsylvania State University Press, 1977.

't Hart, P. "Irving L. Janis' Victims of Groupthink." *Political Psychology* 12, no. 2 (1991): 247–278.

Volkan, Vamik D. *The Need to Have Enemies and Allies.* Northvale, NJ: Jason Aronson, 1988.

Wangh, M. "The Nuclear Threat: Its Impact on Psychoanalytic Conceptualizations." *Psychoanalytic Inquiry* 6, no. 2 (1986): 251–266.

Weber, M. *The Protestant Ethic and the Spirit of Capitalism.* Translated by Talcott Parsons. London: George Allen and Unwin, 1930.

4

The Language of Euphemism and the World of Managed Care: Some Thoughts on Doctors, Patients, Organizations, Ethics, and Culture

"I do not condemn, I testify."

—Maxim Gorky

"It is hard to be a good doctor. The ways we are paid often distort our clinical and moral judgment and seldom improve it. Extreme financial incentives invite extreme distortions."
—Steffie Woolhandler and David U. Himmelstein (1995: 1707)

INTRODUCTION: EUPHEMISM, LANGUAGE, AND CLINICAL REALITY

In the Spring of 1996, I was invited to make a presentation at a forthcoming Oklahoma City conference honoring James E. Hurley, a biologist and inspiring teacher who had been on the faculty of Oklahoma Baptist University for some 35 years, and who had prepared many of his students for medical careers. The symposium title was "Health and Bioethics: Patient-Physician Relationships in the Era of Managed Care." The conference had been organized and sponsored by many of his former students. Dr. Hurley had long garnered the reputation as an exacting taskmaster when it came to scientific and medical thinking. He had long taught that things are rarely what whey seem, or are officially decreed to be, even in the "real world" of medical science. Over the past nearly twenty years, several of his former students had gone on to become "my" residents in Family Medicine. We all became kindred spirits. About a decade ago, I was invited to give a talk on medical organizational culture to a biology class of Dr. Hurley's at Oklahoma Baptist University, in Shawnee, Oklahoma. We met again a couple of years ago at a residency graduation.

When the planning committee for his symposium asked Dr. Hurley if he had any preferences for a presenter, he gave them my name. I was as daunted as I felt honored. Here was a man beloved for his dedication to teaching, to helping others learn, a deeply pious man, one of whose frequent roles in regional theater was Tevye the Milkman in *Fiddler on the Roof*. A century and a half ago, the brooding philosopher Soren Kierkegaard had asked whether there remained any true Christians left in Christendom. In Jim Hurley he would have found one. Somehow my talk at the conference honoring his career and life had to convey this, and its significance in our time as well—or fail utterly. He had asked that I address the nature and meaning of "managed care" for us all, not only for physicians and other healthcare professionals. He gave me my subject—what felt like my calling—to try to understand managed care from the perspective of American culture (and human nature), and in so doing to question some of our widely shared assumptions that take the topic far beyond medicine and into "business as usual."

I wish to begin this discussion of corporate medicine—this book's second "case study" of cultural revolution in the language of business—by placing my argument in the grim spirit of the metaphors "downsizing" and "RIFing" discussed in the previous chapter. Many conscientious physicians have said to me, in one way or another: "Managed care is the downsizing [which is to say the violent rupture] of all clinical relationships and in turn of all clinical medical practice." Many representatives of health maintenance organizations and of preferred provider organizations call on us, hoping to get a "buy in" from our faculty physicians and administrators. In this chapter I inquire into what we are being offered and what we might be lured into "buying into"—a commonly used term that superficially denotes concurrence with, acceptance of, a novel idea. Alas, even agreement with a new form of thought takes the language of financial purchase: We buy what someone else sells. Is this a Faustian bargain, in which we sell our soul for power, prestige, possession?

In the description and evocation that follows of what managed care is about lies a warning about the future nature of physician-patient relationships under the totally regulated world of managed care. If I sound like a clinical Dmitri Shostakovich in Stalinist Russia, it is because my message is despair. The subject of managed care, of corporate medicine, is the triumph of death. We have to stand still long enough to acknowledge it.

Taken more broadly, this chapter is a snapshot of the tenuousness and brittleness of virtually all future workplace relationships: in business, in industry, in government, in education, in corporations, and in those fields where health and mental health caring are supplanted by the packaging, the buying, and the selling of a product called "healthcare." "Managed [health]care" is about having less and less to give. It is about the sense of starving and of being starved, and of being unwilling and unable to give one thing more. There is only room, and time, for taking.

It is my thesis that managed care (and cognate corporate medical terms) is principally about values, about a philosophy of life ruled by images of stark scarcity and lovelessness, a worldview that rests upon inner emptiness, of a life identified with death. If it is a clinical ideology, it is one deeply and widely rooted in its era, specifically in unconscious conflict and its resolution. It is only secondarily, and derivatively, about business, economics, or even biomedicine, although these are its displaced foci and containers. Stated differently, managed care is not primarily about business, but rather business is the *language* or *idiom* through which we live out deeper, unstated values, meanings, feelings, and conflicts. Managed care is officially and ostensibly about economics. Politically, these are what managed care must be about, that is, the shared, obligatory rhetoric of discourse.

Managed care is one among many new "foci of evil" in the dark night of the soul created by the fall of the Soviet Union, the evil empire, our national evil double. Managed care is about implicit as well as explicit priorities. It is about people who count and people who are disposable. It is about figuring out ways of excluding people from various kinds of care, and justifying that exclusion. Not only as individuals, but as and in groups, cohorts, kinds of people: psychologically it is far easier to write off without protest or remorse people as groups than people as individuals.

Managed care is a symbolic, sanitized, form of internal, domestic, warfare. It is about the open public rupture, degradation, and elimination of human relationships, and of the clinical work conducted within them, in the name of cost cutting and profit. At the surface level, it is a means to an end: cost cutting as a means of profit. At a more profound level, it is another kind of means toward a different, more elemental, kind of end. Common to managed care, downsizing, reductions in force, and similar social forms is the wish to get rid of people, to eliminate some groups in large numbers as a sacrifice so that the fantasized group of survivors can be redeemed, live, and be symbiotically restored to the "organization" or the "nation" (see Koenigsberg 1975) as symbolic nurturant maternal figure. Managed care enacts the historically ancient and emotionally primitive wish to purchase life through death. It is magical thinking and magical acting: if one lives, another must die. So, managed care is about dealing with deep anxiety about annihilation, separation, castration, through the medium of healthcare economics.

Now, we do not say this directly to ourselves or to others. *Euphemism* plays the crucial linguistic and ideological variable of mediating deed and wish. Throughout this chapter I shall move backward and forward along the dynamic "chain" from description to phenomenology to defense to fantasy to wish. Managed care is located and operates simultaneously at all these levels.

Managed care is neither primarily about healthcare nor even about business, but about cycles of indulgent excess and privation, of "This-Bud's-for-You" entitlement, to fat-cutting, "lean and mean" sacrifice and penance. The cultural doctrine of one decade is "patients' rights" and increased "delivery of services," and in the next it is "limitation" and "cost containment." A mere two decades ago, as antidotes to physician paternalism and demands for compliance from patients, we were talking about patient autonomy, patients' rights, about greater equality of status between physician and patient. What many metaphorically now call "organizational anorexia" is an attempt to purge ourselves institutionally of greedy overeating (to continue the body fantasy and equation). Despite all the firings and waves of firings, and further, despite the rhetoric of "autonomous functioning groups," there is more administration and administrators, more oversight, than ever.

We treat our reified, projected, organizational body *obesity* with crash fad diets and massive "surgical cuts," that is, with *corporate anorexia* (Uchitelle 1996). But we should not mistake focus for substance, or else we will continue to solve the wrong problems. Managed care is about the overtaking of healthcare by a certain business way of thinking and deciding: but it is the symbolic battlefield on which unacknowledged wars of the soul are waged.

Much of the time in this chapter, I shall consider managed care from *outside* medicine, that is, from the viewpoint of American culture as a whole. A statement about managed care, corporate medicine, healthcare economics, and their ethics is necessarily a statement about core issues in American culture—themselves in turn a part of our species' attempt to grapple with being the human animal, neotenous and long-dependent in our big-brained infancy (La Barre 1954). This broader and deeper viewpoint casts in a new perspective such conventional American biomedical ethical categories as autonomy, justice, beneficence, nonmaleficence, conflict of interest, and responsibility (consider the German word *Verantwortlichkeit*, meaning literally "answerability" to someone's "calling," never merely numerical accountability). We have created a world in which we feel and act as if we have no responsibility toward those categories of people we have made into *non*-persons: those who have been fired during downsizings, those without health insurance, and so on. Part of my task in this chapter is to situate ethics within its culture and to redeem ethics from culture.

One might object that I do not present a logical, impersonal, detached, even scientific, argument; the objection is correct insofar as I attempt to look beneath or behind the official cultural logic to its deeper rationale, one the surface, everyday, logic is meant to conceal. Computer spreadsheets report profit and losses; their ink is blood, and their code is unspeakable brutality. As a clinical medical anthropologist, then, my principal goal in this chapter is to make the usual strange, and to make the strange usual, that is, to ask us to question our assumptions about managed care, a subject we think we already understand.

MANAGED CARE AS JUGGERNAUT AND DISPLACEMENT OF MOTIVES

Managed care is our *juggernaut*; that is, it possesses what appears to be an irresistible destructive force with a life of its own, a force to which we must succumb and adapt. To question it is heresy. We reify it into an alien, independent, oppressive force, as if we were "possessed" by its binding rule. Yet it is only made up of and by people such as ourselves. It is a kind of clinical corporate "Contract with America," except—unlike U.S. House of Representatives Speaker Newt Gingrich and his fellow "Cut Big Government" Congressmen overwhelmingly voted for in November 1994—it is not officially elected into office. Cultural ethoses never are: they are everywhere, permeating all institutional settings. Victims and victimizers constitute a system.

Whatever else might be done with care and caring, they cannot be "managed." The vessel destroys the substance it claims to contain. Caring can be structured, but it must leave room for uncertainty, ambiguity, novelty, surprise. The compulsive lust for total control can teach us nothing but how to dig deeper in a rut of our own ever-deeper cuts. Healing, like science, like music and poetry, like religious revelation, bursts all our boxes, shatters all our idols.

Caring—any kind of caring from an "I" to a "thou" (Buber 1957)—cannot be "managed," its outcome dictated and tightly controlled from the first, its end already fully known and prefigured. In truly caring for another human being, one brings all one knows to each situation, then lets the situation teach what and where and how and when to "do." Caring does not speak in a language of "provider assumes risk" or "customer assumes risk." Caring rests on presence, the risk of personal intimacy and devotion. It cannot be bought, even when the relationship includes some form of reciprocity in the form of fee for service.

Caring under managed care occurs despite the structure, not because of it. At the same time, I do not wish to polarize sentiment and structure, us and them, because we—our fantasies and feelings—are always part of the structure to which we adapt. The structure does not exist wholly by itself. The structure is not altogether "them"; even adaptation to the structure often permits members and employees to express rage and other aggressive wishes with impunity. The organization, "it," is often pretext and excuse. "It" does not have a life of its own separate from the people who constitute it. Often medical corporations have physicians as their CEOs and other upper administration. Clinician bystanders who submit and privately protest have also tacitly allowed the oppressors to take over. They are part of the oppression.

Sincere caring under managed care can properly be seen as a political, moral form of *resistance* (which it has been since the DRG [diagnosis-related group] era of the mid-1980s in hospitals, and occurs in all social forms where physicians feel obligated to "manipulate the system" or social structure in order to help the patient). There can be no caring, only endless distance-making "managing," when all sickness and frailty are the enemy that we would rather be rid of. Their true cost is their reminder of everyone's destiny, no matter how much preventive "wellness" or fitness we possess.

The site or location of "the bottom line" of managed care is not the computer spreadsheet, but in people's hearts. In the several weeks that followed the bombing of the Alfred P. Murrah Federal Building in Oklahoma City, health professionals, and almost everyone else, were guided by an entirely different "bottom line," a different *value*.

On a less dramatic, public scale, some twenty, thirty, forty years ago, physicians throughout the United States practiced a style of charity medicine that would now be virtually unthinkable—one would be thought to be crazy for "giving away" so much. On the one hand, there was a widespread practice of "professional courtesy" extended not only to fellow physicians, but to their families. Physicians took care of one another "without thinking twice." And rarely were such courtesies recorded in the accounting ledger for income tax deductions.

On the other hand, there was a widespread agreement among physicians to absorb the burden of individuals and families in the community who could not afford to pay for medical care. It was seen as a necessary responsibility that went along with being a physician; it was not seen as something especially altruistic, but more a given of life. A frequent figure I have been given is that this amounted to about 15 percent of a physician's practice. Here, as with professional courtesy, many physicians tell me that it was more the rule not to document all this for income tax discount purposes. For all the flaws and excesses of the fee-for-service era, it did not have the bureaucratized closed-heartedness that characterizes corporate medicine. (Ideas in this paragraph crystallized from a phone conversation with Don Cooper, M.D., December 10, 1996.)

THE RESTRUCTURING AND EXPERIENCE OF TIME

Managed care is one expression of a culture-wide redefinition of the way *time* is to be structured and experienced. The only thing that matters is the production line and the immediate short-term profit gained from it. All pasts are erased and become irrelevant. Yesterday's valor and contribution of loyalty now mean nothing. They are nullified by expectations of the present and the future. One is expected to be a dedicated and loyal worker, but is entitled to neither in return. One is "entitled" only to be consumed by the machine he or she serves, and is expected to be loyal to it.

There is no faith, only works, and works can produce nothing but the expectation of more work. The existentialist Sartre surely would have labeled such a circumstance as *mauvais foi*, bad faith. One can never be truly validated; one doesn't really deserve to be in the first place. (On a personal note, only a few years ago, one of my many supervisors chastised me for daring to claim any relevance of my twenty-five years of social science teaching and writing for Family Medicine: "You keeping asking for respect," he said, "but you don't seem to understand that you don't deserve it and never will get it.") Past, present, and future, rather than being part of a continuum of life and in some sense cumulative, become instead totally ruptured. All claims to any past are null and void—a convenient gambit for reducing guilt, shame, obligation for reciprocity, remorse, and any tie of sentiment. Everything is "just business," which is to say, just schizoid. All color is monochromatic. "What have you done for me today? And what more are you going to do for me tomorrow?" are all that count.

One need not be a committed Freudian to hear an oral insatiability and savage, toothy aggression, which joins forces with excremental riddance for all who cannot "fess up" to the extreme capitalist demands of the clinical and every other marketplace. And one need not be a Marxist to recognize a division of labor based almost exclusively on exploitation and exploitability.

MONEY AS OBLIGATORY FINAL EXPLANATION

When we say "Money drives everything," including managed care, we tacitly agree to look, think, and feel no further than literal "money." We say that there is nothing further to think about: "the bottom line" is the final explanation that itself does not require accounting. This is a rhetorical flourish (sleight of word) that makes a word become reality. It is prescription and taboo in the guise of description. It is imperative that insists it is merely declarative. But managed care is not primarily about the economics of cost containment. It is about dread, avarice, greed, rage, hate, revenge, hoarding today because of feared famine tomorrow. It is T. S. Eliot's *Wasteland* of the human spirit. If we worship at the sacred shrine of the bottom line, then we should acknowledge that business has become sacred—and, ironically, bad business at that!

The language ("discourse") of managed care is unmistakable. If we were not culturally under its pall, its drunken influence, we might even regard it as not only stilted, but even a funny, bizarre way to think about sickness, frailty, suffering, and healing. To give but one brief example, in an article on "Outcomes Management: An Interdisciplinary Search for Best Practice," Anne W. Wojner, R.N., M.S.N., C.C.R.N., writes of the need for "critical pathways" as "a tool for practice standardization and outcomes measurement":

> The process of outcomes management involves the enhancement of physiologic and psychosocial patient outcomes through development and implementation of exemplary health practices and services, driven by outcomes assessment. Processes, or interventions, produce outcomes. Favorable outcomes are defined by attainment of specific population goals. (1996: 136)

The words sound plausibly scientific and objective. Yet they are laden with unstated assumptions about value (such as how "exemplary" is to be determined, and by whom), about even what is admissible as a way of thinking about "outcomes." Part of managed care's (and other corporatist models') greatest menace lies in its advocates' ostensible innocence and in its believers' credulity: "We cannot help it. It is strictly a business decision. We have no choice. We have to cut personnel and we have to cut services. That's how we survive as an organization, that's how we get out of the red. And it is for the good of the patient. Aren't patients, too, searching for the best healthcare for the dollar?" It is as if decision makers see themselves entirely as passive victims who are thereby justified and compelled to engage in acts of violence. This language and gesture are designed to obscure the fact that "profit" is a choice; "how much profit" is a choice; "how much I have to generate for my clinic/hospital" is a choice. The compulsion is at one level an illusion, and at another level a mask against greed, ambition, guilt, shame, success, and other motives. Its obligation is displaced if not also projected from the inner world to the outer world, and reinforced by the rationale of shared economic necessity. (At least in a small way, it is given the lie when those occasional organizational leaders, faced by marked corporate income loss, turn the problem over to the collective wisdom of co-workers, and invite them to come up together with alternate solutions to the automatic firing of cohorts of people [a point I owe to consultant colleague Robert Grupe, Ph.D., April 1996]).

But there has been at least one exception, a singularity that compels us to reexamine the rule, and the rapid return to the rule: the bombing of the Murrah Federal Building in Oklahoma City on April 19, 1995. The area of north downtown Oklahoma City was immediately described as a "war zone," and victimized by a "terrorist attack" on the Heartland. With war as the dominant metaphor and experience, the dead were quickly classified as innocent children or as adults as if "soldiers killed in the line of action." The community response was as to wartime. For several weeks, money was no object, to healthcare professionals, to anyone in the wide Oklahoma community who might be a victim of the bombing.

Suddenly, "disaster narratives" competed with, and quickly subdued, routine "organizational narratives." People could not give enough of their time, their medical skills, their blankets and towels, their caring, to those other people whom they defined as innocent victims. Scarcity of caring, including healthcaring, gave way to abundance. Part of that abundance was a freedom to care again. For a blessed month at clinical conferences, there was no talk in the language of "healthcare delivery," but only of "doing everything we can" and "doing what is right," both of which frequently required great personal sacrifice.

Often, healthcare and other professionals did not ask permission from their division heads or CEOs to go downtown to offer help. They simply went, as if by mutual, silent consent as well as according to a formal mass disaster plan. Under these circumstances, what upper management would dare challenge the overriding moral imperative of recovering the war dead and wounded? The attitude of "There is not enough to go around" was temporarily replaced by "We can't give enough away fast enough." Any talk of managed care, which is to say the withholding of healthcare, simply evaporated for a few weeks.

If a mythology of prairie goodness quickly arose out of the bombing response, there was plenty of goodness to give the mythology a fair launch! Abundant personal caring (an emotional, interpersonal virtue) accompanied and sustained the medical care that consisted of specialized skills, techniques, methods, and medication. For a brief time, the fiercely moral and the clinically technical were inextricably wed.

Allene Jackson, M.D., a family physician colleague who has worked intimately with the Office of the Chief Medical Examiner of the State of Oklahoma as a "process consultant" virtually since the bombing, spoke of the "suspension of economics at the time of the bombing. It was a moment of grace. We returned to the practice of medicine, nothing else got in its way. We gave no thought to " 'Who's going to pay for it?' Who cares! Just do it, was how everyone operated. At a certain point we didn't care what the costs were. 'We are doing this for the families,' we kept telling ourselves" (personal communication, September 7, 1996).

Within a month of the bombing and the cornucopia of caring, as mysteriously as the pall of scarcity had lifted, the iron curtain fell again. Then it was as if nothing had happened, as if there were a collective dissociation. In medical boardrooms and case conferences, we were back to our military briefings and debriefings.

If there is danger in romanticizing the response to the bombing, there is equal danger in finding the past flawlessly virtuous and the future wholly wanting in virtue in American medicine. A Currier-and-Ives nostalgia for a never-existent past fits hand in glove with a demonizing of the perpetrators of the future world of corporate medicine: a conglomerate of bad "them," ranging from incurably sick patients, to clinically complex elderly patients, to "bad" administrators. Rarely, though, are physicians (or other healthcare professionals) included on this enemies list, even though in many health plans and organizations, physicians not only provide medical care, but they are also the third party. They are themselves the financially at-risk-for-profit payor. To demonize these physicians would rip away the veneer created by splitting, and reveal that "they" are in fact "us."

For instance, B. J. Haywood, M.D., an Oklahoma City anesthesiologist, suggests that "ethics" in biomedicine may well be a red herring for long-standing dubious practice. Even the content and timing of "ethics" conferences (medical, corporate, and government) are suspect. "It is admirable to talk about ethics, and indeed today the topic is frequently presented. Schools with graduate courses in ethics are placing 'ethicists' in healthcare and corporate positions [including 'business ethics,' HFS]. Is this another hollow gesture to divert attention from the abysmal state of our populace's own level of integrity?" (E-mail, personal communication, September 4, 1996).

Haywood also contrasts the much-discussed topic of "serving two masters" (the patient and the payor) with the more elusive, rarely addressed, sense of threat to the identity and entitlement of physicians: "The real problem with physicians and managed care is an ego and economic one. The physicians are not used to having their orders challenged by anyone. When you combine this with a threat to their income they strike back with exaggerated claims of restricted care" (E-mail, September 4, 1996). Whatever else it portends, managed care promises to set limits on those who have claimed exclusive right to set limits: in patient care it is called "compliance."

Many physician, physician assistant (P.A.), and nurse colleagues have bitterly told me that "managed care is the medical equivalent of downsizing," and "managed care is the downsizing of medicine; many people will be overlooked and lost." Both managed care and downsizing are desperate forms of riddance to preserve some imagined corporate "body." In our dark night of the soul—whether we are CEOs, chairmen, physicians, nurse's aides, or secretaries most recently fired from our hospital or clinic—we are all disposable waste. If not today, then tomorrow.

In recent years many medical colleagues and laypersons have described their horror and outrage at corporate medicine in the imagery of the Holocaust (see also chapter 3). A symbolic equation takes this common form: downsizing = managed care = Holocaust. Whatever its faulty logic, its *cultural logic* is widespread. The Holocaust serves at least two interrelated roles: (1) as a metaphor or image of what it feels like to be involved in managed care (victimization, helplessness, including masochistic defense against aggression); and (2) as an imagined social form or process, the ideology and administration of which parallels the Nazi social program. In the previous chapter on downsizing, I have addressed the first point: one may substitute "managed care" for "downsizing" and arrive at the same inner representations and feelings that are condensed into the metaphor of the Holocaust. I shall address here the second issue. My approach will not be that of Holocaust-as-analogy, but the Holocaust as a parallel psychosocial process, from which, however horrific it was, we can learn at a historic distance about ourselves. I find the arguments compelling, though, as a Jew, also disturbing if repulsive ("How can anything be compared with the awfulness of the Holocaust?," many people insist.) The parallel processes include: rationalization, medicalization, bureaucratization, numerization, technologization, depersonalization, nationalization, and the subtle escalation of the process toward increased deaths. Although the Holocaust and American managed care are not historically, culturally, "the same," managed care can increasingly be seen as following much of the same psychological and organizational processes. American corporate medicine *is not* Nazism, but *the form of thought and deed is harrowingly similar*. Consider, for instance, neurologist Ernest Warner's admonition to American physicians:

> Physicians are really no different ethically and morally than the rest of the population. Once given the ability to kill legally, they proceed down the path. If the controls are loosened, as they have been in Holland recently and in Germany in the 1930's—the same scenario probably will be played out in the U.S. What starts with a capitulation to the arguments regarding futility and prolonged death is moved by economics to terminate "undesirables," who only use resources and do not actively contribute to the economic well being of the state.
>
> How does this bit of history impact on managed care? The issue is similar. If one prevents patients from having DNR/dialysis/ transplants, money is saved. If one can declare these patients as incurable such that further treatment is futile, then life deserves to be terminated. The money saved is shared by the stockholders and the employees (physicians).
>
> Unfortunately, the evolution of the process is usually very, very subtle for the physician. Instead of being the advocate for the patient, to provide the very best medical care at the bedside, he now becomes an agent of a third party, be it the state, Blue Cross/Blue Shield, HMO, etc. (1996: 278)

We blame the "third party" as if it (they) were entirely separate from ourselves, but they are as much physicians' tacit agents as they are ostensibly adversaries. Physicians come to feel oppressed by those who in fact extend and execute their own power.

If, with our perils and parallels with the Nazis, we are "back to the future," in a way, too, we all are also back in the Vietnam War of the 1960s and 1970s: we do not know who is friend or foe; *everyone is a potential "Gook"* who will betray us and kill us off. Supposedly, those in the "workforce" are covered, but only temporarily. Karl Marx's nightmare is becoming ours, even as Soviet communism becomes remote history: people are not people, only "workers" for the collective. We specialize in insecurity, in terror, in death, even if not a single drop of human blood is shed. We justify our actions in terms of economic "bottom lines." But bottom lines are favorite and most widely justified excuses and pretexts, not the causes of our deeds. Bottom lines, downsizing, and managed care are three core euphemisms of our culture, and not only of its medical sector. They are the language of our deception and self-deception.

There is yet another deception in our recourse to economics as the final and ultimate explanation: in part, we Americans speak the supposedly impersonal language of "the bottom line" in order to avoid speaking the far more personal language of "rationing care." If we talked in the idiom of rationing, we would come close to being un-American, to violating espoused values such as equality of access to high-quality care. ("If I can have a kidney transplant, everyone should.") But even the question of the organ availability of hearts is itself a diversion from the deeper, and more disturbing, vision of an entire culture without *heart*.

WAKING UP FROM OUR CULTURAL TRANCE

As I read the voluminous literature on managed care, including some recent Internet communications given to me by J. Michael Pontious, M.D. (personal communication, April 1996), my family physician colleague and supervisor in Enid, Oklahoma, I find that I want to wake myself up from "mush." I keep feeling that I am missing something, that something else is there but hidden, something being unsaid, unfelt—a feeling I have learned to trust in myself just as my physician colleagues have learned to trust it as a crucial part of their clinical judgment. Things do not add up, even if they are supposed to add up according to the Department of Medicine, Washington University (St. Louis) *Manual of Medical Therapeutics*, or in *Harrison's* or *Cecil's* internal medicine textbooks, which are as close as biomedicine comes to sacred texts. I do not understand what I am reading, even though the authors are telling me what and how to understand. What is happening in the House of Medicine feels emotionally 180 degrees from the rationalist, objectivist, legalist, business, word-jungle that is named by the phrases "managed care," "cost containment," "corporate medicine," and their many cognate terms. I get out my stories by Franz Kafka and listen to my music by Gustav Mahler to assure myself I am not crazy.

It does not require a rocket scientist, or even a clinical behavioral scientist, or a visiting Alexis de Tocqueville, to recognize the encroaching presence of "management" and "managed" as noun and qualifying adjective for virtually all acceptable thought and action in American biomedicine. They are the handmaiden, so to speak, of that other metaphor they so loyally, if not often implicitly, serve: "the bottom line" of cost containment, profit, and production. Writers such as G. Gayle Stephens (1984a, 1984b), and Edmund Pellegrino (1994) have recently sounded a linguistic as well as ethical alarm about the automatic, un-self-critical use of business metaphors in biomedicine—and not only in Family Medicine, my two-decade academic home, but in psychotherapy by psychiatrists or clinical psychologists, as well (Brown 1997). Controversies over such clinical ideologies as paternalism, autonomy, advocacy, role negotiation, and satisfaction have all been swallowed up by the "management" image (see Johnson 1995). We want only approaches that "work" inside the glass bubble of "management."

MANAGEMENT AND CONTROL

There appears to be no limit to the horizon toward which the wish to "manage"—which is to say "control"—can be expanded. One has only to attend enough clinical or business meetings, or even to read the "Yellow" or business pages of the telephone directory, to know this. To name but several usages:

    case management (and manager)
    clinic manager
    file manager
    (financial) portfolio management
    information management
    managed care
    patient management
    product line management
    quality management
    resource management
    time management

In rural America, we hear and read likewise of risk management, farm management, livestock management, agribusiness management, pork management, and wheat management. In a world gone virtually out of control, perhaps internally as well as externally, we seem to seek the capacity to rein in and "manage" everyone and everything. Behind management as technique, it is obsession—and dread. Could the belief that we should be able to "manage" everyone and everything be a vice, a conceit, instead of a virtue, a symptom rather than a cure?

I have become enough of an Oklahoman, after nearly twenty years, to believe, following Will Rogers, that if you don't like the weather, wait five minutes and the weather will change. Now, it will take longer than five minutes for the era of "managed care" to pass, but we can be sure that five years or a decade from now, like it or not, we will be speaking yet another foreign language in medicine—but one sufficiently recognizable that currently hidden issues about value and power, life and death, vulnerability and mercy, aggression and love still will remain unaddressed, and the quest for control will take some form!

Whatever the final shape American "healthcare reform" takes, we can be reasonably certain that control-dominated thinking and decision making will prevail—even as we in biomedicine strive to be more politically correct and eradicate patient "compliance" from our lexicon. As healthcare professionals, patients, and public alike, we should wonder what shape the doctor-patient relationship, and the work contained within it, will be asked to take in a world in which patient flow, productivity, volume, and production reports prevail. When physicians become "providers," when patients become "customers," and when medical care becomes a "product line," when even health care becomes a single word, "healthcare," a commodity, a noun, a thing, what do health care and preventive medicine become? The call for insight into our own world of words is preliminary to a call for resistance.

In this chapter, I am arguing that the very vocabulary of managed care is the language of euphemism, that our words-become-flesh are dangerous to everyone—and that the language of managed care is best understood not by reading the latest business magazine or medical economics journal, but instead by reading Lewis Carroll's *Alice's Adventures in Wonderland* and by looking with her through the looking glass.

Lest I be misunderstood, let me say from the outset what must be said nakedly and unadorned: "managed care" is about the creation of a secular-disguised hell-on-earth for the infirm and for those who care for them. It is nothing like what we officially purport it to be about. For example, even if we espouse a new era of preventive medicine and wellness, we are in fact disingenuous, because we are increasingly interested in people as productive capital, not as whole people. People, even healthy people, are good only for the sake of production and profit. It would be dangerously naïve for us to believe that in this corporate ethos "wellness" is intended for "quality of life." "Managed care" is, though, but the expression in a single institution, biomedicine, of the same loveless, angry, scarcity-driven image of life that pervades this American culture of the 1990s. If my talk is about medicine and language, about the power of euphemism as metaphor, it is ultimately not primarily about medicine. It is about our smoke screens and about the fire behind them.

Sometimes, if we listen and watch carefully, an image or word gives away or betrays the deeper meanings, feelings, and fantasies masked by managed care's euphemisms. On such occasions, one hardly needs to interpret: the interpretation is there, manifest. At one Great

Plains hospital's 1996 Christmas party, the invited speaker, a gastroenterologist-administrator, admonished his largely healthcare professional audience to accept managed care as the inexorable wave of the future. It was, he admonished the group, simply a matter of altering their thinking to conform to the changes. To make his point he showed a cartoon depicting a steamroller smashing down one doctor in the asphalt, while another wisely sidestepped his destruction. The caption read: "You can become part of the solution or part of the pavement." Uncharacteristic of prairie decorum, several physicians got up in the middle of the talk and walked out. A week thereafter, a family physician colleague who had been in the audience wrote to me: "Does this [cartoon, attitude] not instill a sense of helplessness? A sort of ultimatum? This doesn't smack of fascism, does it?" (Wesley Andrews, M.D., December 6, 1996, with permission). With managed care, death is unmistakably in the air, on the pavement, and on the screen, as is the smashing of the human spirit in the coercive demand that individual critical judgment be suspended and replaced by group doctrine.

If this chapter offers an organizational and social "diagnosis" of sorts, it also hints at a way out of the impersonal, rationalized world managed care is creating—a way shown for all to see and hear by Oklahomans when a bomb blew up the Murrah Federal Building in Oklahoma City on April 19, 1995. And it is also about why we, as Oklahomans and Americans, swiftly retreated to business-as-usual corporate medicine within only a matter of weeks of the bombing. *We have met the euphemisms and they are ours.* If we have the courage to examine them, they will give us the secret of our own hearts, medical and otherwise.

THE ROLE OF EUPHEMISM

Let me clarify how I use the word *euphemism* in this chapter. Like all symbols, it stands for, represents, something else; it is a substitute and compromise. It condenses many meanings and feelings and intentions, conscious and unconscious, into a single image. It (which is a shorthand way of saying our use of it) directs our attention toward some things and away from others. What distinguishes *euphemism* from other symbols is how it represents that something else, and why people select it rather than other kinds of symbols, such as *simile* and *metaphor.*

Euphemism is a specific form of symbolic operation. Euphemism constitutes a form of masking, of massive deception. It cunningly affirms and loudly negates. Affect (conscious and unconscious emotion) is almost entirely split off from the concept presented in the euphemism. Those concepts that serve as euphemisms have consciously only the narrowest of permissible meanings. (For instance, "the bottom line" is only about economic profit and loss.) If hyperbole exaggerates, euphemism understates so much that it entirely redirects attention from the wish, feeling, and deed, to an entirely sanitized, anesthetized, intellectualized version of the original wish, feeling, and deed.

Euphemism entirely redefines them such that the original is scarcely recognizable (e.g., Orwell 1949). Large becomes small, tiny, insignificant. What isn't is; what is isn't what you think. Confusion is obligatory clarity. Things cannot and must not be called, or felt, what they are. To do so would bring on overwhelming guilt, shame, anxiety, remorse. So, in euphemism the mask is the obligatory face that must be seen. The face is disguised, sometimes the fact that it is the face instead of yet another mask is even not admitted. For instance, in the Nazi language of that colossal euphemism, "The Final Solution to the Jewish Problem," the wish to get away with mass murder is transformed into a dispassionate scientific doctrine that in turn was translated (implemented) into a public health campaign against humans imagined as insects, infectious disease, vermin, infrahuman parasites.

A market and marketplace ideology, together with the language of rational contracts, utterly avoid and dissolve the issues of meaning and suffering into simple business decisions (David Armstrong, comment, Symposium of the International Society for the Psychoanalytic Study of Organizations [ISPSO], New York City, June 14, 1996). The breadth and depth of human meaning disappears into black holes. "Managed care," like the "downsizing" and "RIFing" with which it is strategically associated, denies as even relevant what is toxic to think and feel about: sickness, vulnerability, aggression, decay, dread, despair, death. It "manages" (rationalizes) them out of existence. "The merchandising of meaning fills suffering's void"; "euphemisms are black holes into which meaning disappears" (Yiannis Gabriel, comment, ISPSO, New York City, June 14, 1996). We need to ask squarely, "What do we do when we want to be [organizationally] lean and mean?" (Shelley Reciniello, comment, ISPSO, New York City, June 14, 1996). The unchallenged idea of "Somebody's got to do it!"—that is, the tough, masculine, ostensibly unwanted job of firings, cuts, exclusions from medical care—"is not always or necessarily true," unless we are in the thrall of the euphemism (Robert Young, comment, ISPSO, New York City, June 14, 1996).

THE "CATTLE-DRIVE PRINCIPLE" OVER TIME

I write as one who has had the benefit of conducting continuous fieldwork for three decades in the medical profession. I began teaching and writing during the fee-for-service days. I was already present as a clinical teacher and observer when DRGs (diagnosis-related groups; that is, maximum reimbursement for hospitalization based on diagnosis) were first introduced as a concept, then as an inpatient obligation. I vividly remember the burst of anguish of an otherwise understated, quiet Oklahoma family practice resident during a clinical conference in 1984: "How am I supposed to tell you the value of a human toe!" he protested against the new protocol, which stated how many days a patient with, say, a gangrenous diabetic toe could be hospitalized. Back then, as now, under very differing rubrics of financial incentive, I am familiar with the "cattle-drive principle" of patient care, as one bitter Family Medicine resident described his managed care practice in 1994. I have been a part of the culture that has evolved from there to here. I have been privileged to be allowed to see it from the inside.

Even in the fee-for-service days, those physicians and medical social scientists interested in the patient and doctor's experience of illness, pain, and healing had a difficult time justifying their heresy in the House of God. George Engel (1977) published his now-famous, groundbreaking article in *Science* on the "biopsychosocial" model at a time when such passing fancies as the community and social psychiatry movement and integrative, person-oriented care ideologies were already on the decline—when the "biological" backlash had already begun. Biopsychosocial models were at best good to espouse, so long as they did not interfere with the volume (numbers) of patients seen and income generated. For many physicians, patients were and remain a means—often an uncooperative means—of conquering disease and death, and thereby feeling competent and earning their livelihood. The patient was often regarded as "the enemy" or at least an obstacle, an intrusive "hit" upon the hospital emergency room or ward. Today, "the patient becomes a financial adversary" (Warner 1996: 275). The patient is still an enemy, only a different kind of enemy. In both cases the profit motive was present, if not open.

For instance, in the earlier era, one could hide economically driven decisions behind the "need" (ostensibly for the patient's good) for laboratory tests, procedures, additional hospitalization, return visits, and local medical community standards. "I've got to make such-and-such gross income to pay my overhead and keep my practice going" entirely shielded the rarely articulated value of and entitlement to a high standard and style of living. A thematic line running through fee-for-service to corporate medicine is physicians' own ambivalence toward including the thought, let alone the articulation to the patient or the public, that they are in medicine for a good livelihood as well as good patient care (Stein 1990, 1995). In training and practice settings alike, unresolvable battles rage over charge tickets, laboratory slips, diagnostic and procedure coding, over who's responsible for what, or who forgot what (administration versus nursing)—if emergency rooms or operating rooms were run like this, every patient would be dead! If the profit motive drives healthcare practitioners at least in some respect, we act as if it doesn't, that at best it is imposed from outside, from some "them"— even if it is our own billing office down the hall in another building. Put in a formula: for many physicians, medicine is a business that cannot be acknowledged to be a business. This conflict between giving medical care and receiving some form of remuneration had been silenced long before "marketing" and "advertising" were introduced into medical organizations. There have long been barriers to discussing publicly whether biomedicine should be a business like all other businesses.

I do not bash managed care and idolatrize fee-for-service. Both are and were steeped in excesses, but *in excesses of entirely different kinds*. And in every era, under every structural arrangement (structures that are not entirely externally imposed, I quickly add), I have seen physicians dedicated to their patients find ingenious ways to "manipulate" disease categories, official hospital and clinical codes (e.g., ICD-9, CPT, DSM-IV, DRG), so as to offer more thorough treatment—to treat the patient rather than the lab results or the business codes.

THE "COLLUSION OF ANONYMITY," CORPORATE REIFICATION, AND THE ABDICATION OF PERSONAL RESPONSIBILITY

What makes corporate medicine in general, and managed care in particular, a far more sinister force than fee-for-service ever was is its ostensibly impersonal, bureaucratic, depersonalized, anonymous nature. People decide even when ostensibly and officially "no one decides," and personal decisions are hidden in group consensus often called protocols, mission statements, strategic plans, decision trees, computer printouts, procedures manuals, and company policy. Decisions can be hidden, and people—decision makers—can hide in the labyrinth of corporate medicine the way no one could hide in fee-for-service. It is ruled by what Michael Balint described in another context as the "collusion of anonymity" (1957), rationalized by economic necessity. There is no sinister, secret cabal, however, no calculated conspiracy by the malevolent few. There is only a tightly rationalized business-as-usual attitude in ordinary organizational decision making groups everywhere. The *illusion* of this groupish anonymity is that no one is truly responsible, because "no one really decides." In this way, envy, jealousy, rage, vendetta, and other negatively regarded aggressive feelings and wishes can be enacted and utterly disguised as impersonal acts on behalf of managing the organization.

We often speak of the needs of "the organization" as if it were a living, real organism, with independent needs. We say that "the organization did this and such," but only people do things, people with intentions, motives, and defenses. Organizations do not, and cannot, "survive" or "die" because they are not living organisms in the first place. Only *reification* makes it seem and feel as if they are. Via projection we cede our own intentions upon organizations, and then seal and conceal our intentions with rationalizations and reifications. In seemingly rational managed care, we inhabit the land of George Orwell's (1949) "Newspeak" of *1984*. Behind evil's veneer of banality (an image made popular by Hannah Arendt) lie personal motivation and choice—and euphemism's hysteric denial of it all. But somewhere, we already know what we don't want to know.

PROFESSIONALIZATION AND DEPROFESSIONALIZATION: ANOTHER FALSE DICHOTOMY

Still another false dichotomy should be addressed in discussing managed care and (or as) euphemism: "professionalization" and "deprofessionalization" in medicine and in other occupations. Perhaps now the *locus classicus* of the former is Paul Starr's book (1982). In managed care and other corporate health practices where policy is dictated from above, physicians often feel they are no longer physicians, professionals trained to have independent, scientific judgment. They become salaried workers, piece workers (especially as envisioned under capitation plans where a physician is paid a set amount for every patient, seen and unseen), laborers, hired guns, and henchmen. The deprofessionalization of skill among physicians and all healthcare personnel leads to the de-skilling of the workforce, and to the reduction of clinical relationships and tasks to least common denominators, the conversion of the treatment of whole people by whole people into early twentieth-century Taylorism. Thus, for instance, a nurse becomes superfluous when any person can be trained, and more cheaply paid, to insert a trachea tube. Integration of the complexity of patients' disease(s) and illness experience is no longer valued. Treatment of "the whole person" is replaced by role fragmentation on the part of healthcare laborers who are trained in skills necessary only to perform one narrowly defined procedure (or at most several), and not even to think in terms of persons and the social situation. Another view of this deprofessionalization is "proletarization" of healthcare givers. In a seminal article, Harry Kormos (1984) warned of this "industrialization of medicine" in 1984, when inpatient DRGs were just being introduced.

I believe that all of the above are true, but that they constitute only part of the story. All victimization requires cooperation and collusion. To date at least, there has not been a literal uprising among physicians and other healthcare professionals in protest to an enforced draconian policy that interferes with the very foundation of all clinical work, the physician-patient relationship. Individual resistance, juggling of CPT (*Physicians' Current Procedural Terminology*) codes in the patient's best interest, is the most we have seen. Healthcare practitioners, above all physicians, continue to see themselves as individuals, loners, and—despite group decision making (Stein 1990)—not communitarian, collective "bodies," especially in areas of dissent.

As individuals and as a group, physicians have used training and practice as a social ladder to the American Dream, as a means of rising in social class, status, and power—as occupational equivalent of immigrant ethnic groups. The professionalization of medicine is not immune to motives that include wealth and power, victimization and vendetta. From the "No Irish Need Apply" to ecclesiastical supremacy in American Roman Catholicism, one can think of many outsiders to mainstream "internal" and "aggressive" medicine who have "made it" (that is, "succeeded," a cardinal American virtue and ambition) and aspirants to power, prestige, and possession, who are at medicine's gates if not its "gatekeepers."

Biomedicine as an organization, no less than the wider culture whose ethos it shares, goes through spasms of inclusion and exclusion. A widespread image from the 1970s was that of increasing the "delivery" of health care: giving more and more to more and more people. (Its political historical core is expressed in the sentiment of the Statue of Liberty: "Give me your tired, your poor . . .") The sense of surplus, of abundance, and of personal entitlement all were part of this way of thinking. Today, "delivery" has largely been supplanted by "gatekeeping," "gatekeepers," "limiting" or "restricting" access to health care, and other images of exclusion. (Perhaps an exclusionist equivalent political historical expression would be: "not in my back yard!", which becomes "not in my clinic!"). Whatever else "managed care" is about, it is a profoundly American way of decision making.

Further, to cite yet another Americanism, biomedicine—seen as a whole and not in terms of distinct disciplines, specialties, and subspecialties—is often called from within a "guild" or "fraternity." Alexis de Tocqueville taught us from his visits to the United States in the 1830s how groupish we are, despite our strident individualism. American biomedicine can be characterized as what anthropologists call a "secret society," organizations that are guardians of secrets, often secret knowledge and lore, within a larger culture.

In short, the threat posed by managed care to physicians' professionalism is a threat not only to individual, scientific decision making, but to an American way of wealth and social control, of boundaries, of insiderness and outsiderness. If to be a healthcare "professional" has its undeniable virtues, it is not without its vices. Alas, even the seemingly straightforward notions of being a professional and of diminishing professionals' power in healthcare are *euphemisms* for less-than-benevolent thought and deed. Getting, holding onto, and losing privilege and identity are agendas and panics that lurk beneath the surface of both poles to the dispute. The battle over entitlements is waged over and through clinical euphemisms.

METAPHORICAL ATROCITIES: WHAT'S IN A WORD?

The following eloquent passage by Edmund D. Pellegrino, an eminent and profound physician-philosopher, implicitly weaves metaphorical atrocities into a single fabric. He begins by describing his

> revulsion for the metaphorical atrocities now displacing the once honorable title of "physician." Those metaphors are drawn from business, industry, economics, commerce, and the marketplace. Like all metaphors, they identify one thing by another. To be sure, metaphors are the yeast of creative writing. Used too often, and unthinkingly, we soon mistake the metaphor for the reality. We forget a metaphor is only the product of and a stimulus for the imagination, not a substitute for reality.
>
> The greatest peril I see in all the talk about healthcare reform is that physicians and even patients might begin to believe that physicians really are "case managers," "fundholders," "gatekeepers," or "clinical economists" and should relate to each other in that way. If they do, physicians will surely lose the final moorings of their professional integrity. Physicians might then feel exempt from their traditional ethical imperatives and place the blame on the system for their own moral defection. Needless to say, to protect themselves against such physicians, patients will have to adopt the precautions of the marketplace. Instead of trusting in the physician's ethical commitments, they will have to be guided by the principle of *caveat emptor*. (1994: 505)

In a similar vein, in an article entitled "The Patient-Physician Relationship: Covenant or Contract?," physician James T. C. Li draws our attention to language, intentionality, and the consequences for patient care:

> No patients exist in a market-driven practice of medicine—only consumers for whom the watchword is caveat emptor.

A great danger to the practice of medicine is the transformation of physicians to interchangeable, dispensable workers accountable only to their employers and the financial performance of the institution that employs them [a role change and denigration that extends to nurses and in fact to all healthcare professionals, HFS]. In this setting, physicians and healthcare are simply commodities—cold and without compassion. The greatest danger, however, is *not* loss of the physician's autonomy, degradation of the profession of medicine, or transformation of healthcare to a commodity. The greatest danger is transformation of the *patient* to the status of commodity. (1996: 918)

Finally, and most recently, psychologist Laura S. Brown, in her address upon receiving the 1996 Award for Distinguished Professional Contribution from the American Psychological Association, writes in a similarly urgent, prophetic voice, of

an inherent ethical imperative to question some of the most recent social constructions of psychotherapy. Such constructions are those that define psychotherapy solely or primarily as the delivery of carefully rationed units of "medical necessity" to "covered lives" owned by large conglomerates that use the word *health* in their names as if they hope to obscure that the health they're truly concerned about is the fiscal health of their stockholders and CEOs, that is, the phenomenon of managed mental health care. (1997: 449, quotation marks and emphasis in original)

Here, Pellegrino, Li, and Brown independently not only offer a description but also sound an alarm and make a clinical judgment (one with which I concur) about metaphor and power in the healing professions, biomedical, psychological, and so on. They implicitly ask the question: In whose image is medicine to be taught and practiced? It is necessary also to examine a third area: the persuasiveness, the plausibility, of medical metaphors and of their associated power arrangements, and of the timeliness of such persuasiveness. I suggest that knowledge—including the knowledge that regulates the physician-patient relationship within corporate medicine—is situated within and contained inside the metaphor. Or, to use another spatial view, *corporate clinical knowledge is an extension of the metaphor*. In a culturally real sense, the metaphor generates the knowledge. Those people in power promulgate the metaphor to gather and consolidate their power. Those people who believe in the metaphor help to establish and sustain those who claim the power. The power to define goes in both directions.

To understand metaphor is to understand the worldview that underlies the common words we hear and read every day. For instance, in a recent article in *American Medical News*, titled "New Life for Long-Dormant Law" (Johnsson 1996: 1, 51), Saul Morse, vice president and general counsel with the Illinois State Medical Society, is quoted as saying, "Where doctors are obligated to the employer as well as the patient, they create a significant risk of being put in both legally and ethically untenable positions. . . . That is a large part of the concern that we've always had with the corporate practice of medicine" (Johnsson 1996: 51). We need to situate this criticism within the wider, never-directly-spoken wish behind the euphemism: *"We don't want patients; we want payors."* Patienthood conjures regression, dependency, frailty, mortality; but to pay, to have money, conjures life, youth, productivity, immortality—but *lifeless life*.

The war of metaphors is a conflict over core values, over worldviews, over entire philosophies of life, over internal versus external constraints, and over internalization versus resistance. Sometimes the conflict is between two or more individuals, or between two or more organizations; sometimes the conflict is within one person, and is evidenced by contradictory utterances in different moments of a conversation. At other times, one will speak (or at least seem to speak) for one value, and a colleague will "correct" him or her, saying that he or she "really" means the opposite.

For instance, at a late-1996 primary care conference, one physician said of managed care: "You say [at enrollment time] you'll take care of patients, and then never do it. The less patients you see, the more money you make." Another physician commented about the meaning of "patient education" in HMOs: "Patient education is really marketing. You lure them in by saying 'We'll give you everything [in health care],' and once they're in you deny them just about everything they ask for, saying it's not covered in their plan." Yet another primary care physician, one known for his devotion to his patients, said, "We're paid *not* to see patients, but we need patients for residents in our program." A colleague jumped in to clarify what he had just heard: "For our outside guests in this conference who don't know you, I want them to understand that you really care about patients." Yet another physician expressed his conflict between inner values and outer constraints: "We're told to get more covered [insured] *well* lives in your [medical] practice. I don't like it." "We live in a cost containment environment," emphasized another physician participant, "and we have to realize that we don't have the luxuries of fee-for-service days."

What we are to make of conversations and conferences like this (that do not only occur in medicine, but that reflect crises of values in most, if not all, organizations) is that, in the least, struggles over metaphors reflect deeper ambivalences over values. The spread of corporate medicine to larger and larger conglomerates of institutions and personnel is not merely a simple moral matter of the takeover of "good" clinicians by "bad" corporate executives, of the sacred inside by the profane outside. If there is resistance, there is also collusion. If metaphors are imposed, they are also adopted as one's own.

THE VALENCY OF METAPHORS AND EUPHEMISMS: WAGING WAR THROUGH WORDS

Euphemisms and other cultural metaphors can be classified not only as "present" or "absent," but also in terms of their current emotional "valency" (to borrow a term from W. R. Bion 1955), that is, how emotionally "hot" or "charged" they are currently. For instance, in a recent article on metaphors in biomedicine, Gerald R. Winslow (1994) draws our attention to the long prevalence of *military* metaphors.

In this way of speaking, disease is the *enemy* which threatens to *invade* the body and overwhelm its *defenses*. Medicine *combats* disease with *batteries* of tests and *arsenals* of drugs. As physicians *battle* illness, they sometimes refer to their *armamentarium*. They also write *orders*. Young staff physicians are still called house *officers*. Nurses, who take orders, also work at *stations*. In the past, at least, they also wore *uniforms* while *on duty*. But as one early author on nursing decorum wrote, nurses should not wear uniforms when *off duty*; then, they should wear "civilian dress" [Robb 1900: 118]. As nurses progressed up the ranks, stripes were added to their caps, and insignia pins to their uniforms. Sometimes their orders even called for them to give *shots*.

The language of military discipline pervaded much of the literature of nursing and medicine early in this century. One nursing leader wrote: "Carrying out the military idea, there are ranks in authority. . . . The military command is couched in no uncertain terms. Clear, explicit directions are given, and are received with unquestioning obedience" [Perry 1906: 452]. (Winslow 1994: 3)

Although the military metaphor has been present for over a century in American biomedical practitioners' thinking about the nature of their work (a metaphor closely tied to the competitive sports metaphor, but in the war metaphor aggressive impulses and wishes come even closer to consciousness and are more ego-syntonic), its emotional appeal has intensified since the early 1990s with the collapse of the Soviet Union, the threat of nuclear winter, and the end of the Cold War (see Stein 1994). Its object is no longer only the defeat of disease (if not, through compliance, defeat of the will of the patient also), but the defense and offensive against enemy corporate hospitals and other institutional "alliances." The domestic, internal, enemy is all of us, no longer only scapegoated pariah groups, but everyone. No one is immune any more, no mothers or their infants, no fathers or their sons.

A crucial question is: What is the war being waged against? For its focus changes over time. The wish to attack and kill changes its objects. In the 1960s, we had the War against Poverty as well as the undeclared War against North Vietnam. Since the discovery of microbes, biomedical physicians have waged wars against diseases. Today, we are in the midst of a war against cost, and the symbolic killing off of people from insurance rolls, because that is the means of winning that war (Seth Allcorn, personal communication, June 24, 1996).

Let me extend the current military metaphor of managed care's endless "competition" for organizational "survival" through alliances and competition. Viewed as *political (not only clinical) ideology*, managed care, corporate medicine, integrated healthcare delivery systems, and similar terms can be understood as the *colonization* of healthcare practitioners, patients, families, and communities by insurance companies, administrative organizations, and federal government. Two classes of people are created—neither of whom related specifically to healthcare per se: *the colonizers and the colonized, the conquerors and the conquered, the managers and the managed, those who control and those who are controlled.*

But human reality is more complicated than the image of two distinct piles of people, victims and victimizers, as for instance Raul Hilberg (1992) writes about Jews, Germans, and other national groups in the Nazi Holocaust. Further, as Daniel Jonah Goldhagen (1996) has documented for Nazi Germany, it turns out that many "bystanders" were willing, if not eager, "executioners." Even under more "normal" seeming, less extreme, cultural circumstances, the purely passive, innocent bystander is a widespread illusion. Passivity is not without motivation. Without internal collusion, no terror can take place. One needs to understand the intrapsychic and group dynamics of acquiescence and victimization as much as the oppression and colonization. Further, Hilberg (1992) draws careful attention to the interlocking triad of perpetrators, victims, and bystanders. Without a loyal corps of bystanders who turn a blind eye to the dance of death, the perpetrators would have no victims. And there are more quiet perpetrators (and, as Goldhagen shows [1996], more avid, eager, ideologically committed, and undisguisedly enthusiastic butchers) than we dare think. The same is true of the success of managed care. There is increasing internal and external pressure to "buy in" (collude, but in dollar sign language) to the managed care philosophy, to merge one's personal "stake" as physician with "stake" of the corporation, to define oneself as a "stakeholder" and participate in "risk sharing" with the organization. Here, one could not be further from the earlier language of patient "advocacy," "patients' rights," "the personal physician," "beneficence," "justice," "nonmaleficence," wherein persons and intimate relationships are—at least in espoused ideal—the foundation of clinical practice, of task performance. Ironically, in this dehumanized system, both "bad" patients and "bad" doctors can easily be "terminated." Euphemism abounds in the war against "bad" physicians, patients, and organizations alike.

THE WAR ROOM ATMOSPHERE OF AMERICAN BIOMEDICINE: THE PENTAGON, THE MOVIES, AND BIOMEDICAL BRIEFINGS

In medical academic and corporate departments, within recent years, many meetings and even clinical conferences have taken on the atmosphere of military "war rooms" replete with style and artifacts of presentation: maps, slides, graphs, overheads to the front, the speaker in impeccably clean, knee-length, button-down white lab coat, his face constantly scanning the entire group before it returns to the slide or the overhead projected on the screen, pointer or extended index finger pointing to strategies to raise the patient population, to arrange alliances and coalitions between hospitals and between healthcare corporations. The CEO or chairman stands as a three-star general before his lieutenants, presenting battle stations, plans to take positions, and additional plans for occupation of enemy territory once the invasion is complete. For instance: "If this clinic [department, medical school, hospital] is to survive, we have to capture patients . . . capture the market . . . capture the patient pool."

One CEO admonished his physician faculty: "We need to capture as many healthy patients as possible in our medical practice, so we don't have to spend money to provide medical care. That's how we keep health costs down. We need to find a way to sign up only young, healthy, employed people with good insurance! The sick people can find somewhere else to go!" The group burst into laughter.

The language and demeanor are of war. With the Cold War over since 1990, we are now reconstructing NATOs and Warsaw Pacts within our national borders. With the "socialists" defeated in Eastern Europe, we now become the collectivist enemy ourselves in making "corporate" the highest good. Curricula, clinical rotations, goal setting, even patient care are discussed in the language and with the dire urgency of a military campaign, the price of which is victory or defeat, the gain or loss of vital territory (separation, annihilation, and castration anxiety condensed into one), life or death. At such meetings, authority is rarely questioned. The enemy is clear. Any doubt raised within the group would place the doubter in danger! We are in the realm of "groupthink" (Janis 1982). Within this armed and hostile camp the practice, policy making, and teaching of patient care takes place.

CORPORATE MEDICINE: HOW TO LOCK PATIENTS INTO OUR MEDICAL PLAN

An undistinguished event occurred in Oklahoma City one day short of the third month after the bombing. It differs markedly from the generous and unreserved attitude and response of the medical community that took place in the wake of the bombing. It resembles the hundreds of faculty, department, curriculum, and even clinical meetings I had attended locally and nationally over three or four years prior to the bombing. A woman was making a presentation to a clinical primary care medical department in which she was describing and promoting a new region-wide corporate plan, "Wheatland Health Plan" I shall call it. The following fragments are taken from my notes during her presentation and the clinical practitioner group's response:

> How do you lock people into their health plan? They can change health plans four times a year. So how do you lock them in? . . . What can you do with a kid's ear in the middle of the night? We *have* to take children [in our HMO and medical practice]. Kids are a way of bringing in other family members. We need to educate the parents not to come to the ER. We've got to tune-up triage. How do you field patients who fall between real emergencies and nonemergencies?

Shortly thereafter, she said in a literally changed voice: "Speaking as a mother, my kid had strep throat this last Friday. There was little weekend care available for him [in my HMO]." She illustrates, among other things, the split between two roles and their competing values: that of HMO marketer and that of mother; the wish to limit access to healthcare for other parents' children and the wish to increase access to healthcare for her own child.

Her language and nonverbal behavior (change in voice) illustrate what Lifton (1986) described in a more extreme instance, that of Nazi doctors in the concentration camps, as "doubling," a defensive compartmentalization of opposing aspects of the self. This defense draws upon "splitting" of self- and object-representation and of affect (emotion, conscious and/or unconscious), the result of which is an either/or world of all-good and all-bad people. In the Third Reich, the very doctors who could spend their entire workdays selecting those who were to be slave laborers and those who were to go immediately to die in the gas chambers could, in their off-working hours, be loving, devoted husbands, fathers, family men. Through dissociation of these two "selves," heavily buttressed by intellectualization, rationalization, and ideology, there was no inner conflict, no guilt.

One may infer a similar split and doubling in the corporate medical presenter, except here, the doubling occurred in the same external social space rather than between "work" and "home" contexts. Her shift in subject matter and tone of voice accomplished the same dissociation as Lifton described: both between facets of herself, and between children whom she unconsciously wished to exclude from care and those whom she wished to include. Perhaps needless to say, the self- and role-compartmentalization that occurs among decision makers and implementers of "downsizing" operates according to these same unconscious mental principles (see the previous chapter) as this executive enacted.

There is an additional, broadly historical split here as well: this entire salesmanship conversation or "discourse" simply wouldn't and couldn't have taken place in the Oklahoma City region with respect to the victims of the bombing, their families, especially the children, the rescuers, and the broader community, in the first several weeks of late April and early May. A different mental set, characterized by unleashed, unbridled generosity and compassion, had then prevailed—and soon was promptly withdrawn.

The bureaucratic self-deadening or "psychic numbing" (Lifton 1979, 1986) that had preceded the outpouring of grief and relief in the shadow of the bombing was now restored, repaired, firmly in place. The magical escape from death by identification with it now puts the bombing and its genie back into the bottle. As before, we now glibly spoke in academic departmental, outpatient clinic, and hospital administrative meetings of how many "covered lives" (insured) a physician or a practice should have. What we don't address directly is how many *uncovered lives* (the neologism is my own) we as a society also require. The quasi-military "war room" atmosphere prevails. We make war on our own. Ultimately, the distinction between the covered and the uncovered is arbitrary. Those covered one day could be uncovered the next. All are in danger of being at risk; all feel naked and marginalized.

I turn to an independent "confirmation" of this interpretation, one from over a year and a half later. On October 2, 1996, I made a presentation titled "American Medicine and Managed Care: Why Ethics NOW?" to the medical and administrative staff at Integris Southwest Medical Center, Oklahoma City, Oklahoma. During that talk, I posed a question to the group, which they answered via their body language. I was discussing the concept of "covered lives," specifically, workplace-based, medically insured people. I said that, as physicians, nurses, administrators, and other hospital staff, they could rely on what is called "hallway [medical] consults" and "professional courtesy" (the waiver of financial charges to healthcare colleagues seen as patients). If, however, they could not, would they feel that if a catastrophic biomedical illness, a chronic disease, or a major psychiatric disorder were to befall them and their family, their healthcare insurance was adequate to provide good medical care and to avoid their being wiped out financially? Were they, in other words, "at risk," even though they held steady, even substantial, income-generating jobs in the healthcare professions? In that case, then, the only truly "protected" people are those who are somehow independently wealthy.

Many members of the audience shifted nervously in their seats, nodded their heads forward and back, while maintaining good eye contact with me. We briefly discussed what for me was a disturbing hunch. I was testing for myself a then-still-new notion of mine that I have come to reiterate in virtually every presentation on corporate medicine: the ordinariness, among the wage-workers or salaried employees and the unemployed alike, of a common sense of vulnerability, exposure, that one is "good for something" if one performs wage-work and is healthy. The official and widespread popular image of two distinct groups of people, the "covered" and the "uncovered," is a cultural fiction strengthened by euphemisms such as the term "covered lives" which supposedly distinguishes the protected from the unprotected. The supposedly safe, in fact, are and feel unsafe. Several participants in that seminar, and in succeeding ones, have thanked me for acknowledging their predicament and their anxiety—for giving voice to what isn't supposed to be true, let alone articulated.

THE LANGUAGE OF EUPHEMISM: THROUGH A GLASS DELIBERATELY DARKENED

The world of managed care is a world of meaning, a meaning that can be known through the interweaving of key metaphors, constructs, images, which become inescapable, almost palpable. It is the same with managed care as with foreign-sounding places during wartime—World War II, Vietnam, Desert Storm, Bosnia. Words we could never pronounce, places we never knew, become companions on our landscape. They are a part of mealtime, everytime. We come to take them for granted. They are a part of us, no longer altogether external to ourselves. What are some of the key ideas that make up the linguistic web of understanding of managed care, or of corporate medicine?:

assumption of risk
at risk
the bottom line
buy-in
capitation
case management
case manager
consumer
cost/quality ratios
coverage
covered lives
customer (relations)
customer satisfaction
evidence-based research
financing organization
gatekeeping (gatekeepers)
guidelines
healthcare marketing
health care industry
inpatient optimal recovery
integrated delivery system
management organization
marketplace competition
medical marketplace
medical supplier
one-stop shopping
outcome measures
patient flow
production reports
provider
quality assurance (CQA, QA, and TQM)
quarterly (hospital, clinic) production
resource management
risk sharing
sales

salesperson

scientific management (Frederick Winslow Taylor's early 20th century concept)

stakeholder

subscriber

Further, one could sort or group these terms into a number of sub-categories, and one could also heuristically explicate each term separately. For instance, "outcome measures" refers to "the ultimate reduction of healthcare delivery to an input/output matrix where the lowest amount of input can be calculated to achieve a standardized and—need I add—socially or corporately derived acceptable outcome" [Seth Allcorn, personal communication, June 24, 1996], thereby constricting meanings admissible to physician-patient relationships and decision making. My main point here is that *connotation*, not denotation, is the key to their meaning; and connotation is context, including the environment that consists of the other terms. The terms are more than discrete members of a list. Each is a part of the other. They are nodes of a world.

CULTURE AND PREVENTIVE MEDICINE: TWO PRELIMINARY TEST CASES

Several physician and P.A. colleagues in Family and Preventive Medicine, and in Occupational and Environmental Medicine, have expressed to me both privately and in clinical group settings their hope and belief that in the era of corporate medicine, managed care, and capitated reimbursement, the patient's culture(s), community(-ies), workplace, and the like will all be taken more seriously, because they are all part of "life-styles," and life-style is going to be a key to preventive medicine. "Our day has finally come," they say. "Public health, wellness, fitness, community medicine will finally prevail." Further, my colleagues hope that for the first time, preventive medicine and public health will fare better than stepchildren in the treatment-dominated world. Patient care via preventive medicine is thus a means to status enhancement and to the accumulation of wealth and power, a ladder of succession that recapitulates and plays out in a new institutional setting old, but current, ethnic and religious patterns in America. What appears at first glance to be "medical" is in fact very American: the wish to be "top dog," and for the "winner [to] take all," if only temporarily, until the anxious winner becomes an anxious loser again.

My concern is less theory than practice: very specifically, that we will at best be co-opted (seduced) by an organizational culture whose leaders—physician and non-physician alike—are interested in culture and preventive medicine principally for profit's sake. They will exploit clinicians' good will and innocence, even as good physicians will at the same time attempt to co-opt managed care categories in their patients' behalf. If their motives will not be transparent, their disingenuousness will be. Preventive medicine, wellness, fitness, and ergonomics that are only, in the Kantian sense, a means to cost reduction and profit rather than an end will ultimately short-change programs in preventive medicine, because they too cost too much, when viewed from the vantage point of short-term corporate profit. And even if "incentives" shift so that employers and insurers cast more of their fate and dollars with preventive medicine, it will be because of economic opportunism, not opportunity.

Preventive medicine is dangerous if ill-motivated, because it ultimately exploits healthcare practitioner, patient, and community alike; because what it ultimately prevents is care, intimacy, availability. It is driven primarily by the fear of facing suffering—one's own or a patient's—in the guise of preventing suffering. It "prevents" guilt, shame, anxiety, identification, *in the caregiver*. It will be yet another sham whose time has come, ostensibly in the name of keeping people healthy and productive in the workforce, but demonstrably for healthcare practitioners', executives', and insurance companies' stockholders' pocketbooks and portfolios, and for their power and status ambitions. Preventive medicine and clinical care of illness will lapse in fiduciary responsibility what they will make up in profit—ostensibly for the patient's and population's own good.

The advocacy and expectation of a new golden age of preventive medicine is bogus, so long as the main motive is profit, which amounts to not seeing patients. Under capitated systems (that is, payment per head) each "provider" assumes risk and will presumably be motivated to keep the patient healthy, which is to say a productive member of the workforce, which in turn narrows the vision of personhood down to the category of "worker." The core incentive is profit (which it has been all along, but now is explicitly), and the patient or employee is a means to that end.

The never-stated emphasis on this type of preventive medicine will be scorn for and fear of suffering and pain. It is akin to many nationalists' celebration of only the healthy, the firm warrior body, and their contempt for any infirmity. Preventive medicine here becomes fear of patienthood, fear of the decline that will be the final fate of us all.

Interest in patients' culture(s)—which anthropologists and other social scientists have been urging since early in the twentieth century—will fare little better, even though, as many physician colleagues have said to me: "We have to get interested in patients' cultures." The question, however, is *how* we express that interest, and *what* we do. Permit me two personal examples. In late winter 1996, I spoke by phone with Robert Like, M.D., a family physician who had for a decade and a half helped spearhead the Task Force on Cultural Issues in the Society of Teachers of Family Medicine. Our report was about to be published in the Society's journal. Neither he nor I was especially enthusiastic about how the HMO era might receive and implement our curriculum and practice recommendations. Dr. Like and I both worried that an oversimplification of culture would lead to stereotyping ethnicity, race, nationality, religion, occupation, community, and so forth. We feared that, for all our good intentions, we had developed something that could be quickly abused once it was out of our hands. It could become an extension of what compassionate physicians disparagingly call "cookbook [or 'protocol'] medicine" or "medicine by protocol," according to which, say, each ethnic group would be allotted a page of "recipes" (protocols) on how to treat and interact with all its members. We feared subverting the inquisitive spirit of cultural sensitivity, of the painstaking effort to understand another human being, by turning it into some quick, methodologically deceptive, packaging to be manipulated by "buyers" and "sellers." In the process, culture, like every other personal meaning, would be violated and distorted beyond recognition. In turn, this boundary-blurring distortion would become official truth imposed upon patients as "their" cultural reality.

It will be recalled that another "cookbook medicine" was performed in behalf of the Third Reich by its physicians for the sake of organizational and national improvement. The chief financial officer (CFO) of a large, urban health sciences center whom I quoted earlier said to me in May 1996: "Managed care is the same as Dr. Josef Mengele in the concentration camp. It says to people waiting in line: 'You go to the left; you go to the right.' You live; you die." The embeddedness of official clinical decision trees in their larger culture could not be more clearly articulated.

My second vignette comes from closer to home. In the mid-1990s, one of my current physician supervisors asked me to develop a questionnaire having a maximum of four to five questions which, when answered, would convey enough rich information to a primary care physician to tell all about the patient's culture relevant for clinical purposes. I dared not even try to comply, even as he demanded that I do! The assignment is in spirit akin to many HMO's streamlining of all covered counseling and psychotherapy into a handful of visits, as if by a few sessions, the manipulation of "suggestion," and some magic psychotropic bullets, entire lifetimes—including those now further assaulted by the need to hold jobs that have good medical benefits—are to be collapsed and remolded in a few brief hours. Through an admixture of identification with the aggressor, careerism, opportunism, and moral cowardice, many therapists and physicians are rewriting human biology, neoteny, and development, so as to rationalize the brevity of therapy and the *mutual abandonment required by clinical totalitarianism* (David Pingitore, personal communication, 1995). Understood this way, culture and personality become caricatures that we are not allowed to recognize as such.

The culture to which we need pay more attention is the culture of managed care (that is, managed care *as* culture) and its larger national culture in whose shadow these two vignettes fall as warning. Here, sickness is punishment for falling from wellness' productivity, and treatment is punishment to restore the fallen, nonproductive workers to productive grace. Illness and treatment are moral failure and moral restoration, respectively, a far cry from Talcott Parsons' classic "sick role" model. If physicians have always been asked to be agents of social control via the regulation of dependency, today all health practitioners are being asked to be both moral police and agents of subtle eugenics. But here, as earlier in the chapter, I do not wish to overdraw the portrait of victim and victimizer too sharply, because the larger social policy is one elected to political office to "downsize" government and to wage a scorched earth campaign against our own.

To use another metaphor, that of the Hebrew Bible's confrontation between the prophet Elijah and the high priests of Ba'al: if, with minor protest, we allow the priests of Ba'al to set healthcare *policy*, should we be surprised and righteously indignant if we are required (and secretly wish) to practice *idolatry*?

ATONEMENT, INSIGHT, GRACE: SOME CONCLUDING THOUGHTS BEYOND THE GLARE OF MANAGED CARE

Many historian and psychoanalytic colleagues have noted that a large part of the Soviet, now Russian, elaborate memorialization of the "Great Patriotic War" (World War II) against the Nazis is meant to deflect their own and others' attention from the terror, rage, guilt, and anxiety that comes from remembering the extent of their own suffering under their own leader, "little father," Comrade Josef Stalin. It is far more bearable to draw attention to "This is what the evil enemy did to us" than to acknowledge "This is what we did to our own," "This is what we allowed to happen," or "This is what our own trusted leaders did to us" (e.g., Volkan 1988). A decade or a generation from now, American historians, physicians, policy makers, and the public will have to face with respect to managed care what the Russians over forty years after the death of Stalin are only beginning to realize: In the name of goodness, *we* allowed this to happen; *we* and our ancestors were part of it, as perpetrators, victims, and quiet colluders (see Hilberg 1992).

The legacy of bloodless downsizing and managed care is a legacy of blood, one that makes profit and production and wage-work the measure of life. It is officially the only measure of worth. It will be our own Great Lie somehow to live down, to rationalize, to falsify the past. One does not need to ask, "How could so many Germans have *not* known about the Nazi Holocaust (1933–1945)?"—we have our own answer to our own times to shed light on self-blindedness. We need to choose how we wish to be known and remembered. As what? Innocence is rare if not illusory; collusion is more the order of the day. It is never too late to admit that we are wrong and to atone. To admit that there are no simple villains and victims in this grisly business. And to make amends to those millions of once-essential workers now injured and betrayed.

Where, then, do we go from here? The choice of one excess to correct another only perpetuates the underlying cultural problems. Both fee-for-service and managed care are ways of disguising healthcare practitioners' financial interests, one by their delegation to the clinic or hospital business office, another by their delegation to upper administration and insurance companies. An open acknowledgment by physicians and other healthcare practitioners of their conflicting values (money and medicine) will help lift the veil of secrecy and will help to heal the split or "double standard."

But such acknowledgment is not enough. Only a medicine ruled by *grace* can fathom both suffering and healing, and can transcend the clinical fads and ideologies that distract us all from the fragility and resilience that are the essence of human existence. If I may conclude with a paraphrase that takes us to the heart of the matter, consider chapter 13 of the first letter that St. Paul, an incorrigible letter writer, wrote to the folks in Corinth. The paraphrase would begin something like this: "Though I speak with the tongues of providers and managed care, and have not love, I am become as sounding brass or a tinkling cymbal."

REFERENCES

Allcorn, Seth, Howell Baum, Michael A. Diamond, and Howard F. Stein. *The Human Cost of a Management Failure: Organizational Downsizing at General Hospital*. Westport, CT: Quorum Books, 1996.

Balint, Michael. *The Doctor, His Patient and the Illness*. New York: International Universities Press, 1957.

Benedict, Ruth F. *Patterns of Culture*. Boston: Houghton Mifflin, 1934.

Bion, Wilfred R. "Group Dynamics: A Review." *New Directions in Psycho-Analysis*. M. Klein, P. Heimann, and R. Money-Kyrle, Editors. New York: Basic Books, 1955: 440–477.

———. *Experiences in Groups*. New York: Ballantine, 1959.

Brown, Laura S. "The Private Practice of Subversion: Psychology as Tikkun Olam." *American Psychologist* 52, no. 4 (April 1997): 449–462.

Buber, Martin. *I and Thou*. Ronald Gregor Smith, Trans. New York: Scribner's, 1957 [1925].

Engel, George. "The Need for a New Medical Model: A Challenge for Biomedicine." *Science* 196, no. 4286 (April 8, 1977): 129–136.

Freud, Sigmund. "Group Psychology and the Analysis of the Ego." *The Standard Edition of the Complete Psychological Works of Sigmund Freud*, Vol. 18. James Strachey, Trans. London: Hogarth Press, 1955 [1920]: 69–143.

Goldhagen, Daniel Jonah. *Hitler's Willing Executioners: Ordinary Germans and the Holocaust*. New York: Knopf, 1996.

Hilberg, Raul. *Perpetrators, Victims, Bystanders: The Jewish Catastrophe 1933–1945*. New York: Aaron Asher Books, 1992.

"How Good Is Your Health Plan?" *Consumer Reports* 61, no. 8 (August 1996): 28–42.

Janis, Irving. *Groupthink*. Boston: Houghton Mifflin, 1982.

Johnson, Thomas M. "Patient Management." *Family Medicine* 27, no. 7 (1995): 460–462.

Johnsson, Julie. "New Life for Long-Dormant Law." *American Medical News* (American Medical Association) 39, no. 17 (May 6, 1996): 3, 51, 55.

Koenigsberg, Richard A. *Hitler's Ideology: A Study in Psychoanalytic Sociology*. New York: Library of Social Science, 1975.

Kormos, Harry R. "The Industrialization of Medicine." *Advances in Medical Social Science*, Volume 2. Julio L. Ruffini, Editor. New York: Gordon and Breach, 1984: 323–339.

La Barre, Weston. *The Human Animal*. Chicago: University of Chicago Press, 1954.

Li, James T. C. "The Patient-Physician Relationship: Covenant or Contract?" *Mayo Clinic Proceedings* 71 (1996): 917–918.

Lifton, Robert Jay. *The Broken Connection: On Death and the Continuity of Life*. New York: Simon and Schuster, 1979.

———. *The Nazi Doctors: Medical Killing and the Psychology of Genocide*. New York: Basic Books, 1986.

Orwell, George. *1984*. New York: Harcourt Brace Jovanovich, 1949.

Pellegrino, Edmund D. "Words Can Hurt You: Some Reflections on the Metaphors of Managed Care." *Journal of the American Board of Family Practice* 7, no. 6 (1994): 505–510.

Perry, Charlotte M. "Nursing Ethics and Etiquette." *American Journal of Nursing* 6 (1906): 452.

Robb, Isabel Hampton. *Nursing Ethics: For Hospital and Private Use.* Cleveland: E.D. Koeckert Publishing, 1900.

Starr, Paul. *The Social Transformation of American Medicine*. New York: Basic Books, 1982.

Stein, Howard F. *American Medicine as Culture*. Boulder, CO: Westview Press, 1990.

———. *The Dream of Culture*. New York: Psyche Press, 1994.

———. "When Money and Medicine Mix: A Tale of Two Colliding Discourses." *Mind and Human Interaction* 6 (1995): 84–97.

Stephens, G. Gayle. "The Medical Supermarket: Futuristic or Decadent? Part I." *Continuing Education for the Family Physician* 19, no.5 (1984a): 243–245.

———. "The Medical Supermarket: Futuristic or Decadent? Part II." *Continuing Education for the Family Physician* 19, no. 11 (1984b): 600–610.

Uchitelle, Louis. "Layoffs Are Out; Hiring Is Back: Consultants Are Abuzz; Growth Is Route to Success." *New York Times* (Business Day section) June 18, 1996: C1, C6.

Verrilli, Diana, and H. Gilbert Welch. "The Impact of Diagnostic Testing on Therapeutic Interventions." *JAMA* 275, no. 15 (April 17, 1996): 1189–1191.

Volkan, Vamik D. *The Need to Have Enemies and Allies*. Northvale, NJ: Jason Aronson, 1988.

Warner, Ernest G. "Ethics and Morality vs. Managed Care." *Journal of the Oklahoma State Medical Association* 89 (August 1996): 275–279.

Winslow, Gerald R. "Minding Our Language: Metaphors and Biomedical Ethics." *Update* 10, no. 4 (1994): 1–6.

Wojner, Anne W. "Outcomes Management: An Interdisciplinary Search for Best Practice." *AACN Clinical Issues* 7, no. 1 (1996): 133–145.

Woolhandler, Steffie, and David U. Himmelstein. "Extreme Risk—The New Corporate Proposition for Physicians." *New England Journal of Medicine* 333, no. 25 (December 21, 1995): 1706–1707.

5

Trauma and Its Euphemisms: Reflections on Mourning and the 1995 Oklahoma City Bombing

INTRODUCTION: THE UNLIKELIHOOD OF EUPHEMISM

On the face of it nothing would seem further from a characterization of the response to the April 19, 1995, bombing of the Alfred P. Murrah Federal Building in Oklahoma City than euphemism. The outpouring of local, regional, and national generosity became instantly legendary. Via television it was there for all to see and hear worldwide. Oklahoma's disaster preparedness plan was marveled at and widely adapted—hurling a challenge at, if not inverting, the national image of Oklahoma as quaint, friendly, flat, backward, rustic, anachronistic, boring, and ignorant. Indeed, "old-fashioned" personal relatedness, not professional training and expertise per se, was what made the rescue, recovery, and rehabilitation of a city come about.

There was public acknowledgment that, under conditions that felt like war, siege, and terrorism, there was "a bottom line" of values deeper than the avowed bottom line of business and profit. Plenty replaced scarcity, in attitude as well as in goods and services. People could not give, sacrifice, enough. For a few weeks, the buck stopped far from the dollar sign.

Yet, as I hope this chapter will depict, the "face of it" is only the beginning of understanding. Deep-seated organizational, linguistic, and cultural forces shaped the response to the disaster and almost immediately gave the cataclysm its meaning. Euphemism will be shown to play a crucial role in this re-shaping and re-feeling of what was for those throughout the region a defining event. Part of what made so enormous an event so definitional in magnitude was the fact that it was experienced as nothing "like" any other trauma, tragedy, or disaster. In sum, I shall explore how the trauma of the bombing became *symbolically elaborated*, specifically *euphemized*, and *how euphemism was used in this mythologizing*.

Destructive as tornadoes and floods are, they are culturally expected even as they strike unexpectedly. There is even something exciting as well as terrifying about them. In the least, they are "ours," part of prairie psyche and pride as well as climate and geography. The bombing was so overwhelming precisely because there was nothing else with which to compare it. It was unimaginable. It utterly violated the prairie sense of place. There was no intellectual or emotional "place" for such an event in the conventional scheme of things. The bombing conflated "here" with "there," outside with inside. It lay outside the range of the expected experience and environment (Hartmann 1958). Euphemism became one way of absorbing the singularity of this trauma into prior group experience.

But there is more: euphemism also became a central mode of unconsciously condensing the foreign into the familiar, the new into the old, the novel into the expected. Almost instantly after the blast was recognized to have been caused by a bomb rather than a natural gas leak, the search for outside terrorists began: at first for "Islamic fundamentalists," and later for members of "white militias." There was an urgent effort to distinguish between "them," the terrorists, the violent, evil perpetrators, and "us," the innocent victims. But violence—behind the closed doors of the home, on the highways, at competitive sport events, especially football—was endemic to Oklahoma culture long before the bombing. The "new" violence became a way of displacing and projecting attention from the embarrassing, yet fiercely defended, "old" violence of home and hearth where people were still regarded as owned possessions and private property. It quickly became part of the social burden of euphemism to help protest that what *does* happen here now was imposed, rudely foisted on us. Unexpected violence could be talked about; expected violence could not dare be mentioned in the same breath.

Euphemism helped to bridge the revulsion of what "they did to us" and the enforced silence over what we have long done to ourselves. Euphemism helped Oklahomans, and, more widely, people of the Great

Plains and even of the entire country, to "manage" the trauma by erecting an impenetrable border in space between victimizers and victims, and an equally indomitable fortress in time between the era before the trauma and the new age forced upon us by the bomb. Outrage at violated innocence helped to fend off the painful realization that what can't happen here does and has, though in far less spectacular a magnitude.

In the public response to the bombing of the Oklahoma City Federal Building, as in public attitudes toward more ordinary social forms such as the family and organizational downsizing, one can see a kind of *symbolic equation* at work: *"We do violence to our own [in the workplace, in the sacred family]"* is transformed via projection into *"They do violence to us."* Good and evil are split and projected along the lines of "us" and "them," "inside" and "outside." And if the split does not correspond entirely to how people feel, it corresponds to how people feel they can express and articulate their feelings. Reality, in turn, "complies" with our projections.

To put the whole episode in the language of Western Judeo-Christian religion: the sacred had been desecrated, had been made profane, defiled. The sacred inside had been contaminated by the profane outside. The cultural, political, and religious rite of cleansing would consist of a decontamination and restoration of the borders of sacred and profane. But, at the unconscious, or at least out-of-awareness, level, the sacred was in fact profaned long before the bombing. "We have been violated" is easy to say; "We also violate, even before we were violated" is not only difficult to acknowledge, but taboo. Evil was already inside: that is what is most intolerable, even inconceivable. That is why we resort to euphemism: to keep us from thinking and feeling what we are on the brink of realizing.

Much as a discussion of the Oklahoma City bombing does not aesthetically "belong" in the same place as a discussion of organizational downsizing and managed care, it indeed does rightfully belong as a test case of their way of thinking and way of doing. As the drama unfolded from weeks into months, I wondered: How could we, in Oklahoma City and the state of Oklahoma, of all places, conceive of reinstating managed care as a clinical philosophy, of continuing corporate layoffs, and of proceeding with dislocating reengineerings after all that we had seen and done here? Business-as-usual had to mean, I began to surmise, to some degree at least, internal cultural violence as usual. As participant observer and member of the Oklahoma City and State communities, I saw first-hand the shift in emotional valence and wondered how it was possible. How could we not learn, at a profound emotional, even moral, level from this experience? What was I missing? Euphemism helped provide the cue to understanding.

A DISASTER AND ITS LANGUAGE: WHAT KIND OF EVENT WAS IT?

Within a matter of days following the bombing, an entire vocabulary was already in place to describe and bound the horrific event in space and time. Central among these words were: heartland, innocence, innocent children, immunity, violation, healing, closure, community, generosity, victims, survivors, terrorists, faith, briefing, debriefing, and "This doesn't (can't, couldn't) happen here." The words and phrases were not used in isolation. They quickly congealed into a "semantic environment," a cultural grammar, a kind of prairie quilt, each term implying the other, and together conjuring a gaping hole as much interior as exterior.

These words and phrases came to co-define the parameters of discourse, the "disaster narrative" or "crisis narrative." They became part of an interlaced fabric, a prairie quilt, a new "skin" of words and phrases, that coalesced into the core story line of the event: the core story line of many workplaces, of a city, of a state, of a nation, and even worldwide, with Oklahoma envisaged in terms of friendliness, hard work, prairie, and expansive sky.

Soon image replaced event, even as the image supposedly constituted the event. Sense of place became synonymous with place itself. The unimaginable had now somehow to be imagined. For many, the question became how to restore the cultural ideal, how once again to blur the cultural self-image with supposed daily reality of the peaceable prairie. How, many wondered, could we recover the sacred agrarian space from the profanation, the desecration, inflicted upon it? Euphemism, heavily armed with denial, projection, and intellectualization, became a crucial tool by which to jerry-rig meaning and sentiment in the complicated mourning that followed the bombing (Volkan 1981). Euphemism became a central tool of adaptation to the fact that violence of so unprecedented a magnitude had erupted on workplaces that symbolized, among other things, protected childhood (the daycare center), federal bureaucracy and authority (the federal building), and the final cultural reserve for supposedly traditional, agrarian values (the heartland).

This chapter inquires into *what kind of event the 1995 Oklahoma City bombing was*, and how euphemism helps in our understanding of the meanings and feelings that soon emerged and reconstructed and defined the event itself. I wish to emphasize at the outset that this chapter is not about the bombing per se. It is about what the bombing can teach us about organizational and wider cultural euphemism. It is about *violence in the workplace* (and far beyond) and about *the language of violence* (Diamond 1997). If I omit much, it is because the bombing and its trauma per se are not my focus: euphemism is.

Inclusion of a discussion of the bombing of the Oklahoma City Federal Building in a work on organizational euphemism is compelling on several grounds: (1) euphemism came to define much of the workplace-and-wider cultural event; (2) for a brief while after the bombing, the whole worldview presupposed by managed care and downsizing euphemisms was suspended, only to be restored soon with a vengeance; and (3) the "violence in the workplace" (and beyond) that the bombing exemplified soon was mystified and silenced by euphemism. The Oklahoma City bombing is a "test case" and "natural experiment" in the era of downsizing and managed care for at least two reasons: (1) because of the swiftness with which compassion and charity came to dominate medically related decision making, and (2) because of the swiftness such abundant compassion could be cast off and a return to business-as-usual (which is to say, downsizing and managed care) take place. For, in Oklahoma City and in the far wider American sensibility, the bombing came to be part of the same cultural story as downsizing and corporate medicine.

Eerie as it may at first seem to make any association at all between the bombing and more ordinary corporate trauma, I shall approach the aftermath of the bombing much as I have attempted to understand traumatic organizational and healthcare change. As earlier, my approach will be via euphemisms that fall into recurrent words and phrases, and that ultimately are unavoidable. Members of the cluster are part of the same cultural fabric of meaning and feeling, stated and unstated, conscious and unconscious. The cluster comes to define, to portray, even to replace the event itself.

To better orient the reader to the remainder of the chapter, I offer a rough figure that can serve as a linguistic map. I ask the reader to pay attention both to the clustering of terms (similar to my approach to downsizing and managed care in the previous chapters) and to the evolution or emergent sequence of terms.

THE EVENT AND ITS IMMEDIATE AFTERMATH

At 9:02 A.M. on April 19, 1995, a truck bomb exploded in front of the Alfred P. Murrah Federal Building in the north end of Oklahoma City. One hundred sixty-eight people were killed (seventeen of whom were children in the Murrah Building's child care center), about 500 more were injured, and some 300 buildings sustained major damage. Initially, buildings within a 78-square-block-area sustained some damage.

BEFORE THE BOMBING | AFTER THE BOMBING

"You can't break our spirit."
Loss of innocence
War zone
It can't happen here.
Violation
Heartland
Terror hits home
Victims/Survivors
"Foreign terrorists"

Rescue - Recovery
Mourning
Healing
Coming Together
Sense of community
Support
Love
Faith
We Remember
Proud to be an Oklahoman

Closure
Get over it
Return to normal
Back to work
Grit
Backbone-spine

Seedlings from the "Survivor [Elm] Tree" in Murrah Building parking lot given to bombing survivors
[Taxonomy of:]
"Those who were killed, those who survived, and who were changed forever."
"Oklahoma Standard of Response" (to disaster):
Selflessness, compassion, community, etc.
"Healing is a process, not a destination."
Finalists selected in memorial competition

Downsizing
RIFing
Reengineering
Restructuring
Reinventing
Outsourcing
Managed Care
Provider/Customer
Product Lines
Managed Change

Lowering of American flag to half-mast

EVENTS

19 April 1995, Bombing of Murrah Federal Building

23 April 1995, Prayer Service at Oklahoma State Fair Grounds

23 May 1995, Demolition ("implosion") of Murrah Building

4 July 1995, Raise American flag to full-mast

19 April 1996, 1st anniversary

31 March 1997 Beginning of McVeigh trial in Denver

19 April 1997, 2nd anniversary

3 June 1997, McVeigh Convicted

14 June, 1997 Death penalty handed down

TIME LINE

Nearly two and a half years after the explosion, most buildings in the twelve-square-block-area around the Federal Building remain abandoned and boarded up. Two have been demolished. Few of the small businesses have reopened.

A chain-link cyclone fence, densely decorated with faded wreaths, flowers, teddy bears, T-shirts, poems, and letters, encloses the green lawn where the building once stood. One street has now been permanently closed to traffic. But the area is largely deserted, except for the steady stream of reverential visitors, virtual pilgrims to a shrine. In the surrounding area, plywood remains king. In the news, various memorials are mentioned, but little more. Time is frozen here, where time only a few blocks south scurries with the daily pace of business and big plans for downtown and the adjacent area ("Bricktown") redevelopment.

In a letter to the editor of *The Daily Oklahoman* (Oklahoma City), Mary Anne Perry wrote on April 8, 1997, "The area around the bomb site resembles Sarajevo [referring to the ethnic war in the former Yugoslavia]. The value of our property is at an all-time low" (1997: 4). The imagery of war and war zone is a recurrent theme in the mental reconstruction by Oklahomans of the scene after the bombing. The response to the bombing makes cultural sense if the bombing is construed as an act of war or of its equivalent, terrorism, upon the federal building, the city, and upon the Heartland region and the geographic repository of idealized American (including work) values.

What happens to the sense of space and time—to a workplace, to a building, to an urban region, to a state, to a nation—when a cataclysm of this sort takes place? How do its people digest and metabolize it? What do its people "do" with it? And how can what we learn from it be transferred to other cultural work settings? An understanding of the work of euphemism helps to answer these questions.

TRAUMA, LANGUAGE, AND EXPERIENCE

I shall begin with the *experienced* world of Oklahomans: "We had no warning; it was entirely unexpected; this kind of thing doesn't happen here in the Heartland; we were overwhelmed by it, in shock." Even if, at another level of discourse, there are plenty of cultural contradictions to these claims (e.g., the idealized, pastoral, Evangelical Protestant ethos of nonviolence of North American prairie culture versus the reality of family brutality and children's death), *the study of their trauma begins with what people make of their world when what is not supposed to happen here in fact does*. Trauma is an intolerable break in the world as it should be. It is a break in the aesthetic order of things. It is not only about material reality, but also about reality as inner representation. It is about self-image and the group-image of the world, a projected world, not only the actual world (Hallowell 1955; Hartmann 1958; Berger 1996). It is about the intolerable break between what the world should be and what it unmistakably is (see Krystal 1985 and Rangell 1976 on the concept of "stimulus barrier").

What, in turn, is the social unit of trauma in the bombing? Who is a "victim," a "survivor"? Who was wounded? And how is woundedness defined, and by whom? What is its cultural geography, its map, its demographics, its extent, its boundary? What is traumatized—and who defines or decides whose hurt "counts"? One might begin with those people who were physically killed, injured, or maimed by the bombing, their families (and how, even, is family to be construed?), and those rescuers, recoverers, firefighters, police, and many types of professional emergency medical and demolition personnel who had direct contact with the devastation, the blood, the stench, the mutilation. Further, the traumatized might include the outside rescuers, such as professionals from the Federal Emergency Management Agency (FEMA) who came to Oklahoma City from all over the country to help supervise recovery, only to find themselves emotionally unprepared for *this* kind of disaster, and then to find themselves emotionally rescued by the Oklahomans' hospitality and camaraderie, and then after two weeks to leave it all after their job was done, and return to families and workplaces that could not relate emotionally to their life-changing experiences. In some instances the unit is locally geographic; in others it is not.

One then might go so far as to draw the boundary of the trauma as that nation. But then, in the light of the worldwide fantasy of Oklahoma in the films *The Grapes of Wrath* and *Oklahoma!*—which embody the twin extremes of the state's image, humiliating and glowing, respectively—was the bombing not also a globally symbolic event? A cartoon first published in *The Oregonian* (Portland, Oregon, April 21, 1995, two days after the bombing), and later republished in *Newsweek* (December 25, 1995–January 1, 1996), depicted the bombed-out Murrah Building in the background. Surveying the wreckage, one person asked the other, "How many hurt?"; the other replied, "260 million Americans."

David Rogers, M.D., a family physician faculty colleague who had joined the Family Medicine Department in Oklahoma City after the bombing, said to me: "I was in Arkansas at the time. I saw it [the bombing] as a tragedy, a senseless loss of life. To you all, it must have been a violation of a sense of community. It didn't happen in my state, but in yours. [pause] But in a way, we're not used to terrorism here, so it's a violation of our country" (September 24, 1996). The reconsidered boundary of self (of fusion of the membrane of self and group) and vulnerability, from state to nation, is as clear as it was poignant when he discovered it for himself: the moment "them" became "us."

Finally, the unit of trauma is historical and temporal, as well as spatial. Oklahoma serves as a repository of American idealization and romanticization, an island of cultural wholesomeness ("Heartland," innocence), a place of living nostalgia. It embodies the long-lived invincibility fantasy of "fortress America," a powerful island, blessedly isolated, removed geographically from the European (Asian, or African, or other alien) continent(s).

As an event that cannot be digested and metabolized, which is to say fully mourned, the bombing assumes the form of an introject that is felt as a haunting presence. It becomes an obligatory gift for the next generation to keep alive (Volkan 1988), even as part of that gift is also the duty to bring "closure"—that is, to repress disturbing emotions and "get on with life."

Traumas such as group military defeats and political humiliations are retrospectively written and rewritten, becoming mythologized into what Volkan (1991) felicitously calls "chosen traumas." Likewise, triumphs are subsequently elaborated into resplendent "chosen glories" that far surpass the exultation, relief, or lasting achievement of the original event. The Oklahoma City bombing contained elements of both: especially the attempt to reverse shame into pride for how the disaster was "managed."

TRAUMA, COMMUNITY, ORGANIZATION, AND CULTURAL BASELINE

From the vantage point of a linear, cause-and-affect reading of history, we are tempted to ask about what traumas "do" to the peoples they visit. This approach, while productive, is at best a partial and incomplete truth. People weave even the worst cataclysms into the ongoing flow of events. They wrap a new event into the blanket of meaning and expectation. In so doing, they incorporate it into their sense of time and place. Thus, we must add what people *do with* traumas to what traumas *do to* people. We *adapt to* trauma, by *adapting with* culture (organizational, family, religious, and ethnic). At some level we know this. When we say (1) that a cataclysm terribly ruptures a community's social fabric (cause-and-effect, from outside-in), we also know, if only implicitly, (2) that people themselves define the nature of community sentiment and organization that define the social membrane that can be violated in the first place.

If disaster is the experience of rupture, of disruption, to that sense of community reified into a social unit, then disaster, while perhaps heuristically distinct, is in practice inseparable from community. *Community* (from workplace to city to state, region and nation) *implicitly defines what would shake it to its foundations,* and thus what would constitute a disaster or trauma. How a community would absorb a "shock" to it defines shock in terms of community.

Only our motivated reifications prevent us from recognizing this. Or put differently: what is ruptured is not things, but our reifications. We play a crucial part in what happens to us. Let me turn now from theory and abstraction to example: Oklahomaness-as-community, and the place the bombing came to occupy mentally in that community. My point of departure is downsizing. Not only are hospitals, universities, and corporations undergoing massive "downsizings," euphemism for mass firings or layoffs, but in the early 1990s politicians began to call for the widespread use of employee downsizings to reduce the workforce in city, state, and federal budgets. Although the bombing in Oklahoma City can be construed psychologically as an altogether unique, unprecedented, exceptional event, a terrorist attack on the American Heartland, it can likewise be viewed as an extreme and literal expression of the widespread American wish to get rid of "big," "bad," "greedy" paternal government, one symbolic expression of which was the Federal Building in Oklahoma City. Hatred of Federal government quickly fused with hatred of our own. The governor of Oklahoma, an almost constant presence for over a week at the bombed-out site in Oklahoma City, had resoundingly called for downsizing of his own state government.

A similar cultural contradiction wages over the value of children. Ideological, religious, and often maudlin appeals to "family values" and the outrage over the deaths of "innocent children" in the bombings occur in the same culture that often turns a blind eye and deaf ear to children's deaths in the home. Oklahoma children are "at risk" in their homes, families, schools, and communities, and not only from outside terrorists. Let me situate this epidemiologically. The Oklahoma Institute for Child Advocacy, a nonprofit organization, gathers data on the welfare of children in Oklahoma and publishes an annual report. Their 1997 report states that, based on data from the Oklahoma State Department of Health, "Oklahoma's infant mortality ranking relative to other states slipped from 29th to 33rd during the most recent year (1993) measured" (1997: 11). Further, "During this past year [1996] the proportion of Oklahoma child abuse and/or neglect actually confirmed continued to worsen to a record high (from 12.8 to 13.5 per 1,000 children in the community), with comparable rates also worsening in the majority (45 of 77) counties" (1997: 13). "A higher proportion (13.5 per 1,000) of children are confirmed to be child abuse and/or neglect victims

than were in the mid-1980s (8.5 per 1,000), with such rates also worsening in the vast majority (60 of 77) of Oklahoma counties during the
same period" (1997: 13). "A total of thirty-four children died from child
abuse and/or neglect in FY 1995" (1997: 13), which is to say twice as
many as were killed in the 1995 bombing. The local and national image
of the "Heartland" differs markedly from the less palatable, covert
reality contained in these numbers and in the heated rhetoric about
disposable, downsizable people in government jobs. The Heartland harbors its own heartlessness, as well as a magnanimous heart. True,
these day-to-day, often hidden, and unchampioned deaths are not in
magnitude or symbol "the same" as the blowing up of the Federal Building. But the emphasis on "innocence" and prior "immunity" and the
rush to "closure" suggests a denial and repression of the horrors inside
the culture. An ethos of nonviolence that makes anger itself unthinkable, let alone inexpressible—because, among other things, it is un-
Christian—makes internal cultural violence literally unimaginable,
except at such culturally sanctioned places as football games and other
organized sports. The bombing becomes an occasion for the return of
the repressed.

To say this does not so much impugn Oklahomans' legendary generosity during this terrible event as it places that generosity frighten-
ingly close to other, competing values, fantasies, wishes, and feelings,
which is to say, ambivalence. To mourn our loss of safety we must also
mourn the state and national mythology that perpetuates our *lack* of
safety, and alas, our *lack* of innocence. Consider as euphemism the
notion of "innocence" and of innocence violated in the bombing. If Oklahomans humbly pride themselves on being a kind of buckle in the Evangelical Protestant Bible Belt, Oklahoma is also high in teenage
pregnancy, wife beating, child beating, and family-related child death,
all conducted "behind closed doors" of patriarchal family inviolability
and privacy. There is a disingenuous protest quality (" 'they,' not 'we,'
do this heinous kind of thing") to the outrage directed toward *outsiders*
who would dare harm our children. The terrorism that cannot be publicly discussed, the terrorism that begins at home but cannot be labeled
as such, is now safely displaced onto and focused on outside terrorists.

SENSE OF PLACE AND THE UNTHINKABLE

The bombing in Oklahoma City is not only the local subject of Oklahomans' imagination, for Oklahoma and Oklahomaness occupies a special place in the American national consciousness as well. At bottom
the "unthinkable terrorist act" in Oklahoma City signifies a fantasized
injury to the previously inviolable and sacred heart of the national body

called America—a body that, no matter how ruggedly individualistic we insist we are, is the symbolic, symbiotic, mother, from whom we do not wish or cannot bear to separate.

According to this national fantasy of the nation-as-body, New England is the intellectual, rational "head" of the country. By contrast, the West represents the instinctual, undomesticated wildness of Americans. What of Oklahoma, and more broadly the Heartland? What is its place in the body fantasy of America? The bombing was an attack upon the heart, that is, the cardiovascular pump, which keeps the nation's circulation of meaning, of "tradition," alive and vital. It is the place where, if anywhere in the United States anymore, people still have heart, still care about each other, and still value personal relationships over the dollar. The bombing threatened the death of meaning to the entire nation (Becker 1962). The rural grain and cattle belt, the "Heartland," the soul of the land, serves as the still-beckoning conscience, a place and a value center to which all candidates for national office appeal and to which shrine they visit and pay homage (if not Oklahoma, then Nebraska, Iowa, Kansas) to claim personal continuity with Jeffersonian democracy. Many friends and colleagues call it "God's Country," which they proudly distinguish from the "Devil's Country" of the urbanized east and west coasts (Stein 1987).

The metaphor of "immunity" is part of, and extends, the biological, organismic fantasy: that groups have bodies just like those of people. If the Heartland can be diseased, what is the fate of the rest of the national body? (Perhaps I should state the obvious: that these fantasies of birth, death, separation, growth, and decay apply to and occur in corporations, offices, industries, and other workplaces as well.)

Whatever else "Heartland" connotes and condenses into a single image, it is also the heart, the place that has "heart," the last frontier and remnant of honest sentiment, of close, cooperative community, an island of caring and giving in a national sea of callousness and indifference.

Oklahoma's reputed "loss of innocence" is equally America's loss of innocence as it is embodied by and deposited in the idealization of the prairie, the Great Plains, its families, its espoused values, its official wholesomeness, its burden of history. Consider, as an example of Oklahoma's role in national fantasy, the following letter by Jan Edry in Acton, Massachusetts, published in the May 3, 1995 edition of *The Daily Oklahoman* (Oklahoma City):

> Dear friends in Oklahoma, you are our hearts before they became hardened by the city and by life. You are our trust before it was violated. You are our smiles before they became a rarity. You are our warmth and humanity before we became cold and unmerciful.

To us, you are our bread. You are the drawl that we, with our Boston accents, would love to have. You are cowboy hats and boots, barbecues, square dancing and beautiful open country beneath a vast, starry sky. You are a musical.

You are hay bales and barn raisings. You are our neighbors and friends and represent all that we would like to be if given the chance. We love you.

You are us, OKC. We grieve deeply for your loss. We are there with you and will continue to be until your loss—our loss—is atoned. (1995: 6)

This letter articulates poignantly how cultural geography plays a personified, even bodily, role in local, regional, and national fantasy. That role in national fantasy—that is, who and what the people of the Heartland were expected to be—helped solidify the euphemisms that sustained the utter incredulity that the bombing could dare take place. The magnitude of the bombing was unprecedented—yet the violence was uncanny and not altogether alien. Somehow, the foreign was already the familiar—and had to be made foreign in order to be made tolerable.

A close physician friend and colleague, a man from rural Oklahoma who a decade ago was one of "my" residents (apprentice-trainees following medical school), passed me in the clinic hall a few days after the bombing and said teasingly: "Now *you* look like one of those suspicious characters they showed on television. Are you sure you're not from the Middle East?" We both knew he was "just kidding," teasing in a typical male Oklahoman style of affection, but I felt a little banished as I sensed his self-protectiveness. If only in momentary jest, he had banished me to one of "them," and (via introjection) I keenly felt foreign to a world I had thought to be mine as well as his.

Almost immediately after the bomb explosion and in the days that followed, many Oklahomans defiantly proclaimed to the world, "You can't break the spirit of Oklahoma!"—the spirit of self-reliance, of inexhaustible mutual support, and of resilience in the face of disaster. "The spirit of Oklahoma" became a rallying point after the disaster, and remains so at the time of this writing. As Oklahomans, they were also speaking for the wished-for seamless image of the violence-torn *nation* as much as for the *state*. But the defiance was a protest against the realization that something had been broken, and broken by *some* outside force.

At the April 23d Prayer Service (called "A Time for Healing") held at the Oklahoma State Fairgrounds Arena, Cathy Keating, the State's First Lady, said, "A hundred hours ago our state was a quiet and happy place." Governor Frank Keating later said, "Never in the history of our

country have Americans witnessed such senseless barbarism. It has
been suggested that those who committed this act of murder chose us
as their victims because we were supposedly immune, the Heartland
of America." Many speakers at the service, and countless other Oklahomans in the days immediately after the bombing, spoke of our
mourning "the loss of our sense of safety that was once Oklahoma."
President Bill Clinton said of the bombing, "This terrible sin took the
lives of our American family." It is acceptable, even preferable, to speak
of how others take our lives, but not how we take the lives of our own.
The rhetoric of euphemism about the bombing makes it unlikely and
unnecessary that we realize that Oklahomans, and other Heartlanders,
have long been unsafe from our own: that the imagined safety never
existed.

ADAPTATION TO TRAUMA: BEYOND THE LANGUAGE OF CAUSE-AND-EFFECT

What people do with what happens to them is a process of adaptation.
Just as a disaster can, via regression, unmask personal childhood conflicts, calamity can also intensify and make clearer (as well as serve as
a symbol for displacement of) current adult emotional, psychosomatic,
organic, and family suffering. Both of these dimensions have been made
clear to me through lengthy applied organizational fieldwork in the
Office of the Chief Medical Examiner of Oklahoma, and in the Family
Medicine clinics of the University of Oklahoma Health Sciences Center
in the years since the bombing. It does injustice to those whom we are
trying to understand and to help via consultation, and to theory as well,
if on a priori theoretical grounds we discount either the unmasking of
the past or the horror of the present.

The very nature of "cause," and the very significance of the "event,"
require careful exploration. For Oklahomans, the effect of the
Oklahoma City bombing was officially supposed to be over, with "closure" (emotional finality) achieved by "healing," largely born of "faith"
and of the community generosity. "Real men" (and women) do not brood
in long shadows; they get on with life, "walk on down the road." Largely
in the form of euphemisms, these concepts and vague notions enforced
(and not only by that master linguistic culprit, "the media") cultural
fictions and in part prevented the very healing that they claimed to
accelerate.

Most of my professional biomedical and mental health colleagues in
Oklahoma, like their lay counterparts, are, as one health educator said
to me in October 1996, "sick of hearing about the bombing and want to
get back to normal without being reminded of the bomb, especially by

the media. When I hear about it, it either sounds like we're boasting about how well we did, or moping around in a 'poor me' self-pity. We don't need either of them." His is a common attitude, in part rooted in a keen (culturally shared) sense of shame (1) at calling attention to anything outstanding one did, which separates one from the common consensus, or (2) at publicly exposing weakness and requesting help.

Throughout Oklahoma culture (Stein 1995a, 1995b, 1995c, 1996; Stein and Hill 1993), the emphasis within two weeks following the bombing was back-to-work, get life back together, "suck-it-up" toughness, "no whining," "self-reliance," being "strong," "controlling your emotions," and renewed pride in being Oklahoman from having "survived" yet another calamity (the legacy from the Great Depression, the Dust Bowl, tornadoes, hailstorms, frequent floods and droughts, crop failures, college sports' and county commissioners' graft scandals, bank failures, and now the bombing). If the bombing is a unique event, it also is woven into the cultural fabric of victimhood, survivorship, and defiant resilience. Indelible memory is inseparable from brazen indifference. At least in part, adaptation (even when it is maladaptive) is cultural compliance, a process partly rationalized and enforced by euphemism.

In this regional culture, as with an organizational culture I described in an earlier chapter, to be called a "survivor" is to be accorded the highest cultural compliment, that of being a person of "true grit." Survivorship without complaint or whining, true cultural manliness, is a hard-bitten stoicism, but one with a sternly masochistic undertow wherein one revels in the very tribulations that test survivorship. For survivors of the bombing, the only culturally acceptable form long-term mourning may take is what might be called "tough grief." It thus makes a kind of grim cultural sense (one of turning a passive experience into an active one) for a new B-2 bomber to be christened at Tinker Air Force Base, Oklahoma City, on September 14, 1996, as "The Spirit of Oklahoma." Taken together, these virtues—as an ethos—of true grit provide a bulwark against grief, weakness, anxiety, guilt, shame, and doubt. The "inability to mourn" (Mitscherlich and Mitscherlich 1975) is rationalized into the necessity *not* to mourn as a sign of manliness and womanliness. In minimizing the trauma, in trying magically to return in time to the world prior to the trauma, we in fact assure its repetition. "Survivorship" as cardinal virtue rather than mere fact requires the circumstances that are to be endured and outlived.

Around a year to a year and a half after the bombing, in many medical clinics, corporate offices, academic offices, and the like, there grew a collective sense of great apprehension, of foreboding, filled with agitation and the inability to concentrate. The fantasy circulated that someone would soon kill himself or herself, would kill someone else,

someone would have a heart attack or divorce. People waited for the
first one to "crack," to "go crazy." Some people even revealed to me the
transparent notion that "It was as if there were a bomb in our midst
waiting to explode"—and it took little insight on my part to tell them
that, in large measure, the future they dreaded had already occurred
in the past. Thus at the individual and group level, the trauma is internalized, even as great effort is made consciously to gain distance
from the bombing and "get back to normal."

A close physician friend and colleague described the abrupt mental
reorganization within a month of the bombing in such terms as "being
tough, strong, the John Wayne–type, the 'I can handle it' attitude, a
'keep a lid on it' style, fiercely self-reliant attitude that 'We're back in
charge now' when we darn well know we weren't." If the disaster was
"a total loss of control," an unrecognizable world of "broken and fragmented things, utter chaos," as one Oklahoma City physician put it,
the insistence that "healing" had been accomplished and "closure"
reached signified the reclamation of control—a magical return to the
moment before the bomb exploded, a reversal of terror, humiliation,
guilt, and anxiety. The attempted return to business-as-usual was part
of this abrupt closure.

BRAVURA, RAGE, AND SHORT-CIRCUITED MOURNING

One expression of mourning, and a means of containing that grief, is
a still widely displayed motor vehicle bumper sticker that reads (as of
October 1996), in large letters, "Proud to be an Oklahoman." A blue
ribbon is draped across the silhouetted State. It was as if the bombing
and the community outpouring of love and generosity immediately afterward somehow vindicated Oklahomans' poor collective self-image
(representation), what many Oklahomans themselves have labeled as
their "inferiority complex." Through tragedy, shame could once again
be overturned into pride (football and other fiercely competitive sports
being the primary means to achieving this under normal cultural circumstances). Oklahomans basked in the almost redemptive, vindicat-
ing, national acclaim Oklahomans received for their deft response and
generosity in the immediate aftermath of the catastrophe. People until
recently thought to be "dumb, friendly, backward Okies" now stood at
the forefront of disaster planning; they became the model, not the
laughingstock, of others. At the second anniversary Remembrance Cer-
emony on April 19, 1997, and after, Oklahoma speakers referred
proudly to the "Oklahoma Standard" of response to disaster.

The part Oklahoma and America plays in Oklahomans' fantasy life,
and the converse, cannot be underestimated. Nor can the "manage-

ment" of shame on this national and interior stage be underestimated. If, prior to the bombing, Oklahoma represented "nowhere," "nothing," "an unknown," and at best "cowboys and Indians," the bombing quickly offered a compensatory image of "social solidarity" felt to be absent in urban Elsewheres and of astonishing competency and sophistication in responding to disaster. In 1989, the Rand McNally *Photographic World Atlas* had omitted Oklahoma, along with North and South Dakota, from its regional maps and photographs. The 1995 bombing made Oklahoma into a global presence.

The bombing and the now-idealized communal response to it put a new Oklahoma image on the map. In an Oklahoma City newspaper article on November 25, 1995, Ron Franz asks, "Can we [Oklahomans] be a national model?" (1995: 7) to replenish America's "social capital" of participation in community activities. "In 1987 [*sic*], we bowled alone. In 1995 we formed a new league" (1995: 7). Shame, pride, pain, and thanksgiving all vie in this emotional "league" to provide Oklahomans a new image. In a way, the disaster proved to be culturally redemptive, at least for a time. Oklahoma became a national model for something new, rather than the ambivalently held bastion of the old and the rustic. Oklahoma became mainstream rather than slackwater.

There was, and remains among Oklahomans, a defiant, cool-rage quality of protest of superiority in the face of calamity. Ostensibly a form of mourning, this cultivated calm is a fortress against the vulnerability of mourning. This response runs parallel to that of Susan Cohen, mother of a twenty-year-old woman who was killed 7½ years earlier in the terrorist bombing of Pan American Airlines Flight 103 over Lockerbee, Scotland. Cohen writes: "Of all the emotions I have felt since Theo's murder, anger is the best. Rage gives me energy. Rage makes me strong" (1996: 50). Rage is a bulwark of integration against the pull of grief's regression and disintegration. It is a defense that requires ever-greater vigilance.

In their pioneering studies of crisis and subsequent psychological adaptation, Devereux (1955) and La Barre (1971, 1972) emphasize that it is not the stressor by itself (e.g., the bombing) that is traumatic, but the defensive constellation with which people attempt to adapt to the event. It is not that the stressor does not count, but that it does not count alone. If the event (itself a spatially and temporally *constructed* configuration) does not stand or "cause" by itself, careful attention to what people "do" with it helps us to understand its unconscious force.

For instance, assaults to one's group (from corporate and hospital, to ethnic and national) "solve" the chronic problem of one's ambivalence toward one's own cultural values, attitudes, beliefs, and roles. One's own negativity is split off, projected onto and into the assailant, who now embodies all of one's hostile, aggressive, "bad" parts. This is not to reduce trauma to wish fulfillment, but to identify such wishes as part of the metapsychology of trauma. We "adapt" to unconscious meanings as they are embodied in reality. Too great a protest of innocence and victimization in the face of group trauma often functions to drown out competing wishes and feelings.

US AND THEM: EUPHEMISM, REWRITTEN HISTORY, AND DISAVOWED VIOLENCE

The expectation that such violence, such brutality, does not occur in Oklahoma—in "the Center," "the Heartland," "God's Country"—but instead, on the evil east and west coasts, or across the ocean (New York City and Los Angeles, Beirut, for example) is the surface skin, so to speak, of a simultaneously local and national idealization of the region as the last living bastion of close families, of civility, of caring community ties, of the reliability of a handshake to seal a business transaction, of an ethic of hard work, of simple, direct morals, and of Jeffersonian agrarian virtues (to own, work, and be of the land). The actual domestic violence, the brutality, the child abuse and molestation, and the neglect "behind closed doors" tell a different tale—one filled with shame and defiant entitlement—one that flies in the face of these idealizing, reality-denying euphemisms.

To understand a people's core metaphors—which serve often as euphemisms as well—is to tap into their world: a world both hidden and revealed. Phrases such as "loss of innocence," "loss of immunity," "victims," and "survivors" quickly became incorporated into the most ordinary conversations among news reporters and among those Oklahomans interviewed. They are desperately guarded half-truths. One local writer stressed to me that this event certainly did not mark the first loss of that supposed innocence: witness, for instance, the ravages of the Dust Bowl in the 1930s, the Edmond Post Office shootings in 1986, the current, unthinkable, presence of teen gangs in Oklahoma City, the random devastation wrought by tornadoes, and the increase in drive-by shootings. Still, his voice is the exception. And, in his enumeration, he did not even mention the 1921 race riot in Tulsa, America's worst, in which whites burned down much of the black community. Nor, for that matter, did he describe the histories of various Native Americans currently or formerly in Oklahoma, ranging from Cherokees exiled to Oklahoma by President Andrew Jackson, to prairie peoples chased out to make room for what became called the "Unassigned Lands" that were "opened" for the late-nineteenth-century Oklahoma land runs.

For most Oklahomans, and for many Americans outside the state, there is the conviction that something has irrevocably changed in and about Oklahoma, that the bombing was singular, a catastrophe unprecedented by anything else, however horrible. And *that* has everything to do with the belief that we who had lived in safety in "America's Heartland" now live in fear—and the question of whether we can learn to feel safe here again.

EUPHEMISM AND THE ENFORCED "RETURN TO NORMAL"

Oklahoma Governor Frank Keating ordered the American flags, flown at half-staff since April 19, 1995, to be raised to full mast on July 4, 1995, America's Independence Day. The weeks of professionals' and the public's awe-inspiring generosity with all of life's essentials, toward the wounded and caregivers alike, were over. The outpouring of compassion, material goods, and services was as short-lived as it was bountiful. On May 23, 1995, the remainder of the Murrah Building was ceremoniously imploded and demolished, and the area leveled, to remove not only the hazardous structure, but the reminder of violation and humiliation. The "Conestoga wagons" so quickly and magnanimously drawn into a circle for mutual aid and (mostly physical) support now went their separate ways. As spontaneously and miraculously as the "community of compassion" (Minow 1996) emerged to respond to the urgency of the crisis, almost as spontaneously that precious communal "we" dissolved. Pressure for premature, once-and-for-all "closure" of the trauma walled off feelings of vulnerability and culpability. In the enforced return to "normal," the fact of vulnerability vied with the wish to go back to invulnerability. The bombing itself became a taboo subject, as did grief. Tears are reserved for anniversary public rituals. A chain-link fence surrounds the perimeter of "The Site," as many now call the leveled grassy area on which the Murrah Building stood. It is a shrine to communion remembered and discarded.

The fence is now sacred ground built upon desecrated space, a poignant, living memorial covered with abundant, and constantly replaced, teddy bears, T-shirts, flowers, wreaths, and letters. People visit it from around the city, state, and country. Their tone is always a respectful hush, as at an American funeral. This hallowed place is as close as this independent-spirited frontier city can come to a symbolic graveyard, a shrine, a place to which mourners from all over the nation can come and focus, and in a way deposit, their grief. Its role is not unlike that played by two widely displayed motor vehicle bumper stickers—often both on the same car or pickup truck—that read in bold lettering "Proud to Be an Oklahoman," and "We Remember." The bumper stickers are marks of public pride and defiance; they also allow their owners to get on with life in their families and workplaces. Several friends have claimed and approvingly labeled the downtown fence as "The Wall," "Our Vietnam Wall." They do not see it as a barrier to their grief, but as a protection of sacred ground ("Would you want homeless drunks and dirty bag ladies sleeping and pissing on the ground at night?" one medical colleague said to me in October 1996). They hope it will be a permanent memorial. Others think that it is an abomination, that the fence prevents working through the grief, by walling off and keeping the very area of the cataclysm off-limits, unknowable, a kind of shared secret and mystery. They would prefer to have an open lawn or park there, much like a cemetery for people to walk through. In either event, the sacred ground has been preserved. A formal memorial, winner of a competition, has been commissioned. Stylized remembering and memorialization has achieved far short of healing, even though we speak in the language of "healing" and "closure."

Examples of grief-cut-short abound, but they only occupy and haunt the periphery of prairie grit. A professional grief counselor colleague and friend, who had worked closely with people physically hurt in the bombing, rescuers, and their families, was peremptorily dismissed in May 1996, by her church-affiliated social service. The "downsizing" or "RIFing" (reduction in force) was explained to her as being financially driven. Those who dismissed her protested to her that they had no choice, since their division of disaster relief had run out of money to support postbombing counseling. She pressed them on their explanation, since money was often shifted between various agency divisions and programs to where it was needed, from one budgeted line item category to another. Money was now to be retained and appropriated for child adoptions, marriage and divorce counseling, and other, more conventional agency categories.

The agency had run out of money and interest to support her thriving work only because their timetable of need differed from hers, and they were in the positions of power and authority to define need, value, and priority. Culturally, her time, and the bombing's, were up. "Closure"—a widely used term to designate bringing a quick and clear-cut end to the mourning period—was, or at least should have been, achieved, and her services were no longer officially needed (because the problem no longer officially existed). Euphemisms such as "closure" and "healing" (as in the admonition: "If you had enough faith in God, you would be healed"), and other ideologies of normative (cultural) pathology, paradoxically place people at additional risk by their imperative of a vow of silence (and silent suffering) apart from stylized ritual occasions, even as those who espouse them insist otherwise (Devereux 1980; Lacan 1979). The defense against the trauma additionally traumatizes. Euphemism stands sentinel as guardian of the wound.

CONCLUSIONS: WE HAVE MET THE ENEMY AND THEY ARE US

Euphemism—that constellation of words and phrases that came to define and conjure the bombing and its meaning—does not serve as backdrop or background to the experience and construction of the trauma, but is part of the very foreground of the drama. We try to master trauma via language that masks it and sets the stage for repetition (Klein 1976; Freud 1955, 1958). Even when people do not directly use or invoke these terms, they presuppose them and the worldview in which they occur. The euphemisms are part of the medium of thought for what is expressed. Words can be absent, even if their sensibility, their discourse, their atmosphere, is present—what in German is called *Zeitgeist*, the "Spirit of the Times."

It becomes apparent that euphemism, which we had thought would protect us, turns out to be one of the chief personal and cultural resistances to working through the trauma and thereby mastering it. It helped to give violence (our own, others') distance by making it alien, foreign, to us. To one colleague what made the bombing most incomprehensible was that it was done by "one of our own [people] against civilians." What was perhaps most culturally disorganizing (emotionally dissonant) about the bombing was that it shattered the emotional boundaries between "us" and "them," between "good" and "evil," between what was done to us and what we did/do to others. It exemplifies the return of the repressed. It suddenly created uncertainty as to where the violence was located. It lay not altogether outside, but at least partly inside; and part of that vast "inside" was profound ambivalence toward the federal government and what it represented.

Euphemism played a vital role in the tripartite process of prebombing illusion, disillusionment, and reillusionment in the wake of the bombing. Partly bolstered by euphemism, workers in the downtown Oklahoma City region, Oklahoma Cityans, Oklahomans, prairie folk, and Americans could reassure ourselves that someone entirely unlike ourselves had done so heinous a crime as violate America's innocent Heartland. Here, euphemism helped sanitize, rationalize, and disavow violence. Further, it justified outrage—and more violence. Euphemism allowed us to focus on the "Heartland" and its violation as a means of displacing, of diverting, attention from the intense disaffection with the federal government.

"Their" violence to us is our own familiar, but defamiliarized, uncanny violence among ourselves, real and wished. Euphemism helps us to avoid realizing that we are the enemy as well as the "they." Our ambivalence toward family, workplace, and federal authority fuels bombs and bombers. We shudder at the terror we first wink at. In the wake of the bombing, many politicians suddenly toned down the strident warrior rhetoric that they had used toward their opponents and opposing positions. Second thoughts always come after the fact, too late to prevent sacrificial tragedy. In trauma's shadow, we flee the vulnerable honesty of grief and inch toward repetition. We condemn ourselves to renewed trauma.

REFERENCES

Becker, Ernest. *The Birth and Death of Meaning*. New York: Free Press, 1962.

Berger, Louis S. "Cultural Psychopathology and the 'False Memory Syndrome' Debates: A View from Psychoanalysis." *American Journal of Psychotherapy* 50, no. 2 (Spring 1996): 167–177.

Bion, Wilfred R. *Experiences in Groups*. New York: Ballantine, 1959.

Cohen, Susan. "Rage Makes Me Strong." *Time*, July 29, 1996: 50.

Devereux, George. "Charismatic Leadership and Crisis." *Psychoanalysis and the Social Sciences* 4 (1955): 145–157.

———. "Normal and Abnormal." *Basic Problems of Ethno-Psychiatry*. Chicago: University of Chicago Press, 1980 [1956]: 3–71.

Diamond, Michael A. "Administrative Assault: A Contemporary Psychoanalytic View of Violence and Aggression in the Workplace." *American Review of Public Administration* 27, no. 3 (September 1997): 228–247.

Edry, Jan. "Letter to the Editor." *The Daily Oklahoman*, May 3, 1995: 6.

Erikson, Kai. "Loss of Communality at Buffalo Creek." *American Journal of Psychiatry* 133, no. 3 (March 1976): 302–305.

Franz, Ron. "Tragedy Spawns a Different Thanksgiving." *The Oklahoma Observer* (Oklahoma City), November 25, 1995: 7.

Freud, Sigmund. "Interpretation of Dreams." *The Standard Edition of the Complete Psychological Works of Sigmund Freud (SE)*. Vols. 4 and 5. London: Hogarth Press, 1953 [1900].

———. "Beyond the Pleasure Principle." *SE*. Vol. 18. London: Hogarth Press, 1955 [1920]: 3–64.

———. "Remembering, Repeating, and Working Through." *SE*. Vol. 12. London: Hogarth Press, 1958 [1914]: 145–156.

Hallowell, A. Irving. *Culture and Experience*. Philadelphia: University of Pennsylvania Press, 1955.

Hartmann, Heinz. *Ego Psychology and the Problem of Adaptation*. New York: International Universities Press, 1958 [1939].

Klein, George S. *Psychoanalytic Theory: An Exploration of Essentials*. New York: International Universities Press, 1976.

Koenigsberg, Richard A. *Hitler's Ideology: A Study in Psychoanalytic Sociology*. New York: Library of Social Science, 1975.

Krystal, Henry. "Trauma and the Stimulus Barrier." *Psychoanalytic Inquiry* 5 (1985): 131–161.

La Barre, Weston. "Materials for a History of Studies of Crisis Cults: A Bibliographic Essay." *Current Anthropology* 12, no. 1 (1971): 3–44.

———. *The Ghost Dance: The Origins of Religion*. New York: Dell, 1972.

Lacan, Jacques. *The Four Fundamental Concepts of Psycho-Analysis*. New York: Norton, 1979.

Minow, Martha. "Commentary on 'Suffering, Justice and the Politics of Becoming' By William E. Connolly." Presented at the Roger Allan Moore Lecture, May 11, 1995. *Culture, Medicine, and Psychiatry* 20 (1996): 279–286.

Mitscherlich, Alexander, and Margarete Mitscherlich. *The Inability to Mourn: Principles of Collective Behavior*. New York: Grove Press, 1975.

Modell, Arnold H. *Psychoanalysis in a New Context*. Madison, CT: International Universities Press, 1984.

Niederland, William G. "The Problem of the Survivor." *Journal of the Hillside Hospital* 10 (1961): 233–247.

Ohman, J. Cartoon of the bombed Oklahoma City Murrah Federal Building. *Newsweek*, December 25, 1995–January 1, 1996: 94.

Oklahoma Kids Count—Factbook 1997. Oklahoma City: Oklahoma Institute for Child Advocacy, 1997.

Oliner, Marion Michel. "External Reality: The Elusive Dimension of Psychoanalysis." *Psychoanalytic Quarterly* 65 (1996): 267–300.

Perry, Mary Anne. "Letter to the Editor." *The Daily Oklahoman* (Oklahoma City), April 8, 1997: 4.

Rangell, Leo. "Discussion of the Buffalo Creek Disaster: The Course of Psychic Trauma." *American Journal of Psychiatry* 133, no. 3 (March 1976): 313–316.

Shatan, Chaim. "Unconscious Motor Behavior, Kinesthetic Awareness and Psychotherapy." *American Journal of Psychotherapy* 17, no. 1 (1963): 17–30.

Stein, Howard F. "Culture Change, Symbolic Object Loss, and Restitutional Process." *Psychoanalysis and Contemporary Thought* 8, no. 3 (1985): 301–332.

———. *Developmental Time, Cultural Space: Studies in Psychogeography*. Norman: University of Oklahoma Press, 1987.

———. *Listening Deeply*. Boulder, CO: Westview Press, 1994.

———. "When the Heartland Is No Longer Immune: The April 19, 1995 Bombing of the Oklahoma City Federal Building." *Psychohistory*

News: Newsletter of the International Psychohistorical Association 14, no. 3 (1995a): 2–4.

———. "The Rupture of Innocence: Oklahoma City, April 19, 1995." *Clio's Psyche* (A Quarterly of the Psychohistory Forum) 2, no. 1 (1995b): 1, 12–15.

———. "Reflections on the Oklahoma City Bombing: War, Mourning, and the Brief Mercies of Plenty." *Mind and Human Interaction* 6, no. 4 (1995c): 186–199.

———. "Oklahoma City Aftermath: Trauma, Time, and Adaptation— A Psychohistorical Montage." *Clio's Psyche* 2, no. 4 (March 1996): 92–95.

Stein, Howard F., and Robert F. Hill, eds. *The Culture of Oklahoma.* Norman: University of Oklahoma Press, 1993.

Terry, Jack. "The Damaging Effects of the 'Survivor Syndrome.'" *Psychoanalytic Reflections on the Holocaust: Selected Essays.* Ed. S. A. Luel and P. Marcus. New York: Holocaust Awareness Institute, Center for Judaic Studies, University of Denver, and KTAV Publishing House, 1984: 135–148.

Troy, Frosty. "Sooner Killing Fields." *The Oklahoma Observer,* April 25, 1995: 1.

Volkan, Vamik D. *Cyprus: War and Adaptation.* Charlottesville: University Press of Virginia, 1979.

———. *Linking Objects and Linking Phenomena.* New York: International Universities Press, 1981.

———. *The Need to Have Enemies and Allies.* Northvale, NJ: Jason Aronson, 1988.

———. "On 'Chosen Trauma.'" *Mind and Human Interaction* 3, no. 1 (1991): 13.

6

Conclusions: Can We Transcend Euphemisms in Organizations, and Beyond?

OPENING VIGNETTE

Several years ago, I was standing around in a large seminar room, talking with a managerial colleague after a formal conference had concluded. I forget what topic we were discussing, but I remember saying to her, "I want to think out loud with you for a moment"—at which point a trainee passed us, interrupted, and snapped at me with a mischievous grin: "Don't you know, you're not allowed to think aloud around here except in organizational process groups!" These "process groups" had long been a biweekly safe haven in which corporate trainees at various levels of skill and status met to talk about the difficult personal, emotional side of workplace life, relationships, decision making, administration, and leadership and subordinateship. It was a refuge, but also a designated region in space and time in which participants could try on and rehearse scenarios for future organizational encounters and decisions. The "support," "griping session," "bitching session," and "ventilation" were prelude to some emotional as well as strategic problem solving.

Several years later, this same trainee who had once been guarded, bitter, even cynical, now serves as a cochief apprentice upper manager for her corporation. She has taken as one of her main tasks the process of trying to make every conference, every committee, every meeting a place that is emotionally safe enough for people to think aloud, to risk being wrong as well as right, to be creative, to be playful, to be themselves. As part of her leadership or "management" style, she tries to correct the emotionally numbing and terrorizing organizational atmosphere in which people were afraid to not know the "right" answer, to be wrong, to admit it, and to make public fools of themselves by replying "I don't know" to a question from a person more senior in the corporate hierarchy.

Her style and behavior represent what I mean by trying to *transcend organizational euphemism's strangle-hold of silence, secrecy, of not making waves, and of going with the flow.* She refuses to be complicit with the manufacture of smoke screens. Over the years she has taught me about euphemism's deadly silencing of honesty, openness, of real feeling and of critical thought. She has also taught me about the courage to do better than her teachers, superiors, supervisors, and "role models." Although she risks all by scenting-out and exposing euphemisms much as a bird dog pursues a hidden covey of quail, she also takes the chance of helping her organization to unmask, address, and perhaps even solve underlying, pervasive problems, rather than leave them to fester and worsen in the name of stability, security, and image—that is, facade.

She knows that to be open and direct cannot make things worse (although we usually fear it will), but can only make clear and public what is secret and private. Which is to say, it will make many people uncomfortable, but necessarily so if problems are to be faced and solved rather than further masked.

Our masks blind us to ourselves as well as hide us—not only to others, but from ourselves. They interfere with our ability to learn from experience. A workplace that prohibits and inhibits "thinking out loud" ultimately sacrifices morale, enthusiasm, creativity, productivity, and even long-term profit for the sham of appearance and for the frightened security of "belonging." My managerial colleague reminds me that *euphemism is ultimately the guardian of our own incarceration.*

Euphemistic "Newspeak" is the guardian of our organizational self-betrayal. It is our frightened "No Exit"—even as we wait to be fired. We lie to cover our lies; we enshroud our euphemisms in even thicker layers of euphemism. The study of organizational euphemism, then, is the study in cultural deception and self-deception, and their grim consequences.

EUPHEMISM, AGGRESSION, AND THE PROBLEM OF EVIL

In this concluding chapter, I take certain liberties of interpretation and extrapolation that I have declined—or tried to decline—earlier in the case studies of corporate downsizing, of managed health care, and of the Oklahoma City bombing. I shall look for generalizations or "lessons" for organizations and for consulting with organizations, for history, for American culture, and for understanding human nature. I began this book with a study of workplace distortions and deceptions in language, and I end it by recognizing the complicity of culture and unconscious in the work of evil—evil both as means and as end in itself.

In this book I hope to have at least created a doubt in the reader's mind that organizational euphemisms are a *solution* to problems, even as we fervently believe them to be the only solution. Conversely, I hope that the reader is by now considering euphemisms to be a *problem*, a dangerous kind of solution, a symbol and symptom of some problem, a self-deception and coerced group deception. Corporations, industries, hospitals, universities, government agencies, churches, nations, all spend decades and billions of dollars trying to solve the wrong problem—wrong not only because reality is misperceived cognitively, but worse, because of the emotional investments, the motivations, organizational members have in misperceiving and in mystifying the problem a certain way (Stein 1996). Furthermore, euphemism is both a symptom and symbol. In each of the three case studies, euphemisms clustered into recurrent groups of words and phrases. Taken together, they constitute a culture-specific syndrome, a patterning or configuration of symptoms of a problem or disorder. Euphemism endangers our health even as it guards our defenses.

I am aware that at a certain level, euphemisms *feel* like a solution to members of a workplace. We have a stake in our self-evasions. They make us feel good, whole, at least temporarily. I concede this, and I hope that I have at least acknowledged it and given it some respect: we have the defenses we need. But I hope I have also shown that our defenses, implemented by such linguistic ruses and ideologies as euphemism, ultimately do us in, even as we think they protect us. Euphemism as a way of thought, together with the behaviors euphemism expresses and imposes, is more a protection racket than a source of quiet security.

This book has explored the elusive work of the human imagination (conscious and unconscious dynamics) in building and perpetuating workplace worlds upon the infrastructure of euphemism. More broadly, this book has traced the operation of euphemism as symptom, defense, wish, and misplaced solution. It has long been the fate of workplace organizations and of whole societies (1) to solve the wrong problems and to pursue the wrong solutions; and (2) to be so ambivalent toward their own values, beliefs, and roles that they create and formulate problems in such a way that they cannot be solved, although their solution is hotly pursued (for instance, the endless "war" on alcohol and drugs [see Heath 1996; Stein 1993; Devereux 1980; Nuckolls 1997]). I have shown how euphemism both helps the wrong problem to be solved and perpetuates the misunderstanding of the very nature of the problem!

This book has studied the unpleasant, often sordid, side of life in work, and our attempts through language to make it more palatable. It has inquired about why, where, when, and how we use euphemism to express ourselves and to structure the world of work. It has studied power and powerlessness, and explored the quest for control and the feeling of being out of control. It has situated the human body and the experience of the body behind the words (Koenigsberg 1975, 1986). (In *The Anatomy of Human Destructiveness*, Erich Fromm described a twenty-two-year-old man who insisted that everything in life was "shitty," but said proudly of himself, " 'I am an artist of destruction' " [1973: 341].) This book has described euphemism as the rationalizer (handmaiden) of destruction. It has mapped mystification and self-mystification in organizations—and made a plea for demystification for the sake of morale, human dignity, and the productivity and profitability that surely follow from it.

When I began this book, I had no inkling of where I was going to end up: that the nature and function of euphemism in workplace organizations and culturally far beyond them would compel me to address what philosophers, psychoanalysts, and theologians have called "the problem of evil." The exploration of organizational downsizing, of corporate healthcare and of the long-term aftermath of the Oklahoma City bombing led me to this unlikely but unavoidable—and in retrospect, not surprising—place (see also Freud 1961; Fromm 1973; Volkan 1988). I began by seeing in workplace euphemism the subtle workings of human aggression in the workplace. Later I viewed euphemism in terms of such metaphors as functional/dysfunctional and healthy/unhealthy work environments. I end with a realization of the vast work that *evil*—a specialized and malignant form of aggression—plays in supposedly rational workplace organizations and in groups far beyond their scale. I have come to *recognize in organizational euphemism the face of organizational evil*, an evil self-disguised as masked good (see Adams and Balfour, 1998). Evil is no mere instinctual saturnalia, a *Walpurgisnacht*-like disinhibition of aggressive drives. It is a desperate attempt to contain and organize a dissolving world by the destruction of the other who is experienced as violating one's own boundaries. At the same time, it feels morally justifiable, even urgent.

I arrive at the philosophical "problem of evil," and the language of evil, precisely because they engage my emotions as well as my intellect as I try to comprehend the often incomprehensible experience of the workplace organizations. Nothing less will do. The scope of human destructiveness done under the cloak of euphemism has taught me that the more social scientific, engineering, language of "functional" or "dysfunctional" organizations, and the more metaphoric medical language of "healthy" or "unhealthy" workplaces, are simply too sanitized, too thin, too euphemistic, to convey how life is experienced internally in downsizing, in managed care, and after the Oklahoma City bombing. We know too much to shrink from words that match the depth of feeling.

Much as the word *evil* can be misused—as in scapegoating—it is so powerful in connotation that it engages the reader's imagination (part of the dynamic unconscious and consciousness) and is thereby congruent with the subject matter. I count on the fact that the word is so steeped in history and laden with the reader's own mental associations that the sadistic pleasure of evil may be evoked, and the subject of this book be understood from within. In a way, to speak openly about evil is the psychological opposite of speaking through the fog of euphemism.

From mass political atrocities to depictions in literature and cinema, evil is the perverse joy at the suffering of others through their systematic degradation into the status of nonhumans (in psychoanalytic terms, "part-objects," that is, split-off aspects of oneself). One can only do terrible things to people (literally, terrorism) after we have first made them less-than-human. But no matter how compelling, even paralyzing, the experience of evil, it is not a separate, external power. It is "us" as well as "them." Despite how we experience evil, the demonic is not an independent agency. We reify evil, make it into a thing, an entirely "other" psychological or spiritual force, in order to disembody it from ourselves and externalize it. We manage to keep it, but at a safe distance.

Building on the work of Hilberg (1985, 1992), Staub (1989), and Alford's own earlier study of evil in workplace organizations (1990), Alford courageously describes the political psychology of evil, of a particular kind of destructiveness: "Whatever evil is, it is not *just* going along with malevolent authority. It is identification with malevolent authority, finding pleasure and satisfaction in joining with its destructiveness" (1997: 2). Alford draws our attention to the overwhelming quality of the experience of evil—which is why we so often imagine evil in terms of the demonic or demonic possession. The German word *Schadenfreude*, joy at the suffering of others, captures evil's quiet, smug glee. Further, through processes of identification and ego-adaptation (Parin 1988), one can engage in, indulge oneself in, and abstractly justify acts as if they were "not one's own." We gloat in our momentary reprieve. We hate in monumental proportions, and pretend we do not hate. We turn our frightened vulnerability into a vicious offensive, and attack others whom we make vulnerable in our place.

The excessiveness of boundary violation that defines evil and its power is a beyondness that is as much sought as dreaded. The "doom and dread" (Alford 1997: 12), "the experience of powerlessness before terror" (1997: 12), also excites to thrill in action. One can think of it in terms of turning a passive experience into an active one (Freud 1955), of creating dread where one has experienced and dissociated it, of becoming an executioner where one feels deep down already to be imminently executed. The terrorized becomes the terrorist.

To allow oneself to be "possessed" by evil—which is ultimately no more than to succumb to one's deepest wishes—is magically to overcome the "dread of limits, of mortality, of meaninglessness, of vulnerability and loss" (Alford 1997: 13). To do evil is to become the very doom one most dreads. It is to defeat death by identifying with it. A discourse on organizational and wider evil must begin with the recognition that "evil is, or can be, fun; if it were not, people would not do it" (Alford 1997: 15).

The work of euphemism is to create the delusion that there is no perverse pleasure in hurting, only necessity in getting the job done—well done. Through euphemism, irrationally based pleasure is transformed into rational mandate and protocol. At least for the moment, one does not feel the doom that led one to evil and euphemism in the first place, or even feel the doom of those whom one has condemned. One is doing "just business," or "just my job," or "nothing personal . . . it's just the bottom line." What at first appears to be the "banality of evil" in bureaucracy (Arendt 1964) turns out to be just another clever excuse to inflict pain: the "banality" argument about evil turns out itself to be an exercise in euphemistic reasoning! Philosophical notions of evil's banality, of its source in obedience to authority and in capitulation to group pressure (organizational conformism), are yet further cozening self-deceptions used to justify inflicting brutality and to hide one's own deeper motivations—which include hurt and vulnerability.

From the study of euphemism, it seems that the sadistic joy of doing evil does not consist altogether simply in the discharge of a biological drive. Whatever else this study of organizational cultural euphemism teaches us, it shows us that hatred and destructiveness are not simple. *The perverse pleasure of destructiveness is inseparable from the perverse rationality of that same destructiveness.* This is not euphemism's only paradox. The enforced betrayal of the vulnerable, frightened "true self" occurs via the strutting, strident assertion of the equally frightened "false self." The joy of evil takes place where joy has been renounced. He or she for whom all hope has been destroyed must destroy all hope.

The condemnation, the "sentence," is an unstated part of the single-mindedness. Greed cannot sate emptiness, for it fills the cravings of the false self, while leaving the real self to starve. Betrayal by others begets self-betrayal, which in turn begets betrayal of others. That is part of the tragedy of short-term bottom-line chasers. It can only lead to further chases, to vicious cycles, never to fulfillment or resolution.

Euphemism is as devastating an instrument of human destructiveness as is any bomb—and it has often been used to justify the degradation and murder of millions of human beings. The use of euphemism as described in this book is only more subtle than an explosive. It is an unstated presence in the current increase in, and fascination with, "violence in the workplace." It is a silent, well-employed, partner in the degrading work of bullying, goading, harassment, terror, and terrorism in the workplace.

What are the implications of this study of euphemism in the workplace for organizational culture (management) theory, for management and consultation methodology, and for practice? We need to ask: if a long-standing organizational problem, perpetuated in part by the mystification performed by euphemism, were to be solved, *what would be lost, not only gained*, by the people involved? Such a viewpoint reexamines the conventional wisdom, to the effect of: "Who wouldn't want to solve something identified as a problem that needs to be solved?" (e.g., drinking in the workplace, where it fosters camaraderie, with upper management turning a blind eye, even when they have employee assistance programs for alcoholism).

EUPHEMISM, ORGANIZATIONS, AND HUMAN AGGRESSION

What can this inquiry into the role of euphemism in organizational life teach us about the nature of aggression—in organizations or elsewhere? What can euphemism in the workplace teach us about human aggression? Whatever else they might be, "anger" and "violence" in the workplace are currently popular topics, urgent ones. They are "social cynosures" (La Barre 1946), that is, categories of people or abstractions that attract a great deal of attention. What we *do* about something follows from how we *understand, imagine, define, feel about*, and *construct* that "something." And most often, discussions of workplace anger and violence focus on bombs, guns, knives, and not on those subtle shadings that remove human damage from language and human intention.

What can this study of euphemism in the workplace teach us about human nature, specifically about the nature of human aggression more broadly, and anger or violence in the workplace more specifically (Paul

1978, 1988; Dentan 1988)? The use of euphemism to justify some form of violence against others makes me think that euphemism is part of a larger system of sacrifice and of sacrifice's use of euphemism. The fantasy and wager is that "such-and-such will not happen to me or to my/ our organization if I can make it happen to them." Euphemism is part of the corporate gamble, the merger of self with work-group, to deny death, to make another perish in one's stead.

Another common example of the work of aggression in the workplace, of its role in euphemism and in the service of sacrifice, is the common dichotomy of "oppressor" and "victim." It is too simplistic (though it is tempting and common) to blame upper management, or invisible stockholders, for foisting and enforcing euphemisms in a top-down hierarchical fashion. The creation and enforcement of euphemism goes both ways, and laterally ("horizontally") as well. To say this is not to exonerate leaders, managers, and administrators. Instead, it takes euphemism out of the easy unconscious splitting between all-good and all-bad people. If anger is rampant in workplaces *and* is taboo, it is easy for workers to blame upper management for the presence of euphemism in the first place, and it is equally easy for lower management and for employees to justify their own sadism by insisting that the "bad guys" at the top provoked it.

Many people who wish to focus and spend their rage lie in wait of situations in which it can be justified. Employees can deny their own self-protective "buy-in" (that is, identification) to euphemism if they can insist that upper management forced it on them. Here a subtle, symbolic form of sacrifice takes place: for example, I, as employee, sacrifice one of the "bad" parts of myself, my aggression and its disguises, and keep the inner image of being "good" by offering or sacrificing my badness and depositing it into upper management, act toward them as though they were "bad," and provoke them into acting in ways that confirm my perception. The vicious cycle of projection, identification, provocation, and "confirmation" of fantasy by reality continues.

To borrow yet another metaphor from biomedicine: our solutions or treatments to the problems that euphemism raises are only as good as our diagnosis (or diagnoses). The three studies in this book (on downsizing, managed care, and the Oklahoma City bombing) separately and together affirm my conviction that euphemism's triumph in our business and wider language is a sign of the moral despair of a nation, a civilization, ours. It signifies a failure of love—of inclusion in a shared humanity—not just of nerve. The case studies depict a culture that turns its back on its own heart and conscience, replacing them with a wholesale negation of that heart and conscience. Production and consumption have gone wild. We cannot produce enough. We cannot make enough profit fast enough—no amount of capital accumulation suffices.

We drive hard so that we cannot stop. We consume others, and we are consumed. It does not require a Freudian to detect the unbridled fury of devouring oral and explosive anal rage that takes the form of what Kohut so felicitously termed "chronic narcissistic rage" (1972). In this scorched-earth policy, we destroy ourselves in the process of keeping ourselves and our workplace organizations "competitive" and "profitable." *The perverse pleasure of destructiveness occurs together with the perverse rationality of destructiveness.*

Behind the slogans, phrases, and linguistic clusters of euphemism lies our despair that we, as human beings, as Americans, can ever again be good, honest, fair, hopeful, whole. The American Dream is renounced because its realization feels hopeless. Opportunity is replaced by opportunism, a desperate philosophy of make-all-you-can-as-fast-as-you-can. The only chance we have for hopefulness is to kill all hope and then to place the new, contrived, hope into temporary corporate triumph. Such an ill-begotten phoenix does not stay long arisen from its ashes. It must be brazenly and endlessly touted to be believed—like so many organizational mission statements, strategic plans, goals and objectives, and retreats that are monuments to a falsity that can only be sustained by repetition and enforcement, if not terror.

Addressing identity panics and conversions, Erikson (1968) wrote of the substitution of ideological "totalism" (as in absolutistic, all-or-nothing "totalitarianism") for "wholeness" (a slow, ever-growing, ever-unfinished synthesis) that often characterizes group crisis and the panicky search for instant identity—"closure" in different words. He also wrote of the choice of the "negative identity" and the repudiation of the once-fruitful "positive identity," a literal reversal of the emotional polarity or valency (Bion 1959a) of values. If one cannot hope to attain the ideal, or at least to diminish the gap between the ideal and the real, then one can diminish the anguish by repudiating the ideal altogether. In a different framework, Bion (1959b) wrote of attacking all links of meaning and feeling, attacking even the possibility of linking what must be severed—so that one will not know or feel, or even wish to know or to feel. If there were a link—if we allowed that there be a link— we would feel, for example, sorrowful, guilty, ashamed, responsible, sad, anxious. To abolish the idea of such a link is to avoid any and all of these dysphoric feelings. We would know we were going to die, that we would lose everything we imagine we had gained, and that nothing could prevent it from happening to us.

When we think of recent ideological cultural revolutions, the publicly violent ones of German or Italian fascism, Pol Pot's destruction of Cambodian urban culture, or China's "Gang of Four" are those bloody identity panics that come quickly to mind. But the systematic self-destruction of our own culture under the watchful eye and word of euphemism is no less an ideologized, cultural revolution (Barbara Shapiro, personal communication, 1996). In the language of Winnicott (1958, 1965), the "false self"—conformist, compliant toward others upon whom one depends, and betraying who one really is, what one really feels, and what one really knows—triumphs over the "real self." In its obligatory, compulsive way, it comes to feel real to us, and is ferociously defended to fend off any memory of the real, now dissociated as well as repressed, self. Lie becomes the only truth about ourselves and about the world that we can bear to hear.

BEYOND THE MASK OF EUPHEMISM

There is and can be no simple and easy organizational formula for forgoing and transcending euphemism: no set of, say, six cassettes to listen to, no neatly packaged video, no set of slides or overheads, no workbook, no weekend executive retreat. The "packaging" of the workplace is part of the problem, including the "SWAT team" approach of many consultants and consultant teams. We value only narrowly and linearly conceived outcomes, and suspect all "process." Quick answers should be suspected and rejected—even though our American culture has come to prize and rely on "quick cures" to all problems. The solution is labor intensive: acknowledgment of and working through the resistances to recognizing the presence and "work" of euphemism. Those consultants who will work best with organizations are not "experts" with answers and "spins" before they speak with anyone in the company. Rather, it will be those who listen, wish to listen, best.

"Expertise" lies in a relationship of mutual trust and respect, not in the knowledge and tricks one member of the relationship possesses. The ancient image of the Wounded Healer—now as consultant and corporate leader—comes to mind as psychological antidote. This project has inspired both determination and humility in me. It makes me remember that the purpose euphemism serves is as individual and group self-protection from feeling something terrible—feelings so unbearable that people would do anything to avoid them. And it forces me to realize that any desire I have to be of help, as teacher or supervisor or consultant, must take that individual and group purpose of euphemism as the point of departure.

In these roles, I come to the same conclusion as does Robert Jay Lifton (1979) in his study of the survivors of the atomic bombing of Hiroshima: that I must somehow be prepared to face death, as reality and as representation, if I am to help others to do likewise.

I became convinced that anxious immersion in death imagery is important for psychotherapy or any other important personal change. In that sense renewal involves a survivor's experience: there is a measure of annihilation along with imagery of vitality beyond the death immersion. What must be overcome is not so much repression as chaos or formlessness, on the one hand, suffocating patterns on the other. Only that confrontation with negativity can provide the self-regeneration—the true psychic energy—for change. The self and not the "therapy" becomes agent and basis for change. (1979: 392)

In this book, if my description of euphemism and its contexts is even partially accurate, what does it imply for organizational behavior in the future, especially for the future of euphemism in organizational behavior? Do organizations require self-deception among their members, and in leadership-followership relations, in order to have good morale, productivity, efficiency, revenue, profit? What happens to euphemism under current conditions of massive firings, the scaling down of organizational size (boundaries), increasing concern with staying nationally and internationally competitive, with organizational survival itself (as if a workplace were a biological organism)? What happens to euphemism as organizations become ostensibly less hierarchical and less "tall" hierarchically, more based on autonomous teams or other smaller units, more based on task performance on the part of people who have not worked long together than on long-standing "specialty" groups, and increasingly based on the "virtual workplace" of people working and relating via computer networks? My own guess is that the need for euphemism will increase to fill the void of greater depersonalization, greater uncertainty, greater anxiety.

Euphemism's loud protest of innocence is not itself a sign of innocence, but of protest. Euphemism allows people to disavow the guilt, shame, remorse, and anxiety they would feel by calling it something else. If in using euphemism, workplace organizations, ethnic groups, nations, and religions inflict pain upon others, its purpose is to avoid feeling the pain oneself. It is a form of the age-old sacrifice and the magical thinking that underlies it: if I (we) sacrifice you, then perhaps I (we) will be spared. The difficult solution for organizations already hard pressed to complete tasks and deadlines is to take "solutions" and make a "problem" of it: put in psychoanalytic terms, it is to make what is ego- and culture-syntonic (in keeping with the organization of the mind and group) into what is ego-dystonic. It is to make us uncomfortable, not comfortable—the opposite of the purpose of euphemism. The beginning of recovery from the damage we have inflicted on ourselves and others through euphemism is confession—acknowledgment to oneself and to others—and atonement, alien notions we usually assign to an institution called "religion." The deepest wound we sustain from euphemism is not that it is ultimately unprofitable and unproductive, but that it is wrong. We understand why organizations and whole nations continue to engage in such wrongs in order to understand resistance to insight, but then ultimately in order to transcend such resistance. The three traumas I have described in the case chapters are all emotionally wrenching. It is the trickster's task of euphemism to say it isn't so. But we also see through our sacred lies, at least on occasion. The boundary between oppressor, victim, bystander, and survivor is vague and shifting (Hilberg 1985, 1992). Ultimately, euphemism redeems no one, though it promises much. Its cruel joke is on us all.

Euphemism is a linguistic, and secondarily organizational, monument to what we once called idolatry, the worship of false gods and bogus values. In Winnicott's (1965) terms, euphemism represents the triumph of the "false self" over the "true self," a perverse triumph in which the defensive false self persuades the vulnerable, fragile, frightened real self that what is real, what feels true, is in fact false. In the darkness of euphemism's interior and shared chambers, the "potential space" of organizational and wider cultural creativity is filled with the Hobbesian terrors of persecutory space (Winnicott 1967). One seeks safety in the social torture chamber of self-betrayal. Both Freudian and Marxist "false consciousnesses" reveal themselves to consist of twin facets of the same process. At their worst, through euphemism, as ideological "tag-team" members, they play out the desperate conviction that organizational self-destruction (like that of self-immolating ethnic groups and nations at war) is to be preferred to the experience of the terrible anxiety of their own guilt, shame, rage, betrayal, and ultimate vulnerability. To know and to feel are fates worse than (corporate) mutilation and death. Hatred, and its great rationalizer euphemism, seal over the festering wound of love-renounced life.

In a world governed by euphemism, "spin" is the lord of confabulation. "Spin" does indeed weave a beguiling tale of unreality-as-reality. A properly told "spin" on our organizational, and wider cultural, destructiveness makes unnecessary the horror, the guilt, and the shame at what happened, because it is only good business. But, in the end, this good business is very bad business. Our self-serving euphemisms are in reality boomerangs. The most deceived are the self-deceived. They believe their own "spin."

Organizational euphemism and spin are parts of a vast ideological architecture—one with which Hitler and his master-propagandist Goebbels would have been very much at home. Euphemisms serve as building blocks (or, to use a different metaphor, tools). These blocks create an overarching "spin" or propaganda structure that in turn serves conscious and unconscious purposes of dogma and wish. Although language is not the ultimate object of defense, we come to defend our "spins" as if they were reality itself—and fight for their "reality" as if our biological survival and our identities depended on it.

Bereft of relatedness to one another apart from nostalgized "community," the best we can seem to do is to create temporary corporate islands, each workplace group ready to devour or be devoured by the other. In the "competitive marketplace" of our Social Darwinism, our image of humankind is of a tooth-ridden food chain. Ours is uncontrollable oral rage, an anguished protest above final despair. Just as Nazi and Soviet political regimes turned to their propagandists for reassurance and justification, we turn similarly to our corporate "spin"-smiths for divination and permission. We ask them to sanctify the unsayable.

But woe to every ministry of information or public relations department that believes its own propaganda. Destructiveness is destined to become self-destructiveness. Eventually, the moth and the flame are one.

FROM EUPHEMISM TO MERCY

Where can we as organizational researchers, managers, and consultants possibly go in the face of an unconsciously driven fate such as is the legacy of euphemism? What can we say or do that is not tantamount to massive denial, or to issuing to the masses a kind of psychological pabulum for emotional self-starvation? What is required is what Ralph Cranshaw (1991) calls "the Quality of Mercy," a virtue scarce not only in medical practice and training but, more broadly, in corporate life as well:

What is mercy? It neither has pity's sterile distance and faint aroma of disdain, nor joins compassion's impulsive rush to embrace the afflicted. No, mercy, while appearing to hesitate, pauses to judge carefully both the near and far of anguish, the responsibility for and innocence of wrong. Despite the dictates of reasonable justice, mercy accepts what is as it is, redeeming the insignificant other with solace and support; support that touches with gentle fingers and soft words the body, mind, and heart of suffering. Therein lies the meaning. Mercy is considered intimacy with despair. (1991: 614–615)

Authentic organizational change can begin, I believe, only when we can first despair over what we have allowed to happen in and to our work-places. To embrace that despair intimately is the only "acceptance" worthy of the name. It is no mere acknowledgment and frontier-style "moving on." It is the assumption of total vulnerability, of the implacable realness of "what happened," that at last allows loss and grief—including grief over what and who one has allowed oneself to become.

It is to sit with an overwhelming emotional realization of what happened, not to "do something" to keep from feeling the pain.

To despair over oneself is the beginning of atonement. The kind of organizational leadership required for such psychological—indeed spiritual—*turning* (Buber 1958) is not what we ordinarily ascribe either to visionary "charismatic" or "maintenance"-style (bureaucratic) leaders. But to begin anew and not be haunted by the past, we must acknowledge the atrocities we have committed in the name of business and market. To start, we must first finish: by deep grief. We must reclaim the fragile humanity we have cast off in others and in ourselves. And to do so, we must swim against the swift current of our inclinations. Hatred and the self-protective expression of aggression are easy; vulnerability and love are difficult. We bridge the chasm between euphemism and mercy by repentance (in Hebrew, *Teshuvah*, an interior turning; in German, Buber used the word *Umkehr*). We cannot grieve what we cannot first accept that we have had some part in doing. What we cannot grieve, we repeat—and further shroud in fogs of words. Culture, including workplace culture, is no monstrous juggernaut with a life and will of its own, independent of "its" human participants. Our change of heart *is* culture change. Our repentance releases the strangle-hold of "bottom-line" thinking.

EUPHEMISM AND THE AWAITING TRAINS:
IF WE DO NOT TURN . . .

What if we fail to turn from our compulsive destructiveness "reasoned" away by euphemism? What is the fate of workplace organizations, and more widely of our collective humanity, if we fail to do the psychological work necessary to grieve and to "finish" with the culture we have created and with the enormous damage we have colluded in? Wilfred Owen, the tragic poet of World War I, wrote that "all a poet can do today is to warn." The warning lies in acknowledging as simply and directly as possible: "This is what happened. This is what we have done." And from "this," there must be no postmodernist evasion.

In this book I have limited the discussion of euphemism to the culture of the United States. However, the portrait I have painted is becoming increasingly international. We are in the midst of an unprecedented financial globalization based on short-term "shareholder value optimalization" (Sievers 1997: 27). Euphemism promises to become a widely coveted smoke screen for the elevation of cash flow to the highest value (Sievers 1997). Boundary-less ambition and dread fuel a "cult of the share" (1997: 28) (see Rappaport 1986).

With the ending of the Cold War and the collapse of the Soviet empire, the ideological organization of the world into two psychologically stable camps—together with an ostensibly "neutral" and "unaligned" Third World—has fallen apart. Everywhere, local wars now draw on and enflame bitter ethnic, national, and religious strife. Another form the free-floating anxiety and aggression takes is unbridled *economic* competition: it has become a nearly universal, symbolic war. As all other, once-reliable social forms fail to offer secure immortality (Becker 1973), money alone comes to absorb "the hopes and fears of all the years," as the tender Christmas carol goes.

Compared with today's prospects for human organizational destructiveness, even 18th century British mercantilism did not have such exploitable and expendable human surpluses at its disposal. If economic globalization succeeds, there will be few places to which dependent, occupationally captive populations (Bursztajn 1997) can emigrate or flee. Certainly adaptability and resilience characterize the human species and human history, and worldwide corporate merger and competition will not create a homogenized culture. Still, the question before the international business, governmental, and intellectual community is: To how much should we ask people to "adapt"? Are we not helping to create yet another, now global, "sick society" (Edgerton 1992)? Do we not need to re-think the link between authority and responsibility (not only financial accountability)—not only in the United States, but world-wide? Are shareholders our final constituency, or ultimate ethical authority?

To describe, to interpret, and to bear witness to the work of euphemism is also to sound an alarm. The evocation is itself the warning. The evocation is the face of reality in the face of terrible unreality. It is the redemption of schizoid lovelessness by love, and the redemption of love from frightened hate.

In his posthumous book, *The Drowned and the Saved*, the late physicist and Auschwitz survivor Primo Levi (1988) drew a disturbing parallel between our predicament, our extenuating circumstances, and that of Jews in Nazi Germany. In a study of Chaim Rumkowski, the "ideal dupe" (Levi 1988: 63) and "president" of the Jewish Ghetto of Lodz, Poland, under the Nazis, Levi wrote that

> an infernal order such as National Socialism exercises a frightful power of corruption, against which it is difficult to guard oneself. It degrades its victims and makes them similar to itself, because it needs both great and small complicities. To resist it requires a truly solid moral armature. . . . But how strong is ours, the Europeans [and the world, HFS] of today? How would each of us behave if driven by necessity and at the same time lured by seduction? (1988: 68)

Levi does not shrink from making Rumkowski's moral ambiguity ours (1988: 69). The man who colluded in the deaths of 160,000 Jews in trade for a few years of petty, self-deluding, majesty haunts us—or should.

> Like Rumkowski, we too are so dazzled by power and prestige as to forget our essential frailty. Willingly or not we come to terms with power, forgetting that we are all in the ghetto, that the ghetto is walled in, that outside the ghetto reign the lords of death, and that close by the train is waiting. (1988: 69)

The central lesson of this study of managed care, of organizational downsizing, and of the short-lived grace period filled with abundant good will after the Oklahoma City bombing is that, in the conduct of organizations as in the life of whole ethnic groups and nations, we quickly forget our common frailty. We couch our vulnerability in our grandiosity and contempt. Invincibility is our vilest lie, and its ally, euphemism, is one of dishonesty's most cunning handmaidens.

The psychological "bottom line" is not our spreadsheet, but our panic. We vacillate between the position of Nazis and Jews. There is no quiet familiarity. We are all suspicious foreigners—to everyone, including ourselves.

In all three situations discussed in the preceding chapters, euphemism plays a crucial, complicit role in reasoning away evil's brutality until it *feels* like nothing more than banality. As Robert McCully (1980) has shown from a restudy of Adolf Eichmann's Rorschach Test (projective inkblot) responses, behind what Hannah Arendt (1964) had called the "banality of evil" that occurred under bureaucratic circumstances was in fact a cleverly, unconsciously disguised distraction from aggression. We want to believe that our own organizational and wider social evil is only banality, just compliance with hierarchical "orders" and "protocols." But we know better—which is precisely why we arm ourselves so heavily with euphemism to persuade ourselves otherwise.

Our workplaces and our very national culture have become crowded ghettoes where only the lord of death remains. And no one, absolutely no one, is exempt from the trains.

REFERENCES

Adams, Guy B., and Danny L. Balfour. *Unmasking Administrative Evil.* Thousands Oaks, CA: Sage, 1998.

Alford, C. Fred. "The Organization of Evil." *Political Psychology* 11, no. 1 (1990): 5–27.

————. "The Political Psychology of Evil." *Political Psychology* 18, no. 1 (March 1997): 1–17.

Arendt, Hannah. *Eichmann in Jerusalem: A Report on the Banality of Evil*. Revised edition. New York: McGraw-Hill, 1964.

Becker, Ernest. *The Denial of Death*. New York: Free Press, 1973.

Bion, Wilfred R. *Experiences in Groups*. New York: Ballantine Books, 1959a.

————. "Attacks on Linking." *International Journal of Psycho-Analysis* 40 (1959b): 308–315.

Buber, Martin. *I and Thou*. New York: Scribner's, 1957 [1925].

Bursztajn, Harold J. "True and False Medical Necessity," Presentation at the American Psychiatric Association, San Diego, May 1997.

Cranshaw, Ralph. "The Quality of Mercy." *Journal of the American Medical Association* 266, no. 5 (August 7, 1991): 614–615.

Dentan, Robert Knox. "Reply to Paul." *American Anthropologist* 90, no. 2 (1988): 420–421.

Devereux, George. *Basic Problems of Ethno-Psychiatry*. Chicago: University of Chicago Press, 1980.

Edgerton, Robert. *Sick Societies: Challenging the Myth of Primitive Harmony*. New York: Free Press, 1992.

Erikson, Erik H. *Identity, Youth and Crisis*. New York: Norton, 1968.

Freud, Sigmund. "Beyond the Pleasure Principle." *The Standard Edition of the Complete Psychological Works of Sigmund Freud (SE)*. Vol. 18. London: Hogarth Press, 1955 [1920]: 7–66.

————."Civilization and Its Discontents." *SE*. Vol. 21. London: Hogarth Press, 1961 [1930]: 64–145.

Fromm, Erich. *The Anatomy of Human Destructiveness*. New York: Holt, Rinehart and Winston, 1973.

Heath, Dwight B. "The War on Drugs as a Metaphor in American Culture." In *Drug Policy and Human Nature: Psychological Perspectives on the Prevention, Management, and Treatment of Illicit Drug Abuse*. Warren K. Bickel and Richard J. De Grandpre, Editors. New York: Plenum, 1996: 279–299.

Hilberg, Raul. *The Destruction of the European Jews*. Revised and Definitive Edition. New York: Holmes and Meier, 1985 (1961).

————. *Perpetrators, Victims, Bystanders: The Jewish Catastrophe 1933–1945*. New York: Aaron Asher Books, 1992.

Koenigsberg, Richard A. *Hitler's Ideology: A Study in Psychoanalytic Sociology*. New York: Library of Social Science, 1975.

————. *The Psychoanalysis of Racism, Revolution and Nationalism*. New York: Library of Social Science, 1986 [1977].

Kohut, Heinz. "Thoughts on Narcissism and Narcissistic Rage." *The Psychoanalytic Study of the Child*. Vol. 27. New York: Quadrangle/New York Times, 1972: 360–400.

La Barre, Weston. "Social Cynosure and Social Structure." *Journal of Personality* 14 (1946): 169–183.

Levi, Primo. *The Drowned and the Saved.* New York: Summit Books, 1988.

Lifton, Robert Jay. *The Broken Connection: On Death and the Continuity of Life.* New York: Simon and Schuster, 1979.

McCully, Robert S. "A Commentary on Adolf Eichmann's Rorschach." *Journal of Personality Assessment* 44, no. 3 (1980): 311–318.

Nuckolls, Charles W. *Culture: Problems That Cannot Be Solved.* Madison: University of Wisconsin Press, 1997.

Parin, Paul. "The Ego and the Mechanism of Adaptation." In L. B. Boyer and S. A. Grolnik, Editors. *The Psychoanalytic Study of Society*, Vol. 12. Hillsdale, NJ: Analytic Press, 1988: 97–130.

Paul, Robert A. "Instinctive Aggression in Man: The Semai Case." *Journal of Psychological Anthropology* 1, no. 1 (Winter 1978): 65–79.

———. "Commentaries: Response to Robarchek and Dentan." *American Anthropologist* 90, no. 2 (1988): 418–420.

Rappaport, Alfred. *Creating Shareholder Value: The New Standard for Business Performance.* New York: Free Press, 1986.

Sievers, Burkard. "Cacophony and Organizational Psychosis," Keynote Address to the Conference, "Uncertainty, Knowledge, and Skill." Limberg University/Keele University, Hasselt, Belgium, November 6–8, 1997 (unpublished manuscript).

Staub, Ervin. *The Roots of Evil: The Origins of Genocide and Other Group Violence.* Cambridge: Cambridge University Press, 1989.

Stein, Howard F. "Substance and Symbol." In *Recent Developments in Alcoholism, Volume 11: Ten Years of Progress.* Marc Galanter, Editor. New York: Plenum, 1993: 153–164.

———. " 'She's Driving Us Nurses Crazy': On Not Solving the Wrong Problem as a Consulting Organizational Psychologist." *Consulting Psychology Journal: Practice and Research* 48, no. 1 (Winter 1996): 17–26.

Volkan, Vamik D. *The Need to Have Enemies and Allies.* Northvale, NJ: Jason Aronson, 1988.

Winnicott, Donald W. *Collected Papers: Through Paediatrics to Psycho-Analysis.* New York: Basic Books, 1958.

———. *The Maturational Processes and the Facilitating Environment.* New York: International Universities Press, 1965.

———. "The Location of Cultural Experience." *International Journal of Psycho-Analysis* 48 (1967): 368–372.

Bibliography

Adams, Guy B., and Danny L. Balfour. *Unmasking Administrative Evil*. Thousand Oaks, CA: Sage, 1998.

Adams, Scott. *The DILBERT Principle: A Cubicle's-Eye View of Bosses, Meetings, Management Fads and Other Workplace Afflictions*. New York: HarperBusiness (HarperCollins), 1996.

Alford, C. Fred. "The Organization of Evil." *Political Psychology* 11, no. 1 (1990): 5–27.

———. "The Political Psychology of Evil." *Political Psychology* 18, no. 1 (March 1997): 1–17.

Allcorn, Seth. *Anger in the Workplace*. Westport, CT: Quorum Books, 1994.

Allcorn, Seth, Howell Baum, Michael A. Diamond, and Howard F. Stein. *The Human Cost of a Management Failure: Organizational Downsizing at General Hospital*. Westport, CT: Quorum Books, 1996.

Arendt, Hannah. *Eichmann in Jerusalem: A Report on the Banality of Evil*. Revised edition. New York: McGraw-Hill, 1964.

Becker, Ernest. *The Birth and Death of Meaning*. New York: Free Press, 1962.

———. *The Denial of Death*. New York: Free Press, 1973.

──────. *Escape from Evil*. New York: Free Press, 1975.

Benedict, Ruth F. *Patterns of Culture*. Boston: Houghton Mifflin, 1934.

Berger, Louis S. "Cultural Psychopathology and the 'False Memory Syndrome' Debates: A View from Psychoanalysis." *American Journal of Psychotherapy* 50, no. 2 (Spring 1996): 167–177.

Bion, Wilfred R. "Group Dynamics: A Review." *New Directions in Psycho-Analysis*. M. Klein, P. Heimann, and R. Money-Kyrle, Editors. New York: Basic Books, 1955: 440–477.

──────. *Experiences in Groups*. New York: Ballantine, 1959a.

──────. "Attacks on Linking." *International Journal of Psycho-Analysis* 40 (1959b): 308–315.

Brown, Laura S. "The Private Practice of Subversion: Psychology as Tikkun Olam." *American Psychologist* 52, no. 4 (April 1997): 449–462.

Buber, Martin. *I and Thou*. Ronald Gregor Smith, Trans. New York: Scribner's, 1957 [1925].

The Century Dictionary. New York: The Century Company, 1914.

Cohen, Susan. "Rage Makes Me Strong." *Time*, July 29, 1996: 50.

The Compact Edition of the Oxford English Dictionary. Oxford, England: Clarendon Press, 1971.

Cranshaw, Ralph. "The Quality of Mercy." *Journal of the American Medical Association* 266, no. 5 (August 7, 1991): 614–615.

Dawidowicz, Lucy. *The War Against the Jews, 1933–1945*. New York: Holt, Rinehart, and Winston, 1975.

Dentan, Robert Knox. "Reply to Paul." *American Anthropologist* 90, no. 2 (1988): 420–421.

Devereux, George. "Charismatic Leadership and Crisis." *Psychoanalysis and the Social Sciences* 4 (1955): 145–157.

──────. "Normal and Abnormal." *Basic Problems of Ethno-Psychiatry*. Chicago: University of Chicago Press, 1980 [1970]: 3–71.

──────. *Basic Problems of Ethno-Psychiatry*. Chicago: University of Chicago Press, 1980.

De Vos, George A. "Affective Dissonance and Primary Socialization: Implications for a Theory of Incest Avoidance." *Ethos* 3, no. 2 (1975): 165–182.

Diamond, Michael A. "Bureaucracy as Externalized Self-System: A View from the Psychological Interior." *Administration and Society* 16, no. 2 (1984): 195–214.

──────. "The Social Character of Bureaucracy: Anxiety and Ritualistic Defense." *Political Psychology* 6, no. 4 (1985): 663–679.

──────. "Organizational Identity: A Psychoanalytic Exploration of Organizational Meaning." *Administration and Society* 20, no. 2 (1988): 166–190.

———. *The Unconscious Life of Organizations: Interpreting Organizational Identity*. Westport, CT: Quorum Books, 1993.

———. "Administrative Assault: A Contemporary Psychoanalytic View of Violence and Aggression in the Workplace." *American Review of Public Administration* 27, no. 3 (September 1997): 228–247.

Diamond, Michael A., and Seth Allcorn. "Psychological Responses to Stress in Complex Organizations." *Administration and Society* 17, no. 2 (1985): 217–239.

Dundes, Alan. *Life Is Like a Chicken Coop Ladder: A Portrait of German Culture through Folklore*. New York: Columbia University Press, 1984.

Edgerton, R. *Sick Societies: Challenging the Myth of Primitive Harmony*. New York: Free Press, 1992.

Edry, Jan. "Letter to the Editor." *The Daily Oklahoman*, May 3, 1995: 6.

Eggan, Fred. "Social Anthropology and the Method of Controlled Comparison." *American Anthropologist* 56 (1954): 743–763.

Endleman, R. *Relativism Under Fire: The Psychoanalytic Challenge*. New York: Psyche Press, 1995.

Engel, George. "The Need for a New Medical Model: A Challenge for Biomedicine." *Science* 196, no. 4286 (April 8, 1977): 129–136.

Erikson, E. H. *Childhood and Society*, revised edition. New York: Norton, 1963.

———. *Identity, Youth and Crisis*. New York: Norton, 1968.

Erikson, Kai. "Loss of Communality at Buffalo Creek." *American Journal of Psychiatry* 133, no. 3 (March 1976): 302–305.

Franz, Ron. "Tragedy Spawns a Different Thanksgiving." *The Oklahoma Observer* (Oklahoma City), November 25, 1995: 7.

Freud, Sigmund. "Interpretation of Dreams." *The Standard Edition of the Complete Psychological Works of Sigmund Freud (SE)*. Vols. 4 and 5. London: Hogarth Press, 1953 [1900].

———. "Group Psychology and the Analysis of the Ego." *SE*. Vol. 18. James Strachey, Trans. London: Hogarth Press, 1955 [1920]: 69–143.

———. "Beyond the Pleasure Principle." *SE*. Vol. 18. London: Hogarth Press, 1955 [1920]: 3–64.

———. "Remembering, Repeating, and Working Through." *SE*. Vol. 12. London: Hogarth Press, 1958 [1914]: 145–156.

———. "Civilization and Its Discontents." *SE*. Vol. 21. London: Hogarth Press, 1961 [1930]: 64–145.

Freud, Sigmund, and D. E. Oppenheim. *Dreams in Folklore*. New York: International Universities Press, 1958 [1911].

Fromm, Erich. *The Anatomy of Human Destructiveness*. New York: Holt, Rinehart and Winston, 1973.

Glass, James M. "Against the Indifference Hypothesis: The Holocaust and the Enthusiasts for Murder." *Political Psychology* 18, no. 1 (March 1997): 129–145.

Goldhagen, Daniel Jonah. *Hitler's Willing Executioners: Ordinary Germans and the Holocaust.* New York: Knopf, 1996.

Grey, Mark. "The Failure of Iowa's Non-English Speaking Employee's Law: A Case Study of Patronage, Kinship, and Migration in Storm Lake, Iowa." *High Plains Applied Anthropologist* 13, no. 2 (1993): 32–46.

Grimsley, K. D. "The Downside of Downsizing: What's Good for the Bottom Line Isn't Necessarily Good for Business." *Washington Post National Weekly Edition*, November 13–19, 1995: 16–17.

Hallowell, A. Irving. *Culture and Experience.* Philadelphia: University of Pennsylvania Press, 1955.

Hammer, Michael. "Reengineering Work: Don't Automate, Obliterate." *Harvard Business Review* 68, no. 4 (July 1990): 104–113.

Hammer, Michael, and James Champy. *Reengineering the Corporation: A Manifesto for Business Revolution.* New York: Harper-Business, 1993.

Hartmann, Heinz. *Ego Psychology and the Problem of Adaptation.* New York: International Universities Press, 1958 [1939].

Heath, Dwight B. "The War on Drugs as a Metaphor in American Culture." *Drug Policy and Human Nature: Psychological Perspectives on the Prevention, Management, and Treatment of Illicit Drug Abuse.* Warren K. Bickel and Richard J. DeGrandpre, Editors. New York: Plenum Press, 1996: 279–299.

Hilberg, Raul. *The Destruction of the European Jews*, Revised and Definitive Edition. New York: Holmes and Meier, 1985 [1961].

———. *Perpetrators, Victims, Bystanders: The Jewish Catastrophe 1933–1945.* New York: Aaron Asher Books, 1992.

"How Good Is Your Health Plan?" *Consumer Reports* 61, no. 8 (August 1996): 28–42.

Janis, Irving. *Groupthink.* Boston: Houghton Mifflin, 1982.

Johnson, Thomas M. "Patient Management." *Family Medicine* 27, no. 7 (1995): 460–462.

Johnsson, Julie. "New Life for Long-Dormant Law." *American Medical News* (American Medical Association) 39, no. 17 (May 6, 1996): 3, 51, 55.

Klein, George S. *Psychoanalytic Theory: An Exploration of Essentials.* New York: International Universities Press, 1976.

Klein, M. "Notes on Some Schizoid Mechanisms." *International Journal of Psycho-Analysis* 27 (1946): 99–110.

Koenigsberg, Richard A. *Hitler's Ideology: A Study in Psychoanalytic Sociology.* New York: Library of Social Science, 1975.

————. *The Psychoanalysis of Racism, Revolution, and Nationalism*. New York: Library of Social Science, 1986 [1977].

Kohut, Heinz. "Thoughts on Narcissism and Narcissistic Rage." *The Psychoanalytic Study of the Child*. Vol. 27. New York: Quadrangle/New York Times, 1972: 360–400.

Kormos, Harry R. "The Industrialization of Medicine." *Advances in Medical Social Science*, Vol. 2. Julio L. Ruffini, Editor. New York: Gordon and Breach, 1984: 323–339.

Kren, George M., and Leon Rappoport. *The Holocaust and the Crisis of Human Behavior*. London: Holmes and Meier, 1994 [1980].

Krystal, Henry. "Trauma and the Stimulus Barrier." *Psychoanalytic Inquiry* 5 (1985): 131–161.

La Barre, Weston. "Social Cynosure and Social Structure." *Journal of Personality* 14 (1946): 169–183.

————. *The Human Animal*. Chicago: University of Chicago Press, 1954.

————. "Materials for a History of Studies of Crisis Cults: A Bibliographic Essay." *Current Anthropology* 12, no. 1 (1971): 3–44.

————. *The Ghost Dance: The Origins of Religion*. New York: Dell, 1972.

Lacan, Jacques. *The Four Fundamental Concepts of Psycho-Analysis*. New York: Norton, 1979.

Levi, Primo. *The Drowned and the Saved*. New York: Summit Books, 1988.

Li, James T. C. "The Patient-Physician Relationship: Covenant or Contract?" *Mayo Clinic Proceedings* 71 (1996): 917–918.

Lifton, Robert Jay. *The Broken Connection: On Death and the Continuity of Life*. New York: Simon and Schuster, 1979.

————. *The Nazi Doctors*. New York: Basic Books, 1986.

McCully, Robert S. "A Commentary on Adolf Eichmann's Rorschach." *Journal of Personality Assessment* 44, no. 3 (1980): 311–318.

Meissner, W. W. *The Paranoid Process*. New York: Aronson, 1978.

Mitscherlich, Alexander, and Margarete Mitscherlich. *The Inability to Mourn: Principles of Collective Behavior*. New York: Grove Press, 1975.

Modell, Arnold H. *Psychoanalysis in a New Context*. Madison, CT: International Universities Press, 1984.

Niederland, William G. "The Problem of the Survivor." *Journal of the Hillside Hospital* 10 (1961): 233–247.

Noer, David M. *Healing the Wounds: Overcoming and Revitalizing Downsized Organizations*. New York: Jossey-Bass, 1993.

Nuckolls, Charles W. *Culture: Problems That Cannot Be Solved*. Foreword by Howard F. Stein. Madison: University of Wisconsin Press, 1997.

Ohman, J. Cartoon of the bombed Oklahoma City Murrah Federal Building. *Newsweek*, December 25, 1995–January 1, 1996: 94.

Oklahoma Kids Count—Factbook 1997. Oklahoma City: Oklahoma Institute for Child Advocacy, 1997.

Oliner, Marion Michel. "External Reality: The Elusive Dimension of Psychoanalysis." *Psychoanalytic Quarterly* 65 (1996): 267–300.

Orwell, George. *1984*. New York: Harcourt Brace Jovanovich, 1949.

Parin, Paul. "The Ego and the Mechanism of Adaptation." In L. B. Boyer and S. A. Grolnik, Editors. *The Psychoanalytic Study of Society*, Vol. 12. Hillsdale, NJ: Analytic Press, 1988: 97–130.

Paul, Robert A. "Instinctive Aggression in Man: The Semai Case." *Journal of Psychological Anthropology* 1, no. 1 (Winter 1978): 65–79.

———. "The Question of Applied Psychoanalysis and the Interpretation of Cultural Symbolism." *Ethos* 15, no. 1 (1987): 82–103.

———. "Commentaries: Response to Robarchek and Dentan." *American Anthropologist* 90, no. 2 (1988): 418–420.

Pellegrino, Edmund D. "Words Can Hurt You: Some Reflections on the Metaphors of Managed Care." *Journal of the American Board of Family Practice* 7, no. 6 (1994): 505–510.

Perry, Charlotte M. "Nursing Ethics and Etiquette." *American Journal of Nursing* 6 (1906): 452.

Perry, Mary Anne. "Letter to the Editor." *The Daily Oklahoman* (Oklahoma City), April 8, 1997: 4.

"Prevention of Stress and Health Consequences of Workplace Downsizing and Reorganization" (Announcement 572). Atlanta, GA: Department of Health and Human Services, Public Health Service, Centers for Disease Control, National Institute for Occupational Health, Summer 1995.

Proctor, Robert. *Racial Hygiene: Medicine under the Nazis*. Cambridge, MA: Harvard University Press, 1988.

Rangell, Leo. "Discussion of the Buffalo Creek Disaster: The Course of Psychic Trauma." *American Journal of Psychiatry* 133, no. 3 (March 1976): 313–316.

Richards, A. I. *Chisungu*. London: Faber and Faber, 1956.

Robb, Isabel Hampton. *Nursing Ethics: For Hospital and Private Use*. Cleveland: E. D. Koeckert Publishing, 1900.

Rosenfeld, S. S. "Where to Cut Defense." *Washington Post*, November 17, 1995: A25.

Shatan, Chaim. "Unconscious Motor Behavior, Kinesthetic Awareness and Psychotherapy." *American Journal of Psychotherapy* 17, no. 1 (1963): 17–30.

Sloan, Allan. "The Hit Men." *Newsweek*, Business section, February 26, 1996: 44–48.

Spielberg, Steven, Gerald R. Molen, and Branko Lustig, Producers; Steven Spielberg, Director. *Schindler's List* [Film], 1993. (Available from Universal Pictures, 100 Universal City Plaza, Universal City, CA 91608.)

Starr, Paul. *The Social Transformation of American Medicine*. New York: Basic Books, 1982.

Staub, Ervin. *The Roots of Evil: The Origins of Genocide and Other Group Violence*. Cambridge: Cambridge University Press, 1989.

Stein, H. F. "Culture Change, Symbolic Object Loss, and Restitutional Process." *Psychoanalysis and Contemporary Thought* 8, no. 3 (1985): 301–332.

————. *Developmental Time, Cultural Space: Studies in Psychogeography*. Norman: University of Oklahoma Press, 1987.

————. "In What Systems Do Alcohol/Chemical Addictions Make Sense? Clinical Ideologies and Practices as Cultural Metaphors." *Social Science and Medicine* 30, no. 9 (1990a): 987–1000.

————. *American Medicine as Culture*. Boulder, CO: Westview Press, 1990b.

————. "Substance and Symbol." *Recent Developments in Alcoholism, Vol. 11: Ten Years of Progress*. Marc Galanter, Editor. New York: Plenum Press, 1993a: 153–164.

————. "Organizational Psychohistory." *Journal of Psychohistory* 21, no. 1 (Summer 1993b): 97–114.

————. *The Dream of Culture*. New York: Psyche Press, 1994a.

————. *Listening Deeply: An Approach to Understanding and Consulting in Organizational Culture*. Boulder, CO: Westview Press, 1994b.

————. "When Money and Medicine Mix: A Tale of Two Colliding Discourses." *Mind and Human Interaction* 6 (1995a): 84–97.

————. "Domestic Wars and the Militarization of Biomedicine." *The Journal of Psychohistory* 22, no. 4 (1995b): 406–415.

————. "When the Heartland Is No Longer Immune: The April 19, 1995 Bombing of the Oklahoma City Federal Building." *Psychohistory News: Newsletter of the International Psychohistorical Association* 14, no. 3 (1995c): 2–4.

————. "The Rupture of Innocence: Oklahoma City, April 19, 1995." *Clio's Psyche* (A Quarterly of the Psychohistory Forum) 2, no. 1 (1995d): 1, 12–15.

————. "Reflections on the Oklahoma City Bombing: War, Mourning, and the Brief Mercies of Plenty." *Mind and Human Interaction* 6, no. 4 (1995e): 186–199.

————. " 'She's Driving Us Nurses Crazy': On Not Solving the Wrong Problem as a Consulting Organizational Psychologist." *Consult-*

ing Psychology Journal: Practice and Research 48, no. 1 (Winter 1996a): 17–26.

———. "Oklahoma City Aftermath: Trauma, Time, and Adaptation— A Psychohistorical Montage." *Clio's Psyche* 2, no. 4 (March 1996b): 92–95.

Stein, Howard F., and M. Apprey. *From Metaphor to Meaning: Papers in Psychoanalytic Anthropology*. Charlottesville: University Press of Virginia, 1987.

Stein, Howard F., and Robert F. Hill. *The Ethnic Imperative: Exploring the New White Ethnic Movement*. University Park: Pennsylvania State University Press, 1977.

Stein, Howard F., and Robert F. Hill, eds. *The Culture of Oklahoma*. Norman: University of Oklahoma Press, 1993.

Stephens, G. Gayle. "The Medical Supermarket: Futuristic or Decadent? Part I." *Continuing Education for the Family Physician* 19, no. 5 (1984a): 243–245.

———. "The Medical Supermarket: Futuristic or Decadent? Part II." *Continuing Education for the Family Physician* 19, no. 11 (1984b): 600–610.

Taylor, Frederick Winslow. *Principles of Scientific Management*. New York: Harper and Brothers, 1911.

Terry, Jack. "The Damaging Effects of the 'Survivor Syndrome.'" *Psychoanalytic Reflections on the Holocaust: Selected Essays*. S. A. Luel and P. Marcus, Editors. New York: Holocaust Awareness Institute, Center for Judaic Studies, University of Denver, and KTAV Publishing House, 1984: 135–148.

't Hart, P. "Irving L. Janis' Victims of Groupthink." *Political Psychology* 12, no. 2 (1991): 247–278.

Troy, Frosty. "Sooner Killing Fields." *Oklahoma Observer*, April 25, 1995: 1.

Uchitelle, Louis. "Layoffs Are Out; Hiring Is Back: Consultants Are Abuzz; Growth Is Route to Success." *New York Times*, Business Day section, June 18, 1996: C1, C6.

Verrilli, Diana, and H. Gilbert Welch. "The Impact of Diagnostic Testing on Therapeutic Interventions." *JAMA* 275, no. 15 (April 17, 1996): 1189–1191.

Volkan, Vamik D. *Cyprus: War and Adaptation*. Charlottesville: University Press of Virginia, 1979.

———. "Narcissistic Personality Organization and 'Reparative' Leadership." *International Journal of Group Psychotherapy* 30, no. 2 (1980): 131–152.

———. *Linking Objects and Linking Phenomena*. New York: International Universities Press, 1981.

————. *The Need to Have Enemies and Allies*. Northvale, NJ: Jason Aronson, 1988.

————. "On 'Chosen Trauma.' " *Mind and Human Interaction* 3, no. 1 (1991): 13.

Wangh, M. "The Nuclear Threat: Its Impact on Psychoanalytic Conceptualizations." *Psychoanalytic Inquiry* 6, no. 2 (1986): 251–266.

Warner, Ernest G. "Ethics and Morality vs. Managed Care." *Journal of the Oklahoma State Medical Association* 89 (August 1996): 275–279.

Weber, M. *The Protestant Ethic and the Spirit of Capitalism*. Translated by Talcott Parsons. London: George Allen and Unwin, 1930.

White, Joseph B. " 'Next Big Thing' Reengineering Gurus Take Steps to Remodel Their Stalling Vehicles." *The Wall Street Journal*, November 26, 1996: #1, A13.

Winnicott, Donald W. *Collected Papers: Through Paediatrics to Psycho-Analysis*. New York: Basic Books, 1958.

————. *The Maturational Processes and the Facilitating Environment*. New York: International Universities Press, 1965.

————. "The Location of Cultural Experience." *International Journal of Psycho-Analysis* 48 (1967): 368–372.

Winslow, Gerald R. "Minding Our Language: Metaphors and Biomedical Ethics." *Update* 10, no. 4 (1994): 1–6.

Wojner, Anne W. "Outcomes Management: An Interdisciplinary Search for Best Practice." *AACN Clinical Issues* 7, no. 1 (1996): 133–145.

Woolhandler, Steffie, and David U. Himmelstein. "Extreme Risk—The New Corporate Proposition for Physicians." *New England Journal of Medicine* 333, no. 25 (December 21, 1995): 1706–1707.

Index

About the Author

HOWARD F. STEIN is Professor in the Department of Family and Preventive Medicine, University of Oklahoma Health Sciences Center, Oklahoma City. A specialist in medical, psychoanalytic, and applied anthropology and related fields ranging from rural health to ethnic studies, Stein has observed first-hand the changes that have taken place in health-care and in various other organizations. He is a member of numerous professional associations and author or coauthor of more than 20 books, among them *The Human Cost of a Management Failure: Organizational Downsizing at General Hospital* (with Seth Allcorn, Howell S. Baum, and Michael Diamond, Quorum, 1996) and *Prairie Voices: Process Anthropology in Family Medicine* (Bergin and Garvey, 1996).